C000156739

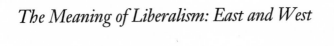

The Meaning of Liberalism: East and West

The Meaning of Liberalism: East and West

Edited by

Zdeněk Suda and Jiří Musil

Central European University Press

Published in 2000 by
Central European University Press

Október 6. utca 12
H-1051 Budapest
Hungary

400 West 59th Street
New York, NY 10019
USA

Distributed in the United Kingdom and Western Europe by
Plymbridge Distributors Ltd., Estover Road, Plymouth, PL6 7PZ,
United Kingdom

ISBN 963-9116-53-X *Cloth*
ISBN 963-9116-54-8 *Paperback*

Library of Congress Cataloging in Publication Data
A CIP catalog record for this book is available upon request

Printed in Hungary by AKAPRINT

Contents

Liberalism in the East

Foreword

When the Swiss journalist Herbert Lüthy stated, commenting on contemporary French society, that "France's clock shows another time", his words were found to be very apt. However, what is true about cultural differences between individual nations must be even more true about those between entire regions, especially if these differences are rooted in distinct political and social traditions of long standing. The West and the East—or, more precisely, Western Europe and East Central Europe—constitute a prominent case in point. Their 'asynchronous clocks' have already caused more than one misunderstanding in modern history— that is, they have created situations in which representatives of the same socio-philosophical persuasion or school in each of the two regions have found themselves talking past each other. It happened, for example, in the memorable year of 1968, between what then passed for the 'New Left' east and west of the Iron Curtain. It would seem that similar communication difficulties have arisen again, after the collapse of the communist experiment, between the spokesmen of the liberal current of thought in the West and their counterparts in the East. Although both claim to be liberals, their agendas and the order of priority in which they perceive the major social, political, and economic problems appear to be quite distinct. The volume which we have the pleasure of presenting to the reader has been put together in order to introduce and to analyze this peculiar phenomenon.

In part one, 'The Contemporary State of Liberal Theory', the principal elements of contemporary liberal theory are exposed. The second part, 'Liberalism in the West', deals with the 'state of the art' of liberal thinking in the West and with the problems and issues with which it is concerned. Part three, 'Liberalism in the East', presents the experiences of liberals in the former communist countries since 1989 and the challenges which liberal-inspired policies have to face there. This part attempts to trace the origins of the differences of the 'frame of mind' which characterize the liberals in the West and those in the East. It also aims to explain the reasons for the difficult fate which liberalism, both as a doctrine and as a political and economic program, has met with in East Central Europe. Its frequent ill-fated confrontations with populism and the unusually virulent type of nationalism endemic in this region will also be addressed in this concluding part.

The editors have chosen to approach the subject from the standpoint of historical sociology. Their intention is not to submit yet another purely academic, abstract, or literary interpretation of liberalism but rather a contextual one. The material is based on, but not limited to, the transactions of the international seminar 'The Prospects of Liberalism in Post-1989 Europe', held in Prague in the summer of 1996 as part of the long-term research and study project 'German Society and Politics in the European Context'. The seminar was made possible by grants from the Central European University and the Friedrich Naumann Foundation, to whom we wish to convey our gratitude.

By Way of Introduction

ZDENĚK SUDA

The volume which we have the pleasure of presenting to our readers is based on the transactions of the international seminar 'The Prospects of Liberalism in Post-1989 Europe', organized as part of the research and study project 'German Society and Politics in the European Context' in Prague, 11–13 July 1996. It is not just a collection of seminar papers, however. As the title indicates, it focuses on a much narrower and more precise topic. Its purpose is to compare and contrast the images which liberals in the West and social thinkers of the same persuasion in the formerly communist-ruled countries currently entertain about the working of pluralist systems and the conditions of their satisfactory performance. However, in order to make sure that the reader benefits fully from these contributions, a brief review of the intellectual scene in which the encounter of liberals from the two parts of Europe is taking place appears necessary.

Liberalism's Credentials

The socio-philosophical landscape of Europe in the 1990s—especially of its formerly Soviet-dominated part—has accommodated four major currents of thought: (i) liberalism; (ii) socialism, sharply divided into two almost incompatible versions, namely, the social-democratic tradition and the remnants of Soviet-inspired real socialism, defeated in the course of the great East–West confrontation; (iii) conservatism, including its extreme offshoot in the form of fundamentalism; and (iv) various forms of populism. Of the four, the outcome of the Cold War appears to have vindicated liberalism most clearly and to have given it the best chance of prevailing. A number of facts underscore its uniquely favorable situation. Liberalism represents, to begin with, precisely the opposite set of political and economic principles, as well as solutions to the major contemporary world problems, as compared to those offered by communism. However, this is not the only justification of liberalism's claim to the title of most suitable candidate for the role of the leading sociopolitical doctrine. The claim is based not merely on the circumstance that liberalism refutes, with overwhelming historical evidence, the communist project of a new type of society. Liberalism also convincingly rejects the underlying sociological and socio-psychological premises upon which this project rested and which communism shared with several other schools of social thought.

In the eyes of liberal critics, the failure of the communist experiment illustrates not only the mistaken nature of the communist blueprint for the reconstruction of industrial societies and the utopian character of socialism in general; it also shows the inadequacy of abstract rational approaches to societal processes. In their view, these processes cannot be interpreted, much less influenced or regulated, by analytical methods borrowed from the natural sciences. Liberals believe they are able to trace this error back to the positivist thinking of the nineteenth century—in fact, back to the period of the Enlightenment. Friedrich Hayek, who is their most articulate spokesman—and, hardly coincidentally, also one of the most revered economic theoreticians in East Central Europe since 1989—links it to the tradition rooted in the work of the French social philosopher Henri de Saint-Simon and his followers, especially Auguste Comte. He thus orients his critique towards a much broader category of social sciences than just Marxian socialism as understood and implemented by Lenin and Stalin; in his own words, his target is 'social scientism', meaning sociology or even the idea itself of social science. In so doing he gives proof of having correctly discerned one of the crucial issues about which the Cold War was waged in the socio-political sphere: that of the 'feasibility' of a better social world brought into being by conscious human action. The perspicacity of the liberals, however, has only set them further apart from all other social thinkers of our time, including those who, in the recent global conflict of ideologies, fought on the same side.

Liberalism and Democratic Socialism

The closing remark in the previous section is valid, to a significant extent, of the representatives of democratic socialism. Most Western liberals are inclined to perceive the West's victory in the Cold War as discrediting, thoroughly and finally, all kinds of socialist theories and programs. Not all who today call themselves liberals would take as radical a position as Hayek does on the issue of planned rational intervention in the social sphere, but there can be no doubt that the liberal camp as a whole rejects socialism, regardless of the means by which it is supposed to be implemented, that is, it also has objections of principle to the policies of socialist parties otherwise committed to the rules of the democratic political process. As far as the liberals in the former communist region are concerned, their perceptions are somewhat different. They are shaped by the particular experience acquired by them in the course of the struggle against communist totalitarianism. They know, better than anybody else, that the Soviet model of communism—so-called real socialism—is economically unworkable and politically insupportable. However, they are prone to attribute its failure to the course adopted in the political arena, that is, to one-party rule, disrespect for human rights, and arbitrary judicial practices, rather than to the nature of the goals pursued—although they, too, view the communist project, as they came to know it under Soviet domination, to be utopian. The fact that democratically oriented socialists were their allies during that time, and on some occasions even paid the bulk of the costs of anti-communist resistance, made some East European liberals consider these socialists as partners in the ultimate triumph over the Soviet-imposed regime and feel that they may have a role to play in post-communist social reconstruction.

Their feeling was reinforced by what they have witnessed, since contact with the rest of the world was renewed, in particular Western liberal circles, namely, distinctive elements of democratic socialism. It seems to them that these elements have come to the fore in the ongoing liberal debate about the role of the state in a free society, and in the admission by certain chapters of the Western liberal school that the present socio-economic system inspired by the principles of liberalism—namely, industrial capitalism—continues to experience serious problems, even after the collapse of communism. Wherever such an admission has been made, the floor has been opened for a discussion of the best solutions to these problems, which for many liberals in the East implies taking into account all proposals or initiatives regardless of their ideological origin, allowing even for those that are socialist-inspired. This is one of several occasions on which liberals in the former communist-controlled orbit and their Western counterparts risk talking past each other. The risk is heightened by the circumstance that many, who in the former communist countries, today identify themselves as liberals have subscribed mainly to the political part of the liberal program, whereas their position on its economic content may not be as unequivocal. This could be seen as a specific instance of the divorce between the two main components of the liberal teaching, a trend which some of the contributors to the present volume believe to have discovered also in the West. In the East, one of its causes is undoubtedly the singular historical experience of the liberals under communism.

'Classical' Western liberals seem unimpressed by the argument that the praiseworthy record of democratic socialists during communist rule, or the admission by the liberals that the industrial market economy is showing serious shortcomings, should in any way rehabilitate socialist theory. They point out that even the social democrats, not unlike their communist foes, commit the cardinal mistake of evaluating the performance of capitalism by comparison with the performance of an imaginary, as yet not implemented, socialist order. Consequently, both their diagnosis of the crisis of capitalist society—however real this crisis may be—and the therapy they propose are invalid. This observation is notable and quite legitimate, even outside the context in which it is made. It represents an important contribution to the debate on ideology and utopia opened in the 1940s by the seminal work of Karl Mannheim. We may also see it as the economic counterpart of the famous dictum by Winston Churchill about democracy being "the worst possible political system—with the exception of all others that exist".

The liberals may claim, *mutatis mutandis*, the same about capitalism, especially after the recent experience with real socialism. They may also point out that the justification of radical social reforms in terms of a comparison of things as they are with what they ideally should be has, as a rule, been characteristic of all totalitarian propaganda—a fact which, of course, can hardly endear socialism, even in its democratic version, to societies that have embarked upon the path of post-communist reconstruction. It would seem, in any case, that the initial apparent advantage which the use of a utopian yardstick may have given the socialists has now been lost owing to the disaster suffered by communism; indeed, we know few things so surely as we know that this order is infinitely worse than that which it purported to replace. This knowledge will determine, for a long time to come, the chances of liberalism and those of socialism to secure popular support. Yet, notwithstanding the undisputed edge liberalism can count upon in this respect at present, its lasting prevalence as a universally accepted world-view is in no way guaranteed; some of the contributions to this collective work attempt to show why.

The Conservative Challenge

A more challenging rival than socialism to liberalism in the post-communist era could be conservatism. Admittedly, this is a current of social thought that is more difficult to define clearly. In a sense, and in some political cultures, conservatism could even be seen as part of the broad liberal stream or, more precisely, as a particular hue of the liberal ideological color. This is especially true when liberalism is primarily understood as an economic doctrine, which tends to be the case in the former communist countries. There the liberal and the conservative perspective and approach to social reality are prone to blend into one. The reader will find in this volume several interesting comments and insights concerning the already mentioned tendency to separate the 'purely political' content of liberalism from its 'purely economic' component. Such a separation would facilitate an even closer rapprochement between conservatism and liberalism, as it would occur in the economic sphere only, somewhat neutralizing a number of significant disagreements in other areas. We will address the most important of them later in this overview; here suffice it to recall that conservatism, one of the allies of liberalism in the Cold War, combated communism on grounds of its own, which often were no more similar to the liberal ones than those of democratic socialism. It could even be argued that, especially if we consider political values and principles, the social democratic opposition to the Soviet-inspired real socialist experiment was more strongly motivated by typically liberal concerns than the opposition of the conservatives. Much of the latter, notably in the countries that had no previous experience of a liberal pluralist polity, was in its essence a manifestation of anti-modernism. 'Building socialism' on the Soviet model was *sui generis* modernization, a Marxist-Leninist substitute for failed or delayed societal and economic development (this, incidentally, was the reason why the communist model, during a particular time period, had such an appeal in the Third World; it was seen there as a short-cut to modernity). The anti-modern element of conservatism would most probably have manifested itself even if the development had unfolded under the 'normal' conditions of foreign investment and a market economy. On the whole, however, anti-modernism has been characteristic of the conservative extreme right-wing—close to fundamentalism in underdeveloped areas—rather than of mainstream conservatism.

Among the former communist societies of East Central Europe, this extreme view can be found only sporadically. The fundamentalist social critique shows extraordinary consistency. For the fundamentalists, communism was only the ultimate phase of the process of modernization which they consider to have been a dead-end from its inception. Their position, therefore, is as incompatible with the liberal one as that of the orthodox communists. The prospects of fundamentalism in post-communist Europe, on the other hand, are negligible, except where it could obtain reinforcement from the quarters of extreme nationalism, as perhaps in Bosnia. For the student of contemporary conservative thought and of its influence on the formerly communist geopolitical orbit, the relation between liberalism and mainstream conservatism is by far the most important. To some it may appear quite intimate but, as we have already indicated, caution is advisable lest we should mistake conservative support for the liberal market economy for an unreserved endorsement of the entire body of liberal doctrine.

An Excursus: American Liberalism Today

It is interesting to note that an oversimplification in the inverted sense, that is, conceiving of a part of liberal political theory as the sum of liberal views and approaches, also in the economic sphere, has been responsible for the peculiar difference of connotation which Europeans on the one hand and Americans on the other attach to the term 'liberal'. In American political parlance, this word stands for everything that in other Western countries would be called 'socially progressive', 'leftist', or even 'socialist'. This shift of meaning is not the mere transfer of a label; it developed quite organically within the same school of social thought stemming from the very logic of liberalism in the specific American environment. The universal liberal principles exported to the 'land of unlimited possibilities' seem to have run up against what was perceived as an impediment to their full implementation, namely, new social inequalities. In the eyes of the

American liberals, who had in no way forsworn their classical European origins, these could not but result in inequality of chances and thus threaten the substance of what has been called 'the American dream'. The threat was perceived particularly keenly wherever wealth and income inequalities caused inequalities in access to education and adequate political socialization, and adversely influenced the level of political participation of the disadvantaged strata, putting the democratic process itself at serious risk.

This perception has inspired the American liberals, since the turn of the twentieth century, to programs and policies that could be interpreted by an outside observer as a sign of their abandonment of the basic liberal tenet requiring the maximal limitation of the power of the state. However, such an impression would not correspond to reality. The intervention by the 'public hand' in social matters came to be viewed by the American liberals as an indispensable initiative in order to re-establish equality of opportunity and to promote social solidarity, thus stabilizing the entire system—not as an intrusion into the private life of the individual citizen that would make him dependent on the state, but on the contrary as an action 'helping him to help himself'. This trend gained particular momentum after the Second World War and made American liberalism the architect of the American version of the welfare state. Thus the American liberals parted company with their European next-of-kin, and the adjective 'liberal' assumed new significance in the American political vocabulary, although the apparent change of position was only partial, limited to the sphere of social policy. Liberals on both sides of the Atlantic continued to subscribe unreservedly to the 'purely political' content of liberal philosophy. The original 'hands-off' approach to social matters was then picked up by the conservative forces, but this happened more or less selectively; it would not be accurate to affirm that the two major camps simply switched places in the American right–left continuum.

The consequence of this terminological disagreement for the subject of our discussion is evident; if we had to assess the prospects of liberalism after the Cold War on a global— that is, not only on a European basis—we would have to address, as far as the United States are concerned, a combination of approaches, initiatives, and programs. In matters of economic policies, we would have to focus our attention on quarters that identify themselves as conservative; in the political sphere proper, dealing with constitutional problems, basic human rights and freedoms, protection of minorities, and so on, we would have to consider individuals and groups generally labeled as liberal. The singular dichotomy of connotation characteristic of American liberalism could also be seen as a symptom of the trend towards the complete separation of the economic component of the liberal doctrine from its political counterpart, which we mentioned earlier. Some of the contributors to this volume deal with this matter in greater detail. However, the American-grown problem resulting from the lack of clarity about the borderline between conservatism and liberalism could be illuminating in another important respect: taking a closer look at it might help us understand what really divides conservatives from liberals, not only in the United States, but world-wide.

The Chances of Conservatism

At present, it is often hard to distinguish conservative attitudes and positions on many issues from those of liberals, especially where problems connected with the post-communist societal transformation are involved. The emphasis on individual responsibility and self-reliance as opposed to state intervention is part of both the conservative and the liberal approach; liberal rejection of ambitious public projects and programs could be defined as conservative as well as liberal; the same is true about the conservative and the liberal view on long-term central planning of all kinds. Yet there is a substantial difference between the liberal and the conservative general perspectives. To be sure, both the liberals and the conservatives are apprehensive of state power and endeavor to stave off its growth. However, while both mistrust excessive social engineering and the concentration of power which it requires, only the conservatives mistrust social change as such. Here the distinction is sharp. Here, too, the American experience could be enlightening. The conservative aversion to social change explains, to a significant degree, the absence of a truly conservative social and cultural tradition in the United States. A society that made progress—that is, social change for the better—into one of its articles of faith, a nation for whom 'later in history' means, by and large, 'better', is not an hospitable environment for the skeptical, conservative frame of mind.

Taking this into account, it will not be difficult for us to recognize that liberalism and conservatism, even in the unique situation of post-communist Europe, are two self-contained social perspectives, despite the similarity of views on some important issues. Thus it can be expected that they will compete for influence or ideological leadership in the years to come. The chances of conservatism do not seem very bright; in fact, they may be even dimmer than those of democratic socialism. There are two main reasons why conservatism is at a notable disadvantage in this contest. First, wherever it could base its appeal on the popular ideas which it shares with liberalism, the credit is more likely to be given to liberalism, since the latter represents a more comprehensive system of thought, better qualified to fill the vacuum created by the demise of communism. Second, conservative antipathy to social change will be a serious handicap in the unprecedented social climate of the formerly communist countries where an all-pervasive systemic change—introduced from above, into the bargain—must be the central objective of any government. In these circumstances, conservatism could hope to compete successfully only if it were able to offer a comparably radical plan of change of its own. Such a plan, however, coming from the conservatives could only be that of a return to the pre-communist *status quo ante*. This would bring the conservative mainstream close to fundamentalist positions, with similarly poor chances of mobilizing the necessary mass support. It appears, therefore, that liberalism has little to fear from the conservative competition.

Populism as Arbiter of Legitimacy

In contrast, populism may prove a rival to be taken more seriously by the liberals than socialism or conservatism. It exhibits a mixture of views and attitudes that is eminently suited to elicit a following in the exceptional socio-psychological atmosphere of post-communist Europe. On the one hand, populists have always been wary of strong central government, centralized administration and bureaucracy, and representative, that is, mediated (as opposed to 'direct') democracy—in short, of all the communist system stood for—and what constitutes the very opposite of the political and social order which the post-communist reconstruction aims at establishing. From this point of view, their stand parallels that of the liberals. On the other hand, however, populism is equally fearful of the dangers of a concentration of economic power, of the monopolist leanings of capitalism, of the possibly adverse consequences of free trade and the globalization of industrial economy, and is definitely less sanguine than liberalism about the beneficial effects of an unrestrained free market. If we add to this list of attitudes the populist commitment to the protection of the 'ordinary man', his interests and economic security, as well as the somewhat lax position of the populists on the perils of the tyranny of the majority in democracy, we have to conclude that opportunities for conflict between liberalism and populism are not lacking.

In evaluating the strength of attraction of both, we must not overlook the circumstance that populism, unlike socialism, is not tarnished by an ambiguous relation to communism. In fact, much of the resistance to the Soviet-imposed regimes in East Central Europe before 1989 was of a populist nature. The Polish Solidarity movement is a case in point. The so-called reform communism that launched the Prague Spring in 1968 was largely revisionist Marxism-Leninism-cum-populism. The political comeback of the revisionist communist parties in Poland and Hungary in the mid-1990s was in significant measure due to populist moods and attitudes prevailing after the initial enthusiasm for unadulterated economic liberalism had passed. However, by far the most powerful asset of populism in its competition with liberalism may be the role which it will play in judging and determining the legitimacy of the social order that is to succeed the failed real socialism. The criteria by which this legitimacy will be measured are—whether the liberals are willing to admit it or not—in principle populist. The new order will be found acceptable or wanting depending on its ability to satisfy the expectations of a just and equitable social system, better than the one which collapsed. The crucial issue will be that of the legitimacy of the new inequalities created by the return to a market economy.

It can be assumed that these inequalities, as far as they represent the outcome of the market process subject to the rule of law, will be accepted if equality of chances is secured for all. Owing to its special position within the spectrum of post-communist social beliefs, populism will act as a kind of watchdog in the critical test liberalism will have to stand, but it is not probable that populist views and goals will completely gain the upper hand—they seem too vague and incoherent. Populism, of course, has offshoots which might develop into self-contained currents and movements, thereby overcoming its incoherence. This most likely would occur at the expense of core values for which the Cold War fought, such as human rights and freedoms. It could be argued that the post-1989 upswing of nationalism, taking at times xenophobic and racist forms, might in the competition between liberalism and populism benefit rather the latter (unless, of course, we recognize nationalism as a rival of liberalism in its own right, which does not seem to be a well-taken position; pursued to its logical consequences, this notion would imply that nationalism has a distinct alternative to offer to the liberal—or any other—concept of the future world order). There appears to exist even a good reason to view the recent nationalist wave as containing populist components or manifestations of populism. To a significant extent, its ethnocentric and xenophobic features emerged as a reaction to the globalization of the industrial economy which had gained new and strong momentum from the removal of international barriers erected during the Cold War. Thus contemporary populism speaks also for the nationalist constituencies, both in the East and in the West. Various right-extremist, fascist or fascistoid groups and centers that feed on ethnic or class resentments and use populist rhetoric might try to achieve similar objectives. They could succeed if the new liberal-inspired socio-economic order fails its legitimacy test, that is, if it does not convince the former subjects of the communist empire about its being more equitable than its predecessor. Can liberalism be trusted to avoid such a failure? If it succeeds, not even populism will be able to dispute its right of candidacy to the universally accepted political doctrine of the post–Cold War era.

Liberalism's Lack of Self-Knowledge

To be sure, being the most qualified among the contemporary social theories to confront the problems of post-communist Europe does not in itself make these problems less challenging for liberalism. Challenging, too, from the start, has been the question concerning which approach to their solution should be chosen. The difficulty here lies in the pluralist nature of liberal social philosophy—a well-known fact commented upon in the various analyses that follow this introduction. There is not one 'orthodox' liberalism but—as cannot be otherwise in a teaching that puts a high premium on tolerance—a motley collection of liberal tenets and beliefs differing among themselves on various points and open to classification in accordance with a number of criteria. One of these criteria could be geo-political, of particular significance in the context of the theme to which this volume is dedicated, that is, based on the distinction between liberalism as it is understood in the broad area labeled 'the West' during the Cold War, on the one hand, and in the formerly communist-dominated part of Europe, on the other. At the time when the choice of the model of liberalism to be applied in the former communist countries was made, the difference between the two was perceived as one of degree of doctrinal maturity, with the liberals in the East playing the role of the junior, less enlightened member of the liberal socio-philosophical college.

In fact, the most consequential distinction between contemporary liberalism as understood and practiced in the East and in the West was created by their long separate historical experience. It is connected with the dramatic and, on the whole, not very successful past record of political modernization in Germany and East Central Europe. It can also be explained by the unique and unprecedented situation in which this region has found itself since 1989. Of the two factors, no doubt the second has been the most important. Paradoxically, it is also the one of which the liberals seem to be least aware—to the point of ignoring it altogether.

The current problems of the transformation process in East Central Europe can be traced chiefly to a misperception which—and this is essential—is part of an oversimplified and erroneous idea about the social and cultural preconditions of a working liberal democratic political system with a market economy. It could also be said—which would amount to the same thing—that it rests on the assumption that all principal preconditions of the establishment (or rather 're-establishment', since 'return' is the word most frequently used in this context) of this system are given in any and all social environments. This assumption will probably go down in history as one of the most fateful errors committed by a school of social theory.

The cause of it certainly rests in the dominant, if not exclusive, role played by liberal economic theory in devising the strategy of post-communist reform in East Central Europe. This theory postulates the psycho-sociological dispositions of 'homo economicus' in every social actor world-wide. According to the neo-classical liberal interpretation, the task of the managers of the post-communist transformation process consisted solely in creating the conditions and incentives for free-market exchange; everything else would automatically follow. For the transformation to succeed, all that was needed was the release of the mechanism of economic reactions supposedly built into the mental outfit of every individual.

The problem with this expectation has not been so much that it does not correspond to reality, but rather that it does not tell the whole truth. The free market may be a necessary condition of democracy but it takes more than just a free market to establish a liberal democratic society. Much more. Here the contrast between the historical experience and the current problems faced by liberals in the East and those in the West becomes starkly evident. The recipe for the post-communist transformation, as developed by neo-classical liberal experts and advisors, would probably have worked quite well in the West, or, for that matter, in any environment in which previous systemic experimentation pursued by real socialism had remained strictly limited to the economic sphere (and did not last as long as it did in the East). This, however, was inconceivable in the case of communism; it would have been a contradiction in terms. In the course of 'building socialism' profound and far-reaching changes were effected in countless sectors of social life, often with the explicit intention of rendering the ongoing economic transformation irreversible.

The Western liberal definers and interpreters of the situation as it existed in the former communist countries either minimized or wholly ignored such changes. To be sure, these were much less obvious than the changes made in the structure of ownership, planning, production, and distribution. In addition to the failure to recognize the impact of several decades of collectivist policies upon the non-economic area, the neo-classical liberal understanding of the problems of the societies that once had been targets of real-socialist experiments was flawed in another, indirect, but nonetheless equally portentous sense: it started from an insufficient knowledge of the necessary conditions of a well-functioning liberal social order as such. It betrayed the fact that the Western liberals did not fully realize what had made their own story such a success.

The Post-Communist Social Laboratory

Recognition of this highlights the value of the experience of the liberals in the East and of their possible contribution to the universal liberal debate. This experience could help fill serious gaps in liberal self-knowledge and correct a number of inaccurate ideas and illusions about liberalism's real strengths and weaknesses. East European liberals do not owe this advantage to their unusual genius. Their wisdom, if any, was paid for dearly. Here we could, as if by an historical irony, use the analogy made long ago by one of the arch-enemies of liberalism, French diplomat and politician Joseph de Maistre. Talking about the lessons of the French Revolution he compared this epochal event with a violent sea storm which may cause tremendous damage but has the beneficial effect of showing to the observer the solid rock bottom which remains unmoved and upon which we can count in all circumstances.

Disregarding de Maistre's position on democracy and liberalism, we certainly have the right to borrow this parallel to illustrate the experience of communism as lived by the liberals in the East. They too, at a terribly high price, have been shown what matters, and what does not, among social relations and institutions when freedom, human dignity, and quality of life are at stake. The same cannot be said of their Western counterparts. Having lived for generations in nearly ideal conditions permitting full development of the liberal political, economic, and social order, the temptation to take these conditions for granted is too strong for them to resist. For some of them, they do not even enter their consciousness, similar to the air they breathe. As a consequence, the very theory of liberal democracy by which they explain the function of the political and economic mechanism of their own societies is incomplete.

This situation is not entirely without irony. The gaps in the awareness of Western liberals concerning the conditions of a well-functioning liberal socio-economic order were especially visibly highlighted when the unique historical opportunity offered itself to build, or, as it is often argued, to rebuild a liberal society 'in real life', after the fall of the Berlin Wall. At that point, their advice or even participation in the rebuilding process was sought. There is no doubt that in a majority of cases this advice proved to be seriously wanting. Those liberal experts who responded to the call for help from the East recommended a more or less straightforward emulation of the Western model by the former communist countries; however, they did not fully realize what this model required for its satisfactory functioning. Their failure provided evidence about the deficient nature of the Western liberal self-image. On the other hand, the unsuccessful Western input in the post-communist reconstitution forced liberals on both sides of the former Iron Curtain to seek more satisfactory answers to the question about the requirements of a working pluralist polity with a free market economy. The encounter of the liberals from the West with those from the East stimulated new inquiries and contributed to the further progress of liberal theory. In several places in the present volume, the reader will find interesting comments on this subject.

What This Book Is About

Liberal experience acquired in the course of the reconstruction process in East Central Europe may also lead to a reconsideration of some Western liberal propositions which have not hitherto been seriously challenged. These propositions deal with the mutual relation and influence of the liberal economic system and the type of polity in industrial societies. The proposition advanced by Milton Friedman that capitalism is a condition—not sufficient but necessary—of democracy can serve as an example. It would have been possible, from the start, to suggest that it is rather the free market, not capitalism as such, that creates a climate favorable to the development of democracy, in that it fosters competition, the political variant of which is pluralism, that is, competition among political views, approaches, and programs (the 'market of ideas'), and thus ensures socialization into a democratic pattern of political behavior. But this is not the main issue nor the only element in Friedman's proposition that is open to debate. If we consider the lessons which the post-communist reconstruction and the attendant, initially unforeseen difficulties have taught us, it might be equally justifiable to ask whether the relationship in which Friedman considers capitalism and democracy to stand—the former as an independent and the latter as a dependent variable—is indeed so straightforward as it appears to him; whether in fact stable liberal democracy is not a precondition of capitalism rather than vice versa. Admitting this would have the advantage for an economist, as well as for a politologist, of avoiding a proximity, too close for comfort, to the Marxist perspective (economic base determining political superstructure). It would also be more in harmony with the historical facts, since the so-called bourgeois democratic revolutions of the eighteenth and nineteenth centuries clearly preceded the expansion of industrial capitalism everywhere in the West. A few of the contributors to the present volume have, on the basis of the recent post-communist experience, understood the two-way dependency of the liberal political order and the free market economy; one of them (Stephen Holmes), has even made it the central point of his discussion.

We are aware that this volume is, for the most part, breaking entirely new ground. The role played by liberalism in the post-communist transformation process and its prospects of asserting itself as a dominant social philosophy in the former communist region, which could ensure its ideological leadership in the world at large, has not yet, it would seem, received the attention which it deserves. At the time of writing, only one major monograph devoted to this subject is known to us, Jerzy Szacki's *Liberalism after Communism* (CEU Press, 1994), which, although it to a large extent deals with the Polish situation and uses chiefly Polish illustrations, comes closest to the problem area we propose to cover and arrives at a number of generally valid and remarkable conclusions. This can be said, for example, about the author's emphasis upon the weakness of the political constituent of liberalism, relative to its economic counterpart, in East Central Europe today, which has special reasons reaching far back into the past. His classification as only 'protoliberal' of most contemporary currents of thought in the former communist societies that call themselves liberal is a valuable contribution to the intellectual anatomy of the political cultures of these societies and a piece of groundwork that will facilitate a number of investigative undertakings. The reader of Szacki's book will also appreciate his insightful hint at the somewhat paradoxical situation of the liberals as they face the task of creating, after the collapse of the communist experiment, not only a new social order but also its basic premises, such as the middle class, entrepreneurs, and civil society, almost *ex nihilo*; this task can be performed only by a strong coordinating center pursuing a detailed long-term plan, that is, by methods which are the very opposite of those advocated by liberal political theory.

Yet our volume intends to address a subject that is both broader in impact and narrower in scope. As already observed, it should provide the reader with some insights into the dialogue about, or rather into two parallel interpretations of, the content of the contemporary liberal message as presented by the liberals in the West on the one hand, and those who subscribe to liberalism in the former communist East on the other. No doubt, it will be the interpretation of liberal doctrine by the latter that will, by and large, determine not only the mode of its implementation in the former communist countries but also its chance of having a lasting impact. This again will be possible only on the condition that liberalism will be perceived there as a theory offering satisfactory answers to the problems resulting from the ongoing process of social reconstruction. However, an agreement, or at least an understanding in principle, between the two chapters of the liberal school would considerably strengthen the position of the liberals in the East. How easy will it be to arrive at such an understanding? There are a number of reasons why it cannot be expected that it will prove to be entirely unproblematic. In the previous part we have touched upon several important points that may be seen differently by the two partners in the dialogue, owing to their specific historical experiences; in the particular context of our discussion, we mean the experience lived during the forty-odd years of the East–West confrontation known as the Cold War.

Geopolitical location exposed the individual currents of liberal thought to specific external pressures and influences which inevitably drove them apart. The Cold War could serve as a prominent example. However, it has not been the only nor the first instance of the liberals in the West and their Eastern counterparts encountering the same social and political problems, but in clearly distinct settings and perspectives, which could not fail to shape, in a different manner, the perceptions of each of them and the adequacy of the available solutions. In the formative years of European continental liberalism, in the middle of the nineteenth century, East Central European societies, notably the German, went through a stormy process of nation-building complicated by the circumstance, characteristic of this region, that these societies had become nations before having created states in the modern sense of the term. They had been, for a long time before, in frantic search of their collective identity and a geopolitical home. This gave Central European nationalism an extraordinarily virulent trait, national values and what was seen as the national interest taking precedence before any other ethical concerns.

Different Historical Experiences: West versus East

Under these circumstances the progress and development of liberal ideas and liberal social philosophy could not be as smooth as in key Western democracies such as Great Britain and France. Moreover, conflicts between liberalism and nationalism could not be avoided whenever the perceived need to safeguard national interests seemed to require the disregard of human rights and freedom. Such conflicts, indeed, have been quite frequent, with nationalism getting the upper hand in most cases. The difficult situation of liberalism in Central Europe is most eloquently illustrated by the story of the creation of the German national state. After the first attempt at building such a state on a liberal basis—by an act of the Frankfurt Parliament in 1848–49—lost its initial momentum and failed, a unitary German State was eventually formed on conservative foundations, by means of 'blood and iron', in 1871. German society obviously preferred a non-liberal—in many respects even an anti-liberal—state framework to the prolongation of the status of 'nation-without-a-state'. The order of priorities in which a stable state structure occupied the highest place determined many fateful German choices in critical moments of later German history, most prominently when the Third Reich replaced the unsuccessful Weimar Republic in 1933. But it has to be emphasized that this value scale was not a German specialty; it was region-wide.

Another challenge to liberalism in East Central Europe was the peculiar notion of national in contrast to individual freedom. In accordance with this idea, a nation living in a nation-state which is sovereign in terms of international law is considered free regardless of the political regime to which it is subject. Thus, again using the example of Germany, the Germans as a nation would be seen as free under Nazi rule, more free, for instance, than under American, British, or French administration after the Second World War, although it was precisely this administration, introduced after the defeat of the Third Reich, that returned to individual Germans their basic human and civil rights and freedom, and freed the German economy from political constraints. The divorce between individual and collective freedom implied here is unique. A reconciliation between the notion of national freedom, as conceived of here, and true liberal individual freedom would be thinkable only if every member of the collective explicitly approves of the prevailing regime and assents to it, giving a blanket endorsement of all its future moves. In this way, however he or she would forfeit their natural rights and freedoms, which are, by definition, inalienable.

The concept of collective freedom and liberal political philosophy, therefore, cannot be reconciled. That this concept nevertheless survives next to the more universal notion of individual freedom in East Central Europe can be documented by another example from recent history. In Czechoslovakia after 1945—and in increased measure after 1989—relations between the two nation-building ethnic groups, the Czechs and the Slovaks, were disturbed by the nostalgia felt by the latter for the short-lived sovereignty of the Slovak puppet state established with the help of Nazi Germany in

1939 and later tarnished by active participation in Hitler's 'Final Solution'. It was remarkable that this nostalgic attitude was entertained in wide circles of Slovak society, including those that never shared the fascist ideology of the Slovak State. This at first sight rather schizophrenic mood was made possible only by the prevalence in the Central European region of the singular dichotomy of individual freedom and national freedom. This unique phenomenon is indicative of the specific socio-philosophical climate in which Central European liberalism has always had to operate, and accounts for a good many of its misfortunes.

Economic Liberalism in East Central Europe

Economic liberalism in the strict sense of the term has had a somewhat uneasy career in East Central Europe. State guidance and state support of domestic industry and agriculture has had a long and rich tradition there, especially in Germany where it was connected with the names of Karl Rodbertus and Friedrich List. The principle of free trade, although its application on the level of the myriad of smaller sovereign German provinces and territories significantly facilitated the constitution of a unitary German state by means of the customs union—*Zollverein*—of 1834, never found any advocate of stature in the entire region. Later development of the various national economies only confirmed this general trend. The economy of the Third Reich, marked by the initiative of the Finance Minister Hjalmar Schacht, was based on extensive state regulation and aimed at self-sufficiency or autarchy. Even the economic policies of the Federal Republic of Germany, succeeding the deregulatory strategy of the Allied administration, was not liberal in the classical meaning of the word. The type of economic system striven for during that period was labeled *die soziale Marktwirtschaft* or 'social market economy', denoting the commitment of the state to intervene in the economic process with a view to alleviating the adverse impact of the market mechanism upon the economically disadvantaged. The approach of the economic leaders in other Central European countries, before these countries became part of the Soviet bloc—that is, before the Second World War—was no closer to classical liberal positions than that of Germany. Here, after all, only countries whose industrial potential had by then been realized come into consideration. This would limit their number to no more than two: Austria and Czechoslovakia. These nations did not subscribe to an unbridled free market and free trade either. As regards other liberal economic principles, Czechoslovakia at that time faithfully observed the canons of monetarism, imposing strict fiscal discipline, which partly aggravated the effects of the Great Depression of 1929 and delayed recovery.

The Prospects of a Fruitful Dialogue

In sum, the histories of liberal doctrine as they have unfolded in the two parts of Europe are different enough to warrant reservations concerning the chances of establishing easy dialogue and understanding between the representatives of the respective regions. Still more obstacles in the way of smooth and steady communication may arise from the separate experience of contemporary post-communist problems and from the different order of priorities in which they see them. In many respects, liberals in the West seem to be concerned about other issues than their fellow-believers in the East. The great liberal debate, started during the Cold War but not directly related to it, about the minimal state or about the extent of the responsibility of a liberal democratic society for the welfare of its members (the communitarian challenge) has on the whole taken place without Eastern participation. It is not easy to arouse the interest of the liberals in the former communist region in this debate because, among other things, the Eastern liberal camp can no more be viewed as a homogenous body than its Western counterpart. This in itself, in consideration of the diversified nature of liberal doctrine, need not be too alarming. However, among the liberal ranks in today's East Central Europe we also find elements that, although they call themselves liberal, often take positions incompatible with liberal principles. This incongruity dates, in large measure, from the period of struggle against the communist system, as we pointed out earlier. At that time, many opponents of the regime, aware that liberalism stood for the very opposite of the program and political strategy of real socialism, identified themselves as liberals or readily accepted the liberal label whenever it was stuck on them as a derogatory term by official propaganda. Therefore, some screening of the liberal ranks in the former communist part of Europe would appear desirable in the interest of more fruitful East–West liberal dialogue.

Yet the source of difficulties that could do most to mar this dialogue is the widespread misperception on both sides of the very nature of liberalism. The unique situation of the former communist societies and the discussion of appropriate policies that could meet their needs brought this misperception very clearly to the fore. On the part of the leaders responsible for inducing economic and social reconstruction, who were—or professed to be—mainly of liberal persuasion, the expectation was often voiced that liberalism as a body of social theory would supply a blueprint by which they could orient themselves. This, however, was not possible; liberalism had no recipe for the successful implementation of concrete policies in the post-communist transformation. In fact, liberalism has not, and never has had, a program of its own, if by that term we mean a set of particular objectives to be reached by political means. Rather, it represents a set of rules and methods by which any objective, with the exception of those that violate basic liberal principles, can and should be pursued.

In the case just mentioned it was the Eastern component of the liberal community that was the most prone to succumb to a misperception of the real character of the liberal doctrine. 'Classical' Western liberals emphasizing value neutrality and the 'ideology-free' quality of liberalism would seem to be more immune to such errors. Nonetheless, even they have entertained an image of liberalism—especially of the conditions necessary for the satisfactory performance of liberal institutions, notably economic ones—which is false, or at least incomplete. This, too, became clearly visible after the collapse of communism, when some of their leading representatives were called upon to diagnose the problems of the former communist societies and help devise strategies for their solution. At that point, it was revealed that Western liberalism overlooks, or takes for granted, a number of prerequisites of a well-functioning democratic society with a free market economy; in other words, that it does not sufficiently know itself. We touched upon this earlier in our discussion, but here we would like to point to a more positive side of the challenge posed to the East–West liberal dialogue by the different perspective and historical experience of the two partners. There are reasons to believe that the test to which the liberal idea has been subject following the end of the Cold War will in the end prove to be rather beneficial. This test highlights and underscores many of liberalism's current problems, most prominently the risk of a divorce between its economic and political components and the possible consequences of such a separation. This brings it home to many liberals in both East and West how inaccurate are their notions of the conditions of the successful operation of the liberal system and of the real potential of liberal theory in everyday politics. Thus it will enrich the contemporary liberal debate to which the Eastern component can also fruitfully contribute.

The Contemporary State of Liberal Theory

Citizenship and Moral Individuality

CATHERINE AUDARD

"It is only through being a member of the state that the individual has objectivity, truth and ethical life."
(Hegel, *Philosophy of Right*, §258)

This chapter is the first draft of a more ambitious project which aims to examine and discuss the relations between citizenship and moral individuality as seen within both the liberal context and the French Republican tradition. Very few political theories would deny the link between citizenship and moral beliefs and attitudes that make up the individual's moral individuality, and follow Machiavelli in saying that political *virtú* is totally distinct from—and even opposed to—the personal virtues that individuals normally develop among family and friends. Most would recognize that the virtues of the citizen proceed from or interact with the ideals of the moral individual and the corresponding dialogical competences (Habermas, Scanlon) that are fashioned within the non-political sphere, but still color the political realm. Indeed, there exist many possible links: citizenship can be seen as a protection for the flourishing of moral individuality and of moral development in the sense of both Rousseau and Mill; or as a constraint on individual freedom and justice which should be kept as limited as possible, as in the libertarian view of the minimal state; or it can be seen as the ultimate expression of moral excellence and virtue, as it is in Aristotle's conception of man as a political animal.

Because this chapter is concerned mostly with the question of the stability of democratic societies, it will question a major assumption in contemporary political theory that connects citizenship to moral individuality, in the sense that stability might be secured not only by the virtues of democratic and just institutions—as Rousseau and Kant thought when talking about "just institutions being fit for ruling even devils"—but also by the impact, through citizenship, of the 'good' of democracy on the development of moral individuality. This is the ground where allegiances and attachments to democracy and to democratic values will be formed by 'good' citizens in the long run. This belief is central to a theory such as the political liberalism of John Rawls, anxious as it is to secure the stability of democratic regimes at a time when modern societies are more likely than not to generate very little agreement on a common and shared good, and when the appeal of democracies will be based on their making few or virtually no coercive demands on individuals. The vulnerability of such a basis for a social and political contract has long been obvious for the critics of liberalism in general, and of Rawls in particular. But, curiously enough, these critics—such as those emerging from the French Republican tradition and from its reaction to Rawls (Ricoeur, and so on)—use similar individualistic arguments when they want to demonstrate why we should support democratic institutions and practices. The vocabulary of the 'good' of citizenship for individuals is similar: the self-respect and dignity of the citizen are the prize for our renouncing our particular will in favor of the general will.

My thesis, following Will Kymlicka's suggestive analysis in his latest book, *Multicultural Citizenship*, is that the poverty of this conception of moral individuality makes it impossible to ground any kind of serious commitment to democracy—a difficulty well underlined by the communitarian critique, especially that of Michael Sandel—but that this should not lead us to abandon altogether an individualistic legitimation of the good polity. What is required in particular is a notion of self-identity—such as narrative identity in Ricoeur's sense—that is rich enough to explain commitments and responsibilities towards the good polity in the long term and to be the source of new specific rights, without necessarily leading to the affirmation of a common good. When such a notion is combined with the idea of democratic citizenship, with a full list of rights and liberties and the conditions of their fair value, then it is clear that an individualistic justification for the good polity does not need to be as fragile and weak as it is in the different versions of liberalism mentioned above.

The 'Good' of Citizenship

The main features of democracies are their appeal to the good of the individual (Pettit and Hamlin) as a basis for legitimation and as an alternative to coercion, and the vulnerability of such a basis when faced not only with conflicts, but with the simple task of surviving the lack of individual commitment and participation in democratic politics. In other words, it is the individualistic dimension of democratic authority which makes it so vulnerable and, sometimes, indefensible—what Pettit and Hamlin have aptly referred to as "the principle of individual relevance" (Pettit and Hamlin, 1989, 8). This is the principle that brings moral individuality into the justification and stabilization process of democratic institutions and practices in contrast to the appeal to authority, tradition, or coercion (Max Weber). What kind of citizens, then, would the members of the political association have to be in order to secure its survival if no coercion, beyond that of the law, is to be exerted? Would they not have to be angels of some kind? What is the source of their commitment to democratic institutions, especially when, as Rousseau said, the general will may quite often go against their particular will and their particular interests? Obviously the answers will differ according to the degree and kind of liberalism we are discussing. My thesis is that, on the whole, a conception of moral individuality and of the 'good' effects that citizenship has on it is necessarily presupposed in the argument for democracy but that, generally, it is not scrutinized closely enough to provide a satisfactory explanation for this moral commitment to democracy.

Let us distinguish three instances of liberal legitimation and see how they share an appeal to the moral stance that defines citizenship.

(i) First, we have the civic republican version, inspired by Rousseau and still alive in the contemporary French political context. What is gained from democratic equality is, for Rousseau, a heroic sense of dignity; the people that once were subjected to a master, however benevolent and peaceful, are now sovereign and freed from the infamy of servility. The prize conquered by the equal rights of citizenship is the freedom to say no, to be oneself, the protection of one's autonomy and of the self-respect that goes within it, in other words, the moral standing implied by the possession of political power and the exercise of basic liberties and rights. Let us use a contemporary phrase and call it 'empowerment'. Rousseau's view is fairly extreme in the sense that the acquisition of sovereignty by people is enough to change human nature and, out of a selfish and limited animal, to make a sociable and rational being (Rousseau). Moral individuality is *created* by citizenship and there is no way back to a non-political moral nature, as was still possible for Locke. The Republic is the mother of virtue, the cure for private vices, and it is on civic virtues that the moral character of the individual can be established.

(ii) Apparently a long way from this heroic vision of the individual moral commitment to democracy, we find the instrumental–utilitarian conception of the good polity. The polity is good if, and only if, it can be proved that the welfare of the individual has been improved, or even maximized. We can talk here of the "good in people" that is brought out by the good polity (Pettit and Hamlin, 1989, 8), which implies that this good is not necessarily what the people themselves would have chosen. But next to this illiberal view of utilitarianism is Mill's version where individual welfare includes moral flourishing and the development of virtues, both personal and political. The utility principle is an overall guide: it points to both material and moral welfare. This was made clear by Mill in his defense of representative government as a means to allow the flourishing of a creative individuality and to protect it from the tyranny of public opinion. The system of rights and liberties is instrumental in the creation of a new individual, free from fear and servility. The utilitarians are, then, very close to the Romantic vision of this new moral individuality and the commitment to democracy is a commitment to self-realization, but not in the extreme fashion described by Rousseau. We have now moved from the liberty of the Ancients to the liberty of the Moderns.

(iii) The Rawlsian answer equally promises self-respect in terms of a 'primary good' that a just and well-ordered society promises its members (Rawls, 1971, §67). The allegiance of the citizen is gained when he discovers the 'good' of the principles of justice and of the well-ordered society, a good so attractive that it neutralizes his anti-social, egoistic instincts, and that is conducive to moral behavior. The citizen of a well-ordered society sees himself and the other citizens as moral persons in the Kantian sense, that is, as ends in themselves who are worth respecting. In that sense, self-respect is a primary good, the social conditions of which the second principle of justice should secure. It is not enough, for Rawls, to affirm the liberal principle of equality of opportunity for all; the 'fair' value of the basic rights and liberties is a necessary complement, if citizenship is to have moral standing. It is on the strength of this recognition of the equal worth of each member's rights that democratic institutions can hope to survive in the long term. But the 'fairness' of the well-ordered society is attractive only as long as it produces individuals with a corresponding sense of justice, as the third part of *A Theory of Justice* shows. And, in the end, for Rawls the Kantian argument seems to be the strongest: once we have the desire to express our 'intelligible character' of autonomous rational beings and we recognize that, as moral persons, we have higher-order interests, the conflict between justice and first-order interests disappears, since it will be contradictory to will to be a moral person and not to accept the necessary constraints of justice.

By contrast to these three liberal positions on the 'good' of citizenship, the communitarian critique tends to put the emphasis on the 'good' of membership in smaller communities and to see citizenship at the level of the nation-state as an empty legalistic and abstract shell. It therefore rejects the possibility of a strictly individualistic legitimation of democracy. The appeal of democratic societies has to be based on their ability to promote and respect sub-national communities—whether traditional or not, or religious or not—so that each nurture a common good, and, in the end, the larger society should be equally anxious to show its attachment to a common unifying good if it wants to create a sense of belonging and recognition among its members. But even if the possibility of state intervention in reinforcing people's allegiance to their constitutive ends remains a real threat and makes communitarian ideas highly questionable for liberals, the communitarians have had the merit of pointing to a basic weakness in a liberal justification for democracy: that is, in its conception of moral individuality and in its understanding of the concept of self-respect.

Moral Individuality and Cultural Membership

A caricature of the communitarian critique would say that liberals are still prisoners of the Enlightenment and of an abstract and ahistorical conception of the self—a characterization which is true but fairly inadequate. We cannot simply turn to a historical vision of a socially determined individual with no say in his institutions and abandon liberalism altogether. If we seriously want to take the communitarian critique into account and still value individual autonomy, as it is expressed in the ideal of a liberal democracy, we have to enrich, not to reject, the conceptions of moral individuality implied in the three versions of liberalism mentioned above. We have to analyze the moral sentiments and the dialogical competences at work in the allegiance to democracy and show how much more complex they are than the simple notions of self-respect, dignity, or awareness of one's own worth. I now turn to that point.

Rousseau, in both the *Discourses* and the *Social Contract*, gives us the version with probably the strongest contrast between the 'good' of citizenship and the evils of the private man—between the civil society and the Republic. His concept of moral individuality is based on its instant creation through the purifying asceticism of the social contract as the act of birth of a new virtuous man. He gives no real explanation for this instant transformation, except the necessity of what Hume called the "circumstances of justice" and of survival, which explains the creation of society in general, not the particular impact of democracy. There is no psychological continuity, no transformation from within because—for him as for the Enlightenment in general—man as a progressive being is the product of experience and education, of the institutional context. The political institutions, the new context created by equal rights, will be enough to create this new moral individuality. The only explanation that he gives for the birth of a moral individuality where previously only interests and egoism ruled, is of a metaphysical nature: the essence of man is freedom and this sacred spark had been nearly extinguished. Now, "without freedom of the will, there is no morality in action" (Rousseau, *Social Contract*, I, 5). The moral commitment to democracy is, then, of a metaphysical and quasi-religious nature: it is the attachment to our rediscovered true essence which has long been hidden behind the monstrosities and deformities of social conventions, as was the case for Glaucus's statue (*Second Discourse*). It is thus fascinating to find an echo of this passionate longing for a 'true self' in contemporary secular France and its justification of the role of the state in educating the citizen.

The role of the state school system in France has undoubtedly been that of an instrument of conversion, of shaping the mentality and the instincts of ordinary people in order to produce 'good citizens', endowed with a moral individuality, a sense of the common good, and of their own responsibility to it. One should pause here and reflect on a striking feature of the Republican ideal, namely the persistent denunciation, in the name of the citizen, of the 'private' corrupted individual or, in Rousseauian terms, of the tension between the evils of the particular will and the 'good' of the general will. The meaning of this conflict can be interpreted in two ways, one philosophical, the other more cultural and historical (which shows that the real difficulty in liberal thought is not where the communitarians see it, for example, in the lack of historical content, but in the hidden illiberal use of this history). At a philosophical—or ideological?— level, this conflict might be understood, in Platonic terms, as the conflict between appearances and sense, and it does not come as a surprise that, in the—compulsory—teaching of philosophy in school, the central feature is always the Platonic Myth of the Cave and of the conversion of the human soul to truth. The aim is to enlighten the ordinary person as to his true nature, and to help him renounce the immediate pleasures and activities of his private pursuits on behalf of his higher interests, those of the sons and daughters of the Republic. Here is what Jacques Muglioni, Chief Inspector of Secondary Schools, wrote in 1993 in a paper entitled 'The Republic and the School': "A human being, characterized by his personal allegiances, identifying himself with particular groups, with collective or individual interests, cannot be a good citizen since *a good citizen, first and foremost, does not belong to anyone*" (my emphasis).[1] And he goes on to say, "but is it the citizen that makes the Republic that makes the citizen? The reciprocal link is only made possible by the school, over and beyond any respect for family, work or community links, even for traditions, however essential they may be. The school is at the service neither of the family nor of the employers. Its only function is to shape the mind, without any consideration for interests or beliefs and to bring it to its highest level of freedom".

There is a lot to comment on here. Beyond the totalitarian tone—"the School has thus an essential link with truth" (p. 77)—one should recognize the will to create a new type of human being, the *citizen*, that is, someone who is no longer a particular individual, devoted to particular pursuits. And here we have the second interpretation of Rousseau's conception. This new type of human being is a citizen, that is, a Frenchman, no longer an Alsatian, a Breton, or a Provençal, no longer alienated by his allegiance to particular sub-national communities. The only context in which moral individuality can develop is that of the unity of the nation. The content of citizenship is the membership of the national community and its reward is national pride and patriotism. What seemed, at first, to be an abstract basis for a commitment to democracy is in fact the very powerful attraction to a tradition and to a historical linguistic community of which one is proud. One learns how to become French through the study of the great writers and figures of the past, not through Socratic self-discovery. This explains why, in the very syllabus of the schools and in the methods of teaching, the emphasis is on general knowledge, '*culture générale*', rather than on personal experience and curiosity, because the latter would be likely to lead to diversity, heterogeneity, anarchy, perhaps, but in any case to a challenge to the forces of unification. It says a lot about the ideology of emancipation according to the Republic that the 'Founding Fathers' of the school system, the most famous of whom was Jules Ferry, should be disciples of Auguste Comte, not of John Stuart Mill! [2] One might be tempted to see the Republic as a totalitarian entity, the enemy of freedom, whereas it has been and still is a political instrument of integration within a civic, not an ethnic nation, where citizenship is the substitute for cultural homogeneity. One is not born French, one becomes French, to paraphrase Simone de Beauvoir. The birth of a democratic community and allegiance to it are made possible by a seemingly totalitarian ideology where the individual seems to be crushed, when in fact it is his local parochial attachments that are repudiated.

The question, then, is: Can there be an allegiance based on the acceptance of these parochial attachments, or does one necessarily have to distance oneself from them to become a citizen of a democracy?

The answer for both Mill, in *Representative Government*, and for the early Rawls, is "no", and they both side with Rousseau and the Republican ideal, even if they express their views in less cryptic language than that of the general will. The civic nation provides the concept *par excellence* for the development of moral individuality, because it is free from the imposition of a shared common good and allows for the possibility of a personal search for the truth and the development of our dialogical competences. This is a personal but troubled and difficult process, whereas parochial local allegiances, in imposing a common good, limit personal autonomy and anxieties. Moral individuality, for Mill as for Rawls, is possibly an obstacle to smooth integration, as it means that we want to live our lives from within and, consequently, we ask to be free to question our beliefs. The kinds of allegiance based on that type of individuality are, by their very essence, reflective, which the communitarians see as a dissolving and sterile attitude (an echo of Hegel's analysis in the *Phenome-*

nology of Mind of 'pure insight' or *Gedanke*). This individuality has been interpreted by Michael Sandel as a "disencumbered self", deprived of any constitutive attachments to its ends. Such an interpretation is mistaken in that autonomy does not mean the absence of given norms or constraints but the possibility of their critical appraisal, in contrast to heteronomy. When both Mill and Rawls, following Kant—and Max Weber—insist on the ability to detach oneself from one's own beliefs and to act upon principles, not according to authority or group pressure, and that this is the hallmark of moral individuality and responsibility, they do not deny the existence of this given context of shared beliefs. This is crucial for the making of the civil nation. If beliefs were constitutive, it would make it impossible to create a political association respectful of both diversity and freedom. The only viable political unity would be one based on a homogenous cultural, religious, and linguistic reality, that of the 'ethnic nation' (Anderson). Why, for instance, are fundamentalist Christians traditionally seen as bad citizens and the Church as a threat to the state from which it would be separated? Because those Christians will always put their beliefs first, far beyond the common welfare as envisaged by the state in the law; for instance, they will never question their beliefs as they are constitutive for their identity, much more than their membership of the nation-state and their citizenship. The point made by liberal thinkers, following Rousseau's intuition, is that the nature of the nation-state as a political association or community is radically different from the nature of the sub-national communities. Rousseau went much further in saying that these communities are obstacles to both the unity of the 'good' polity and the emergence of moral individuality. They are based on constitutive beliefs in a common good. The nation is, in contrast, a community of free and equal citizens who do not necessarily share the same particular good even if they share a common history and 'societal culture'—a nuance which is essential here.

Now, the difficulty is that in stressing the legalistic and abstract definition of citizenship as equality of basic rights and freedoms, liberals seem to forget that citizenship also means membership in a community, albeit not a 'natural' or given ethnic community, but a 'chosen' community (Renan: "the nation is a daily plebiscite"). In the case of Rousseau, the key to the understanding of the general will is the civic nation. The same is true of Mill's individualism when he shows that the sort of freedom and equality that matters exists only within the limits of one's own nationality or 'societal culture', to use Will Kymlicka's expression (Kymlicka, 1995, 76–80). In the case of Rawls, this is, of course, much clearer in his second work, *Political Liberalism*. But, unfortunately, Rawls confuses his reader when he says that the citizen *is* the moral in the Kantian sense. What he should have said is that the respect commanded by citizenship is partly respect for its being a right-bearer, for equality and freedom, partly for its being part of a larger and just society that recognizes these rights and principles of justice within a historical tradition. Failing that, Rawls is placed in Habermas's extremely difficult situation of having to defend an allegiance to democracy on the basis of a 'constitutional patriotism' with no 'mother country' or, even worse, no '*Vaterland*', to speak of.

What is lacking, then, in the liberal concept of moral individuality, as expressed in the legitimation of the 'good' of democracy, is a notion of narrative identity which leads naturally to incorporating the historical dimension of citizenship instead of treating it as an enemy within. Narrative identity can mean that we can choose to identify with particular values, within a tradition and a context, making it our own through our narrative powers, but also modifying these identifications. (An excellent example of this is the narrative identity to be found in Alain Finkelkraut's *Le juif imaginaire*. It should be added in this case that we have to know who is telling the story and, in the case of Finkelkraut, that he rebelled against the 'official' narrative told by the family and the Jewish community it belonged to, and replaced it with a new personal narrative, hence his 'salvation' through literature). We are not instant beings, we possess a kind of 'sameness'—although that is not, of course, pure self-identity, neither is it total discontinuity and atomization. As Ricoeur says in his book *Soi-même comme un autre* we should distinguish between identity as *idem*, strict sameness, and identity as *ipse* or selfhood (Ricoeur, 1992, 140). A narrative concept of personal identity, says Ricoeur, allows us to overcome the contradictions between concordances and discordances, identity and diversity in our character, by moving from the level of the character itself to the level of the narratives it is part of: "it is the identity in the story that makes the identity of the character" (Ricoeur, 1992, 175). The possibility of articulating the many distinct events that make up a life into a narrative is central to moral individuality. This possibility rests on the existence of what MacIntyre calls the 'idea of a tradition' which allows for 'the unity of a human life' in a narrative mode (MacIntyre, 1984, *After Virtue*, chapter 15). Ricoeur recognizes the affinities of his own position with that of MacIntyre (Ricoeur, 1992, 187–88) and it would be interesting to explore further the relation between the two.

To return to citizenship, we now see more clearly how and why it cannot be separated from patriotism, and how the attachment to democracy is the attachment to a community, a history, a culture. In the same way, if we take the concepts of respect, self-respect, and dignity, these have no real meaning unless they relate to a social context of recognition and valuation, the sphere of 'public reason' for Rawls, where we could exercise our dialogical competences. The dignity of the citizen cannot be separated from the pride of being the member of a nation, involving not only shared beliefs, but also institutions (like the American Constitution, the French Declaration of the Rights of Man, or the German Basic Law, and so on) and common respected practices. Self-respect, the social conditions of which are secured by the principles of justice, is, equally, inseparable from self-esteem, from the individuals' mutual recognition of their own worth within their own community of justification and meaning, by reference to shared understandings. In conclusion, we should say that our moral individuality, understood in narrative terms, values cultural membership not as a constitutive good, but, to use Kymlicka's expression, as "a meaningful context of choice". Cultural membership within a nation, because the nation lies outside the normative sphere of a common good (Tamir), or a comprehensive doctrine (Rawls), provides this favorable context. In the liberal concept of democracy, the civic nation allows for a diversity of goals and pursuits within a secure framework of rights and liberties, and "provides a secure foundation for individual autonomy and self-identity" (Kymlicka, 1995, 105).

The Rights of Cultural Membership

If we can accept that an individualistic foundation for the justification and stability of democracy can be enriched and understood in narrative and not only in instrumental terms; if we can follow Kymlicka and Tamir and see cultural membership not as an obstacle, but as a vector of liberal citizenship; it remains to be seen what sort of rights and institutions best embody this recognition within the political realm itself. In other words, should they be specific rights of cultural membership, specific protection of the valuable context of choice it represents, notwithstanding the reluctance of states to recognize its importance? How can the necessary legal and political space be created for a moral individuality to develop that is autonomous, but not self-created *ex nihilo*?

The failure, for the moment, of both the Republican tradition and the liberal concept of justice to generate policies congenial to cultural diversity should not be seen as a final failure. If we look at the historical process that leads from the Declaration of the Rights of Man and the Citizen, in 1789, through the 1848 Revolution in France, to the recognition of the economic and social rights of the worker in the 1948 Universal Declaration of the UNO, there is no reason why new rights should not be added to the list, allowing for new social and historical conditions to be taken into account. Rights being both the condition and the result of political 'empowerment', we cannot hope that the process will be struggle-free. A first stage, before new rights are identified and enacted, is that of the socio-economic struggle. The quest for inclusion is, first, the search for better living conditions and this is where attachments and commitments to democracy are first created, where new bonds are forged. Integration through citizenship has been a powerful vector of social mobility and modernization in the case of France. In that sense, previous rights—to employment, education, culture, knowledge—can be given a new meaning and might open the way to the fulfillment of the needs of moral individuality.

Such a development might be unsatisfactory. Too often democratization is mostly synonymous with social mobility, not with the acquisition of moral dignity and responsibility. An example of such a process has been that of the Frenchification of the peasantry through the workings of the education system and the teaching of the French language. Why, for instance, did the people of Alsace, at the turn of the century, feel so strongly attached to France even though their cultural, ethnic identities and attachments were much more obviously German than French? One reason is that the equal citizenship granted to them by the Republic gave them wider possibilities, opened up for them more opportunities—learning, social prospects, employment, and so on—than if they had remained one of the many provinces of the German Empire. The appeals of modern citizenship counted much more for the majority of people than the protection of a second-rate ethnic identity in an authoritarian empire. The same could be said to a lesser extent of peasants from Brittany, central France, and so on, for whom assimilation through the acquisition of the French language has meant an enormous gain, if only from the point of view of social mobility. One should, then, never underestimate the appeal of assimilation when it means a wider range of basic rights and freedoms, including the freedom to cultivate one's own identity within the framework and constraints of citizenship. We saw earlier that one of the main benefits of integration, according to the French concept of the nation, has been education and the social value attached to citizenship. But does this really make up for the loss of local identities and attachments in the name of access to a new social status and security? What is not present in the idea of the Republic is the moral value of this new-found dignity. The French story has been more one of social mobility, social status acquired through citizenship, than one of personal, moral development. The Republican model, inspired by Greek and Latin antiquity, loves to talk about civic virtues and the value of political participation as the source of moral dignity. But the reality is very different.

The loss of parochial identities and the politics of assimilation have been resented mostly when the content of citizenship has become thinner, when the value of fundamental rights has been eroded, first in their socio-economic dimension (access to education, employment, fair wages, and so on) as in the contemporary case of North African immigrants in France.

It is when the process of assimilation is forced upon the people without the recognition of the different forms of cultural diversity and without the compensation of full citizenship that things go wrong. We should, by contrast, call for differentiated processes of integration. This is why Kymlicka is right to draw a central distinction between two very different forms of cultural pluralism: the case of multinational states, as in France when Algeria was not only a colony, but a '*département*', and when an independent entity was forcefully integrated into the mother country; and the case of polyethnic states that result from immigration and where the quest for inclusion and assimilation is much stronger. Consequently, if new rights should be added and if political life should be modified to accommodate them, three different types of rights should be granted in a differentiated manner. Rights of self-government and federalism could be an answer in the case of a multinational state, whereas polyethnic rights should be an answer to secure a transition between first-generation immigration and full integration. Polyethnic rights are the rights of the individual to be granted legal protection and financial support and solidarity in the exercise of his religious, linguistic, and cultural practices, in the strengthening of the corresponding institutions as long as they are congruent with the principles of justice and with the law of the land. They are the answer to the demands of a narrative identity that could develop within the framework of the nation-state without threatening its unity, and even contribute to it in a positive way. Cultures are never-ending processes of invention and adaptation, as are individual narratives, and minority rights are there to shape and orientate these complex processes, not to fossilize them. Special representation rights might, by contrast, be a threat to the unity of the nation, if they were given permanent status.

For the time being, French legislation has been unable to recognize the need for the protection of minority cultures and the usefulness of such rights to strengthen the attachment of minorities to the Republic. In Rousseauian terms, any diversity is still seen as a threat to the unity of the nation. But, one might ask, if that was the case at the time of the French Revolution, after two centuries of strong state intervention, is the national identity still in danger of being overwhelmed by new waves of immigration? Obviously, the reasons why there is such a reluctance are very diverse and not necessarily acceptable. But, even if a compromise could be found, even if immigrant children of non-Christian origin were provided with the kind of education that they need to become 'good' French citizens and yet to keep in touch with their traditions if they wish to—as has been the case with all previous immigrations in France of Christian or Jewish origin—distinctions should be made within the sphere of minority- or group-differentiated rights: they should always be rights of the individual; they should be conducive to integration in the long run and not a source of division and hostility. This is why the process cannot be hastened and existing rights should be used to their full potential, while using the argument of the needs of moral individuality presented here, rather than the argument based on diversity as such and the so-called fact of pluralism that make Rawls's solution so unconvincing.

Conclusion

The task of political philosophy is to provide arguments and to make conceptual distinctions where previous confusions could hamper legitimate policies or courses of action. It has, therefore, a strong normative dimension. We have examined the ways in which a defense of democratic institutions, of a well-ordered society in the sense of Rawls, desperately needs to be enriched by a narrative concept of moral individuality that allows for both the autonomy and the diagnostic dimensions of personal development. This is not an easy position. Communitarian critiques of liberalism are very attractive, as they echo the urge of sub-national communities to be respected and the recognition that the unity of the larger society is a destructive myth, that we should reconcile ourselves to the conflictual nature of so many human ends, in the sense of Isaiah Berlin's value-pluralism. Still, the task remains to reconcile diversity with freedom on the basis of sound arguments.

Bibliography

Anderson, Benedict. 1991. *Imagined Communities: Reflection on the Origin and Spread of Nationalism*. London: Verso.

Finkelkraut, Alain. 1994. *Imaginary Jew (Le juif imaginaire)*. Lincoln, Nebraska: University of Nebraska Press.

Hamlin, Alan, and Philip Pettit. 1989. 'Deliberation and Democratic Legitimacy', in *The Good Polity: Normative Analysis of the State*. Oxford/New York: Blackwell.

Hegel, G.F.W. 1967. *The Phenomenology of Mind*, trans. by J.B. Baillie. New York: Harper and Row.

———. 1942. *Philosophy of Right*, trans. by T.M. Knox. Oxford: Clarendon Press.

Kymlicka, Will. 1995. *Multicultural Citizenship*. Oxford: Clarendon Press.

MacIntyre, Alasdair. 1984. *After Virtue*. South Bend, Indiana: Notre Dame University Press.

Mill, John Stuart. 1975. *Considerations on Representative Government*. Oxford: Oxford University Press.

Rawls, John. 1971. *A Theory of Justice*. Cambridge, Massachusetts: Harvard University Press.

———. 1993. *Political Liberalism*. New York: Columbia University Press.

Ricoeur, Paul. 1992. *Oneself as Another*. Chicago: University of Chicago Press.

Sandel, Michael. 1982. *Liberalism and the Limits of Justice*. Cambridge: Cambridge University Press.

Weber, Max. 1968. *The Theory of Social and Economic Organization*. New York: The Free Press.

Notes

1 J. Muglioni, 'La république et l'école', *Philosophie politique*, No.4 (Paris: Presses Universitaires de France, 1993), p. 75.

2 See Blandine Kriegel, *L'identité française* (Paris: Editions Tierce, 1985), p. 84, and the reference book on the question by Claude Nicolet, *L'idée républicaine en France* (Paris: Gallimard, 1982).

Liberal Values, Liberal Guilt, and the Distaste for Politics

JOHN CROWLEY

What We Mean by Liberalism

In order to judge the possible relevance of liberalism to the contemporary world, we need at least some agreement on what we mean when we use the word or refer to it. The difficulties involved in doing so are notorious. Etymologically, liberalism is defined by its primary concern with liberty. Historically, such concern is a fair summary of what it has been in its various manifestations, but also a very thin one. Concern for liberty has meant different things in different times and places, partly because of the concrete requirements of politics, partly because of the conceptual instability of the very notion of freedom. Liberty has been defended against a wide variety of threats: absolute monarchy, established religion, the tyranny of the majority, socialism, fascism, communism, state bureaucracy, communalism, consumerism. The defenses all have some claim to be 'liberal', yet may differ sharply from each other. Furthermore, even if local variations in political liberalism could be reconciled philosophically, a profound conceptual difficulty remains. Am I free when I do what I want, or does the answer depend on what I want and why I want it? The conflict between 'positive' and 'negative' conceptions of freedom (to use Berlin's widely followed distinction) is insoluble (Berlin, 1969, 118–72)—as Berlin stresses, the political implications of 'positive' conceptions of freedom may be deleterious, but its value remains. Putting it very crudely: unless one has a very optimistic view of human nature, it is hard to see why what people want (to do) should necessarily be worthy of respect; but conversely, it is hard to see how any external standard of worthiness could be compatible with freedom. Ultimately, as Berlin underlines, attempts to escape from the dilemma (from Kant onwards) merely restate it more starkly. The ambivalence within liberty can be removed only by equating liberty with necessity—which means that it cannot be removed at all.

To define liberty primarily by reference to the liberal tradition is thus an extremely difficult task. Fortunately it is not the only available, or the most appropriate, approach. This chapter will work with a generic conception of liberalism (concern with liberty), checking that it is consistent with parts at least of the liberal tradition, but making no attempt to resolve all the conflicts within it. There is no insuperable difficulty in identifying core liberal values. Since we live in a world that can be regarded as liberal in only the crudest sense—as involving approximately free markets—a critical liberal perspective should be fairly easy to formulate. Indeed, liberalism has historically been characterized by its critical edge—in other words it is defined primarily by the enemies it defines for itself. Yet contemporary liberalism seems timid. The second section of the chapter will suggest that this is not accidental, but related to structural features of liberalism and to the logic of its historical development. Finally, the third section will explore the possible content and relevance of a revived critical liberalism.

The Liberalism of Our Time

Contemporary liberalism is, on the whole, philosophical rather than political. For the purposes of locating and explicating the liberal tradition, this can be misleading. Thus, a major concern in recent theoretical discussions has been the apparently arcane question of whether liberalism is (or should be), in the jargon made familiar by John Rawls,[1] a 'comprehensive conception of the good'. Rawls's point, shared by many other writers,[2] is that liberalism has a core commitment to pluralism, which is inconsistent with any idea of organizing society in order to promote a specific hierarchy of values, even liberal values. Consistency therefore requires that liberals should defend liberalism not substantively but as a second-order political principle of 'neutrality', for public purposes, between conceptions of the good (including liberalism stricto sensu, 'comprehensive liberalism' in Rawls's sense). The reasons for the argument, which is mainly a response to communitarian criticism, will be discussed later. Suffice it to say at this stage that in the core liberal tradition the distinction between 'comprehensive' and 'political' liberalism is meaningless.

It is uncontroversial to say that religion is at the heart of the historical development of liberalism.[3] From the wars of religion of the sixteenth and seventeenth centuries, at least in countries (notably England and the Netherlands) where they produced no clear winner, came the idea of toleration. However offensive a subject's beliefs may have been, eliminating them was less important than keeping the civil peace.[4] To put it more simply: orthodoxy was no longer worth killing for. From the mid-eighteenth century, the questioning of religious doctrine itself (as distinct from its political implications), by applying to it forms of reasoning and standards of proof derived from natural science, changed the character and the consequences of toleration. Instead of being merely politic, it was increasingly seen as intellectually necessary. No truth was ever definitive, and no view, even the most eccentric, unworthy of the opportunity to challenge received wisdom. This did not lead to relativism, however, because of the unquestioned assumption of progress and of the universal application of experimental method. The clash of ideas would produce not chaos but the gradual improvement of human knowledge.[5] In this sense, freedom of thought and of speech is the historical core of liberalism, viewed both as a set of institutions and as an 'outlook' (Barry, 1991a). It also points clearly, in the way it cuts across subsequent distinctions between 'positive' and 'negative' and between 'political' and 'comprehensive', to important contemporary weaknesses of liberalism. Freedom of thought and speech is in the first instance defined negatively. It is freedom from censorship, from compulsory belief, from the constraints of orthodoxy—freedom, in a word, from interfering governments and ecclesiastical authorities. It thus derives less from institutions than from the absence of repressive institutions. Its enemies are prior consent for oral or written pronouncements and punishment for views judged undesirable and, in practice, the insidious restrictions found in countries that pay lip-service to it: discriminatory taxation, limited availability of paper, broad interpretations of libel, use of career incentives to encourage orthodoxy, and so on. By analogy with speech (an analogy sometimes judicially explicit, as in the US) a wide variety of actions also require, in the liberal view, freedom to develop: current issues of sexual behavior and life-style options show the continuing relevance of this agenda.

There are thus in essence three reasons why people should, prima facie, be free to think and do whatever they want. First, there is no external standard of truth (or 'good') by which their choices could be shown to be 'wrong'—not because in some abstract sense truth does not exist but because any truth judgment is necessarily a judgment by someone, who by assumption can have no privileged claim to knowledge. Secondly, no one can in fact, or is entitled morally, to judge consistency between another person's acts and interests. Even paternalistic concern for others is unjustifiable (and, after all, 'paternalistic', generally regarded as derogatory, is only the same as 'fatherly'). Reasons for interference may be advanced, but they must be based on quite different considerations. Finally, generally speaking, the consequences of free thought and action are desirable, as contributing to the progress of human understanding.

The connection between the economic and political aspects of liberalism (as constituted historically) is often regarded as accidental. The previous paragraph shows, however, that Barry's quip that "libertarianism [he has in mind the thought of Hayek, Friedman, Nozick and others] has been well defined as the form taken by liberalism as common sense asymptotically approaches zero" is unjustified (Barry, 1991b, 278). Liberalism provides a strong prima facie case for letting human activity develop. The need to set limits arises from the logic of human interaction: each person's actions affect everyone else's options, and freedom can therefore be threatened not just by constituted authorities but by the deliberate or intended consequences of freedom itself. The so-called harm principle formulated by Mill has been very widely accepted, at least in general terms: society (not the state) is justified in interfering in individual freedom only to prevent harm to others. Forbidding me from killing my neighbor is an infringement of liberty that, on grounds of reciprocity, I should reasonably be expected to accept; and even if I do not, the ban is justifiable as the condition of my neighbor's liberty. While the second reason logically makes the first redundant, the characteristic liberal view is that the two are in fact mutually supportive. Applying the harm principle to the workings of the economy is exceedingly difficult. As Marx recognized and repeatedly stressed, there is a profound and genuine sense in which the free market is free. If one accepts that, broadly speaking, it provides benefits for all involved (it is superior in terms of Rawls's 'difference principle' to other, non-market, forms of economic organization), it would be necessary to identify within it specific harmful transactions. Yet, precisely because a market economy forms an integrated whole, any attempt to isolate a single transaction would be meaningless. In this sense, and at this very crude level, both Marx and Hayek are correct that liberalism and the free market are inseparably linked, and that criticism of one entails criticism of the other. There are of course a number of significant complications, and it is not impossible to formulate a liberal critique of free-market economics, on condition that one regards serious inequalities of economic power (which make the idea of economic 'freedom' meaningless for many economic agents) as produced outside the market, and reflected by it, rather than being exclusively economic in origin. This is not a straightforward task.

Banishing tyranny is an important achievement. Preventing its return is more significant still. There are two ways in principle to entrench freedom: either by ensuring that all rulers be virtuous lovers of freedom, or by ensuring that no ruler, however vicious, could become a tyrant. The political institutions of liberalism embody a clear choice between these alternatives. Rousseau famously asked whether it is possible for the people to govern itself badly, and recorded his emphatically negative answer (Rousseau, *Du contrat social*, II, 12). The French Revolution—often viewed (with questionable historical justification) as the implementation of Rousseau's ideas—provided in the eyes of most liberals conclusive evidence that he was wrong. However repugnant it may be to believers in the perfectibility of human nature, the people *can* govern itself badly. From Tocqueville to Mill and to Schumpeter, the distrust of popular sovereignty runs through liberal thought. In principle, it would be possible for a liberal to fall back on non-democratic procedures for the selection of virtuous rulers.[6] But the claim that any identifiable sub-set of the people could be relied upon to be what the people as a whole cannot be is implausible. Certainly the widely shared liberal view is that prevention of tyranny should be independent of rulers' personal qualities. Thus, because the 'people'—however defined—can govern itself badly, institutions should be designed not to implement sovereignty but to produce good government. In principle, as Marx (following Hegel) powerfully stressed, this is incoherent. In Locke, the non-political basis for politics is unambiguous and coherent: natural law—that is, the will of God—which defines both the purpose and the limits of government.[7] However, once liberalism had come into conflict with the idea of religion (and not simply with established religion), this was no longer tenable. Unless the purpose and limits of politics can be defined within politics itself, immanently, we are left simply with the subjection of politics to the spuriously 'natural' facts of civil society (in fact the morally arbitrary distribution of property that came out of the collapse of the *ancien régime*).[8] Ultimately, liberalism is just a sham: limits to politics imposed purely to prop up pre-political power relations, to prevent politics from interfering with them. Liberalism has consistently refused to accept the force of this argument. As recent contributions from Hayek and Nozick, among others, underline, the debate is not simply a nineteenth-century one. The reasons adduced by liberals are important, and are intimately linked with ignoring the positive–negative and political–comprehensive distinctions now taken for granted in the literature.

The idea can be stated quite simply. History is the development of human potential, and since the highest standard of human excellence is essentially unchanged since antiquity (nineteenth-century liberals were classically trained), development can only mean the broadening and deepening—in a word, the democratization—of human development. Liberals necessarily become pragmatic elitists, not because anyone is by nature better than anyone else, but because some have not yet fully developed.[9] Hence the centrality of education in liberalism. As a consequence, negative freedom is inseparably positive freedom, in the sense that the removal of constraints is a necessary and sufficient condition for human flourishing. Similarly, political liberalism is inseparably comprehensive liberalism. The system of institutions that prevents any dogma (including public opinion) from imposing itself on society is valuable not so much per se as because it is the condition for human flourishing—which is the gradual diffusion of enlightenment. Note that this is not the assumption of a single, identifiable truth that will over time impose itself hegemonically. Mill is very explicit that liberalism enjoins and is based on pluralism. However, pluralism is not universally permissive: truth is necessarily tentative, but error is certain; and erroneous beliefs can only be held by people who are ignorant (for which the remedy is education) or manipulated (for which the remedy is free competition of ideas).

All this can be summarized in one phrase: civil society. Philosophically, although some genuine and important liberals have been Hegelians (Green, Hobhouse, Croce, for instance), this is equivalent to a refusal to take Hegel seriously. Civil society requires regulation: concentrations of power and ignorance (which are two sides of the same coin) must be dissolved and diffused in the name of liberalism itself. What it does not require is radical restructuring by the operation of sovereignty (on the Rousseauian or Jacobin model) or subsumption (Hegelian *Aufhebung*) within a state that resolves its fundamental contradictions. In fact, while civil society involves conflict, it does not have contradictions: the

historical narrative of progress fills the logical (transcendental) gap left by the disenchantment of politics.[10] The power
of these ideas is that they go far deeper than any particular
set of institutions or historical circumstances: something of
this kind is a necessary component of any philosophically
consistent liberalism. (Conversely, this discussion underlines—and I hope explicates—the often noted fundamental
philosophical, and political, incoherence of the Rea-
gan/Thatcher attempt to marry liberalism with conservatism.) Nor are they simply of antiquarian interest. *The
Economist* continues every week to bang this drum with elo-
quence and wit, and to remain genuinely relevant, although
not always popular with those who like to think of themselves as liberals.

To summarize, in a philosophical sense, to be a classical
liberal, in a generic sense, is to subscribe to two basic beliefs:
(i) that human beings are complete in civil society, and consequently that freedom is to be conceived in the terms appropriate to civil society; and (ii) that there is a transhistori-
cal standard of human excellence best exemplified by scientific and philosophical inquiry and literary and artistic creation. Political liberalism reflects these beliefs. Politics is
therefore instrumental to human freedom and excellence,
and government or the state should serve the ends of civil
society (which, to repeat the point, are not arbitrary but
necessary, inscribed within a historical narrative, and ultimately non-contradictory). Characteristic liberal institutions
are designed to promote 'good' government in these terms:
freedom of thought and expression (implying but not limited
to restricted government) contribute simultaneously to the
development of human freedom and human excellence. The
highly variable character of the concrete expressions of political liberalism derives from the widely varying circumstances of its implementation and very unequal confidence in
the truth of the belief.

The Growing Diffidence
of Contemporary Liberals
and Their Three Main Worries

A characteristic feature of traditional liberalism is confidence: confidence in the defense of its own institutions, confidence in the validity of its criticism of its opponents, rooted in its self-identification with history and progress.[11] The opponents of liberalism may be powerful and dangerous. They may even win in the short run. Liberals fear tyranny precisely because it is a genuine risk, and the price of liberty is, of course, eternal vigilance. But anti-liberals cannot be right. Ignorance, superstition, and self-serving cynicism cannot survive indefinitely in a free world.

The most important ideological shift since the classical development of liberalism in Constant, Tocqueville, and Mill is a growing diffidence, tentativeness, even despair, among liberals themselves.[12] The evidence for this loss of confidence is too familiar to require lengthy discussion. The oft-repeated quip that a liberal is someone who is not prepared to take his own side in an argument is unkind but not entirely inaccurate. Cold War politics—seen both as East–West antagonism and as decolonization—illustrated a certain tendency among liberals to regard strong views as reflecting some combination of dogmatism and ulterior motives, and thus to eschew them, thereby perversely leaving the field open to the most dogmatic and cynical of their opponents. Liberalism thus often finds itself defending the status quo, without however being able to provide any compelling reasons for doing so. Indeed, unease about strong views may even lead to the romanticization of cynicism and the power-worship often ascribed to nineteenth-century German liberalism, in which a form of vitalism serves to preserve the dynamic of progress, while dropping its supposedly untenable moral content.[13] A similar tendency, as yet more significant philosophically than politically, is apparent in the contemporary debate between (so-called) 'liberals' and 'communitarians'. Liberal writers—Rawls being in this respect exemplary[14]—seem to grant almost unreservedly their opponents' points about the 'cultural particularity' of liberalism and the deleterious social effects of individualism (Parekh, 1992), while being unwilling to challenge the authoritarian implications of the (admittedly very vague) institutions communitarians appear to favor. The only significant exception to the trend proves the rule (in the strict sense of this much-abused phrase): because of their lack of interest in the foundations of their own activity, economists are largely immune from liberal diffidence. In the West, this is often considered as making them irrelevant. In East Central Europe, it has given them a virtual import monopoly on (so-called) liberalism.

Specifically, liberal diffidence reflects three worries or fears about the relation between the characteristic metanarrative of progress and the core liberal value of freedom.

(i) The golden age of liberalism was pre-industrial and pre-democratic. As the squalid realities of industrial society and mass politics became unavoidable, the classic problem of the 'mob' became central to liberal thinking. In Mill, fear and confidence are still compatible. The problem is defined as keeping liberal institutions safe until education has transformed the mob into a virtuous democratic political community. The snobbery and humanism are held together, somewhat uneasily, by the belief in progress. It did not last. By the early 1900s, the belief that the mob would be a permanent threat to liberty had become commonplace. At best, institutional reform might preserve liberty and the appearance of democracy by keeping the mob (and demagoguery aimed at the mob) out of politics.[15] This is precisely what we have come to call 'liberal democracy'—a contradiction in terms that is generally regarded as pragmatically indispensable. Whether it is likely to prove durable is another matter. Liberalism has long been haunted by the fear that industrialism, commercialism, and mass culture (blind forces that no one controls) will conspire to extend the mob indefinitely, beyond the capacity of any institutional barrier to contain it. This spells the death of liberalism, because it implies either a stark choice between enlightened dictatorship (preserving a space where the capacities of a select few may flourish) and submitting to the tide (abandoning all idea of human excellence), neither of which makes liberal sense;[16] or a reformulation, ultimately anti-humanistic, of the concept of 'human' potential in collective and technological terms.

Liberal fear expresses itself in the key twentieth-century cultural figure of the 'last man'. The idea is basically Nietzschean.[17] The time is close, says Zarathustra, when men will no longer bring forth stars, when a shrunken Earth will be ruled by that most despicable of creatures—by him who is incapable of despising himself. These are the 'last men', and they are a stable equilibrium, a genuine dead-end, something like the philosophical equivalent of the heat death of the universe (not a Nietzschean simile). Their race is indestructible, for they have invented happiness[18]—they are one flock with no shepherd, where none wishes to be ruled, and none to rule. Those who think differently are insane, and go willingly to the asylum. Zarathustra's speech is intended to shame the people into yearning for the *Übermensch* ('super-' or 'overman')—the only way out of the dead-end: but the people, of course, clamor joyously to be made like the last men.

The extent of Nietzsche's influence is not at issue here. His is simply a concise and eloquent formulation of a widely shared prophecy (a dystopia or nightmare). What is interesting is that liberalism offers a rather different twist on the theme. Liberalism is (some kind of) humanism or it is nothing, and it cannot use Nietzsche's anti-humanistic distinction between *Mensch* and *Übermensch*. It is interested, therefore, not in Nietzsche's 'last men' (who, humanistically speaking, are not really 'men' at all), but in the 'penultimate' men—the last to be truly human before the darkness. The central figure thus becomes the siege of the final redoubt of humanity. Depending on one's view of the self-consistency of technological development (the inevitability of either absolute control or self-destruction) this may take two forms—the struggle against Big Brother or against barbarous anarchy—but the basic structure is the same. Orwell, although not a liberal in any doctrinal sense, may be regarded as exemplary (and profoundly influential) in this respect. The working title for *Nineteen Eighty-Four* was 'The Last Man in Europe',[19] and what dies with Winston Smith's 'victory over himself' in the very last pages of the novel is humanity itself, in the humanistic sense (which Orwell shared) of the compossibility of human intellect and common human decency. Henceforth, the O'Briens shall have the intellect, the proles shall have the decency, and 'never the twain shall meet'. The fear that such a future may be a serious possibility also inspires the pessimistic tone of self-conscious liberals such as Hayek (at least in *The Road to Serfdom*—he had become more sanguine by the time of *Law, Legislation and Liberty*) and Schumpeter, as well as the more ambivalent (and sometimes explicitly Nietzschean) Weber.

The liberal fear, in other words, is not simply that the belief in progress might be misplaced, leaving the future open; but that there might be a quite different 'way of the world' in which humanism has no place; that liberalism may turn out to be just a historical parenthesis between the collapse of the *ancien régime* and the rise of some debased form of mass society.[20]

(ii) Liberal pessimism as just described seems to go in cycles. Compared to the dark vision prevalent in the first half of the twentieth century—not solely explicable by the disasters of two world wars, since it predated them—the contemporary liberal climate is much less tragic. In spite of fierce criticism, some version at least of Fukuyama's analysis of the historical triumph of liberalism has, often unenthusiastically, entered into common sense. However, to believe that the world is going in a basically liberal direction, while it keeps the nightmare of the 'last man' at bay, has different implications once the idea of progress (of a value-driven 'History') is abandoned. Maybe liberalism is merely a symptom of 'path-dependency'—of the ability of the nineteenth-century European bourgeoisie (in the words of the *Manifesto of the Communist Party*) "*sich eine Welt nach ihrem eigenen Bilde zu schaffen*" [to create a world after its own image]. If so, the triumph of liberalism is entirely devoid of normative content and, furthermore, liberalism can survive only by a combination of ideological hegemony and military supremacy—a Hobbesian recipe which, again, makes no sense in truly liberal terms. (Anyone skeptical in practical terms about ideological hegemony and military supremacy is simply led back to the first worry.) The prevalence of this worry shows up most clearly in the way in which (most) liberals respond to the multicultural (or communitarian, or relativist) challenge that liberalism is simply another particularism, but one with enough power and money to be able to afford the fancy clothing of universalism. The argument that most people outside the liberal West seem to want Westernization (including, but not limited to, liberalism), and grab it when given the chance—an argument still common in public debate—is widely rejected as unfit for sophisticated consumption. In more technical terms, liberals have generally accepted the principle of 'neutrality' as a constraint on public philosophies, and the criticism that liberalism as traditionally conceived is not neutral because it specifically promotes certain ways of life and norms of human development, and thereby makes it impossible for others to flourish.[21]

(iii) The claim that the success of liberalism is to be explained solely or primarily by liberal power is often regarded as implausibly strong and epistemologically suspect (since it seems to make sense only idealistically or in terms of some kind of conspiracy theory). As a consequence, the second worry is also found in variant form. Liberalism, in this case, is regarded as a genuine component of a 'world-historical' process that is not reducible to it and is in some sense objective; and of which, furthermore, some aspects at least are profoundly deleterious. Recognizing this and remaining a liberal means judging that, on balance, the benefits of liberalism are greater than its drawbacks. Once the issue has been stated in these terms, however, it is difficult to make such a judgment with any great confidence. If one agrees to blame social trends of which liberalism is inseparably part for selfish individualism, the loss of meaning due to the dislocation of traditional cultural systems, the spread of crass consumerism, and so on, it is hard to be certain that significant compensating benefits actually exist. At a deeper level, there is room for doubt whether such a trade-off makes any sense at all. As Berlin repeatedly stressed, the kind of value monism that would allow one to compare the various desirables and undesirables on a single scale contradicts human experience and moral intuition, and seems impossible to defend on any other grounds. How many avant-garde paintings 'make up' for the closure of a church? How many *Finnegans Wakes* 'make up' for the disappearance of a minority language? (Assuming that one does recognize some value in religion and minority languages as components of human flourishing—as most contemporary liberals would, unlike a major strand in historical liberalism which would dismiss such things as superstitious and obsolete.) According to the 'Berlinian' liberal, these questions sound stupid because they are stupid, and yet any kind of 'trade-off' argument requires them to be answered. Therefore the idea of a trade-off is meaningless. Of course, we must act: a minority language must be protected, tolerated, or eradicated—or something in between. But while utilitarianism may be a useful tool of practical reason, it is morally vacuous. Thus, many policy decisions involve putting an implicit or explicit price on human life: most people would regard this as reasonable, while still firmly believing that human life is priceless.[22] For a hard-core utilitarian, this is grossly inconsistent—for a Berlinian merely a tragic fact of life: namely, that morality, by its very nature, is incapable of providing a sufficient and logically coherent basis for practical reason.

The details of Berlin's arguments have aroused considerable debate, but something on the lines of his value pluralism is widely accepted among liberals. It is reflected in the fear that the various individual and social dimensions of human flourishing that liberals care about are not ultimately reconcilable, and that nothing else can meaningfully 'compensate' for the loss of those that are deliberately pruned or unfortunately wither away. The connection with the worry about 'neutrality' is obvious, but this variant—while in one sense less dramatic—in many ways goes deeper. It replaces the clash between liberalism and its competitors by an irresolvable tension within liberalism itself. Rather than a combatant in the 'war of the gods', liberalism thus becomes a battlefield.

To be worried is not necessarily to feel guilty. Nor is the evidence that contemporary liberalism is in some sense guilt-ridden as straightforward as that for liberal diffidence.

Certainly the point is not some purely psychological fact about liberals regarded as a contingent group of individuals. My claim is that there are reasons within the very structure of liberalism—closely related to the worries just discussed— for people subscribing to liberal values to feel guilty about doing so. One specific, and characteristic, feature of this guilt is the awkward status of politics within contemporary liberalism.

The structural difficulty is as follows. If, as just discussed, history casts doubt on the truth, coherence, and viability of the liberal ideal, then, assuming—as many people do—that it is intrinsically attractive, what grounds are there for subscribing to it? At an individual level, a series of perfectly good explanations for liberal faith might be produced: arbitrary personal commitment, crass stupidity, genuine belief in the supposedly discredited narrative of emancipatory progress, the expectation that one is likely to benefit personally from a liberal system. What none of these can do, however, is justify liberalism, even to liberals themselves—except of course the third, assuming a liberal entirely immune from all contemporary worries.

Since liberalism is intended as a public philosophy, incorporating specific institutional principles, and not simply as a life-style, it is called upon to justify itself, and liberals as individuals find their motives questioned. The two issues should be entirely separate, but in fact, because of the erosion of traditional forms of justification, they tend to collapse into one another. Many fair-minded liberals will naturally wonder whether they defend liberalism only because they expect to profit from it. In other words—the United States is the clearest example, but the trend is also visible in Europe, rooted in the post-colonial guilt the French call *tiers-mondisme*—liberalism comes to be stigmatized as the trades-unionism of the OECD chattering classes, and many liberals see some truth in the criticism. Ultimately, but in an odd way logically, this leads to a dead-end where freedom and progress collapse into the defense of public funding for avant-garde art: what one might call the 'Mapplethorpe syndrome' is perhaps the reductio ad absurdum of liberal guilt.

The nature of liberal argument is a further issue. Liberals (correctly) consider as central to liberalism the requirement to subject ideas to public debate, and not to base major decisions on reasons that cannot be shown to be compelling—dogmatism and tyranny being regarded as intimately related, as indeed they have been historically. This is the honorable basis for the tentativeness that inspires so much sarcasm, but tentativeness it still is, and it can produce paralysis in the face of emergencies, even when core liberal concerns are at stake. As a matter of fact, at least in terms of 'high politics', it is hard to argue that liberals have generally performed in the face of adversity any worse than, say, supposedly hard-headed conservatives or communists. Nonetheless, liberals tend to believe otherwise, and as a consequence to feel guilty both about their weakness and about the related sneaking admiration for people with fewer scruples—from Mussolini to Thatcher via Stalin, to summarize things crudely.

To marshal systematic evidence for all these claims would require a survey far more extensive than is possible here, and in addition the basic idea is perhaps not profoundly controversial. The Orwellian generalizations of the preceding paragraphs will therefore suffice for present purposes.

Liberal values are in essence a form of vanguardism: they are the values of a current elite regarded as indicative of future human development. But if human development in fact has no particular direction, they become simply the values of an elite which happens to be in a position of power and privilege. This is what puts a peculiar twist on the traditional liberal stipulation (which, as discussed earlier, made perfect sense in the classical nineteenth-century context) that popular sovereignty should be subordinated to the principle of good government.

Constitutionalism, in its generic form, reflects the fear that tyrants might use democratic processes to destroy liberty. Taking certain things out of politics—by the use of international conventions, entrenched rights, qualified majorities for constitutional amendments, and so on—does not of itself guarantee liberty, but does at least make it difficult for tyranny to advance masked by due process. In principle, there is nothing undemocratic about this. A people conscious of its possible weakness of will might very reasonably choose such restrictions in its own best interests.[23] In fact, however, it rarely works that way. Not only are constitutions usually dictated in times of crisis by (supposedly) providential figures without much reasoned public debate (which would indeed be incongruous in times of crisis)—the actual politics of the constitution are not usually consistent with the idea of limitations on government power as the expression (rather than the negation) of sovereignty. The tendency since the Second World War (in the aftermath of which most European countries acquired new constitutions and the first major international conventions on human rights were signed) has been increasingly to regard constitutions (in the broad sense, including international conventions) as fixed, except in very unusual circumstances, and to extend ever more broadly the range of issues with constitutional status. Political mobilization to reverse constitutionalization (for example, by enacting legislation or amending the constitution to overturn judicial rulings) is regarded by liberals as dangerous, and even downright illegitimate. In theory (as exemplified by the Rawls/Dworkin form of liberal political philosophy),[24] the United States is in this respect an extreme example, although practice is in fact more ambiguous. The trend is clearly perceptible in countries such as France, where the creation of a genuine constitutional jurisdiction is a very recent innovation, regarded even today with deep suspicion by the non-liberal Left which, in the Jacobin tradition, equates democracy with popular sovereignty. The UK, where the liberal suspicion of politics has traditionally found rather different forms of institutional expression, now also seems likely to follow this path.

Rather than a formal political constraint, what constitutionalism thus tends to mean in practice is the entrenchment of liberal concerns that are known to be unpopular and likely to remain so. The abolition of the death penalty is, in all European countries, the best example (and, conversely, points to the peculiarities of the US situation). Quite logically, however, in view of the argument sketched here, constitutionalism is instrumental rather than valuable in its own right. The broader issue is that, in a political system comprising an enlightened elite and an unsophisticated electorate that can easily be led astray, good government is generally best promoted by keeping sensitive issues out of politics and firmly in the hands of the liberal elite. Informal mechanisms, where feasible, are generally even more effective than constitutional entrenchment (and in addition more flexible in policy terms). The management of immigration is a classic case, of which the UK is in many ways the best example.[25] Thus liberals may be led, in logical stages, to a paternalistic version of political authority that flatly contradicts the essence of the liberal conception of freedom. Liberal values and liberal politics are united by guilty ambivalence about their legitimacy. Furthermore, the entrenchment of liberal values *contra vocem populi* gives only a partial view of the effects and meaning of the liberal distaste for politics. If "politics is necessary but should not become serious",[26] all serious issues must be depoliticized. In a perfect world, perhaps nothing would be serious, but more realistically anything wrong with the existing order must be reduced to technicalities or swept under the carpet. As a result, liberalism risks losing all critical edge. Yet recognition that politics may become serious reintroduces the issues of sovereignty, of power and violence, that liberalism purports to neutralize. The pure, asymptotic form of political seriousness is struggle to the death between public enemies (*hostes*, as distinct from *inimici*)—a central theme in the thought of Carl Schmitt which, far more than his unpleasant personal politics, explains liberal discomfort about him. The view (à la Fukuyama) that nothing is seriously wrong with the existing order is neither meaningless nor ridiculous but, as discussed at length earlier, very few contemporary liberals would accept it. To defend the basic institutions (including the constitutive values) of a social, economic, and political order while guiltily denying it any cogent normative justification—which is the effect, if not always the intention, of much contemporary liberalism—is a recipe for philosophical and political irrelevance.

Conclusion

One possible conclusion, therefore, would be that liberalism is indeed irrelevant—that it has nothing to offer to debates about transition from authoritarian or totalitarian rule to democracy, or future developments in currently (more or less) democratic states, or the emergence of a new world order. Because of the depth of the crisis within liberalism—a crisis of which, I have suggested, self-doubt is a major component—such a conclusion would be quite understandable.

Yet it still seems odd. Historically, as discussed earlier, liberalism is most conveniently defined by its enemies. Tyranny, ignorance, superstition, corruption, constrained orthodoxy, denied opportunities—none of these has disappeared from the face of the Earth, and if liberalism was once an appropriate response to them, it is hard to see why it should have ceased to be so. What is potentially valuable in liberalism, in other words, is not so much a positive political ideology, or even a set of institutions (although the kinds of institutions that have developed in historically liberal societies—including the market as well as parliamentary government, constitutionalism, the rule of law, and so on—incorporating experience at least as much as self-conscious design, may often be usefully exportable), as a critical thrust. For this to be mobilized, the structural difficulties discussed earlier must be addressed. Critique requires both a critical position, and a justification for it. Neither anti-democratic elitism nor the myth of progress can perform adequately in this respect, and a revived critical edge is incompatible with any fastidious distaste for politics.

Attempts in recent liberal theory to face up to (and go beyond) guilt illustrate at least three possible critical positions, which are relevant to different contexts of political argument.

(i) Internal critique is the dominant form of current liberalism (although liberals are by no means alone in articulating it). On both theoretical and practical grounds, philosophers as diverse as Rawls, Rorty, and Walzer (ignoring for these purposes the very real differences between them) argue that it is at best a waste of time and at worst meaningless to seek a justifiable critical position outside the system one purports to criticize.[27] Critique should be self-criticism, with the theorist acting as a kind of midwife—the criticism of society in light of what its members think it should be and what it shows in certain spheres it can be. Ultimately, the target of internal critique is hypocrisy, and its canonical argument is 'If you believe x, then you should do y; and if you're not prepared to do y, you should stop pretending to believe x'. What makes it available to liberals is that Western societies are, roughly speaking, historically, normatively, and institutionally liberal, but notoriously fail to live up to their own principles. A society that believes in the equal moral worth of all individuals cannot tolerate widespread racism. A society that believes in the possibility and desirability of the development of human capacities cannot tolerate denial of educational opportunities to significant sections of the population. A society that believes in freedom of speech should not deny it to people simply because their views are unpopular. Where applicable, such a critical position is powerful and valuable.

(ii) The limits of internal critique are, however, narrow. In the absence of normative consensus, it is forced to remain silent, and it is irrelevant outside the boundaries of the liberal tradition. One way out of the difficulty is to relocate the critical position as internal not to a specific set of political values but to a form of political argument. Liberalism thus defines itself in terms of one key component of its historical tradition, derived from the struggle with established religion: the requirement that all arguments should be prepared to submit to hostile public scrutiny—in other words, the requirement of impartiality—in the sense not simply that self-serving arguments are to be excluded, but further that questions should not be begged. Its canonical challenge is therefore: 'Can you justify this to someone who does not already believe it?'. The best-known version of this approach is the discourse ethics of Habermas, but it is also exemplified by attempts to formulate a liberal multiculturalism in the work of theorists such as Taylor and Kymlicka. In practice this tends to work more towards a purified form of liberalism, perhaps relevant beyond the boundaries of the liberal tradition, than towards exacting critique of non-liberal traditions, but the tools are at least available.

(iii) The difficulty with a critical stance based on formalized argument is that its political relevance presupposes the willingness of non-liberals to accept as a norm the principle of impartiality (or of an ideal speech situation), and therefore to try actually to adjust their conduct towards it. Bona fide philosophical arguments might perhaps be manageable in this way, but to premiss one's politics on one's opponents' good faith seems dangerously naive. To avoid this trap requires legitimation to be substantive rather than procedural. Formally, this means returning to the spirit of classical liberalism, but full-blooded commitment to progress or to a transcendental notion of human potential is by no means necessary. It is sufficient for critique to identify human potential that is, as a matter of fact, denied development in the society one wishes to criticize, and to show that some change in social, economic, or political arrangements would be conducive to a greater degree of opportunity. The underlying humanism—the axiom that waste of human potential is never a good thing, though it may for practical reasons be inevitable—cannot be justified to anyone who does not share it, to anyone, say, committed to biological or religious determinism which makes either the idea of generic human potential meaningless or its unequal development desirable. But this fact is not an objection: it means simply that liberals must be prepared to fight for their beliefs, and should recognize that there is nothing wrong in doing so.[28]

Thus, while there are good historical reasons that explain liberal guilt, it should not be regarded as a necessary feature of liberalism. Liberals have a set of core values, basically reducible to the belief that human freedom is not just a good thing in itself but also produces desirable results, and that it is possible to arrange society in ways conducive to such freedom. What they do not have is a straightforward institutional blueprint that, say, countries in transition could simply import. Indeed, all of the characteristic institutions historically associated with liberalism are ambivalent in liberal terms. The free market, limited and representative government, the priority of civil society over the state—all have the potential both to enhance freedom in certain respects and to constrain it in others. This, however, does not spell irrelevance. Designing institutions is a matter of statesmanship, about which liberalism has little to say. But the nagging voice of human freedom, which it is liberals' self-appointed task to transmit, has a vital role to play in preventing the intended or unintended defects of such institutions from hiding behind spurious concepts and fine words.

Bibliography

Barber, Benjamin. 1996. *Jihad vs. McWorld—How Globalism and Tribalism Are Reshaping the World*. 2nd edition. New York: Ballantine.

Barry, Brian. 1991a. 'How not to defend liberal institutions', in *Liberty and Justice—Essays in Political Theory 2*, 23–39. Oxford: Oxford University Press.

———. 1991b. 'The continuing relevance of socialism', in *Liberty and Justice—Essays in Political Theory 2*, 274–90. Oxford: Oxford University Press.

———. 1991c. 'Tragic choices', in *Liberty and Justice—Essays in Political Theory 2*, 123–41. Oxford: Oxford University Press.

Bellamy, Richard. 1992. *Liberalism and Modern Society—An Historical Argument*. Cambridge: Polity Press.

Berlin, Isaiah. 1969. 'Two concepts of liberty', in *Four Essays on Liberty*. Oxford: Oxford University Press.

Bloom, Allan. 1987. *The Closing of the American Mind—How Higher Education Has Failed Democracy and Impoverished the Souls of Today's Students*. New York: Simon and Schuster.

Bohman, James. 1995. 'Public reason and cultural pluralism. Political liberalism and the problem of moral conflict', *Political Theory* 23 (2): 253–79.

Cohen, Joshua. 1993. 'Moral pluralism and political consensus', in *The Idea of Democracy*, ed. David Copp et al. Cambridge: Cambridge University Press.

Crowley, John. 1993a. 'Le vote secret contre la démocratie américaine (1880–1910)', *Politix* 22: 69–83.

———. 1993b. 'Paradoxes in the politicization of race: A comparison of the UK and France', *New Community* 19 (4): 627–43.

Dunn, John. 1969. *The Political Thought of John Locke. An Historical Account of the Argument of the Two Treatises of Government*. Cambridge, Cambridge University Press.

Foucault, Michel. 1966. *Les mots et les choses*. Paris: Gallimard.

Gray, John. 1986. *Liberalism*. Buckingham: Open University Press.

————. 1995. *Berlin*. London: Fontana.

Hampsher-Monk, Iain. 1995. 'Is there an English form of toleration?', *New Community* 21 (2): 227–40.

Hayek, Friedrich A. 1982. *Law, Legislation and Liberty*. One-volume edition. London: Routledge and Kegan Paul. (The page numbering of the one-volume edition retains that of the original separately published volumes.)

Howard, Dick. 1993. *From Marx to Kant*. 2nd edition. London: Macmillan.

King, Preston. 1976. *Toleration*. London: Allen and Unwin.

Larmore, Charles. 1990. 'Political liberalism', *Political Theory* (3): 339–60.

Lavau, Georges, and Olivier Duhamel. 1985. 'La démocratie', in *Traité de science politique*, ed. Madeleine Grawitz and Jean Leca, vol. 2, 29–113. Paris: PUF.

Manent, Pierre. 1987. *Histoire intellectuelle du libéralisme*. Paris: Calmann-Lévy.

McClure, Kirstie. 1990. 'Difference, diversity and the limits of toleration', *Political Theory* (3): 361–91.

Nagel, Thomas. 1987. 'Moral conflict and political legitimacy', *Philosophy and Public Affairs* 16 (3): 215–40.

Parekh, Bhikhu. 1992. 'The cultural particularity of liberal democracy', *Political Studies* 40 (special issue): 160–75.

Rawls, John. 1971. *A Theory of Justice*. Cambridge, Massachusets: Harvard University Press.

————. 1987. 'The idea of an overlapping consensus', *Oxford Journal of Legal Studies* 7 (1).

————. 1993a. *Political Liberalism*. New York: Columbia University Press.

————. 1993b. 'The law of peoples', in *On Human Rights*, ed. S. Shute and S. Hurley, 41–82. New York: Basic Books.

Rorty, Richard. 1985. *Contingency, Irony and Solidarity*. Cambridge: Cambridge University Press.

————. 1991. 'Unger, Castoriadis, and the romance of a national future', in *Essays on Heidegger and Others—Philosophical Papers Volume 2*, 177–92. Cambridge: Cambridge University Press.

Schnapper, Dominique. 1994. *La communauté des citoyens*. Paris: Gallimard.

Strong, Tracy. 1996. 'Foreword' to Carl Schmitt, *The Concept of the Political*, trans. by George Schwab. Chicago: University of Chicago Press.

Tenzer, Nicolas. 1994. *Philosophie politique*. Paris: PUF.

Walzer, Michael. 1987. *Interpretation and Social Criticism*. Cambridge, Massachusets: Harvard University Press.

————. 1988. *The Company of Critics: Social Criticism and Political Commitment in the Twentieth Century*. New York: Basic Books.

————. 1995. 'Are there limits to liberalism?', *New York Review of Books* (19 October): 28–31.

Notes

1 Rawls (1993a), foreshadowed to a limited extent by *A Theory of Justice* (1971), but mainly developed from the essay 'The idea of an overlapping consensus' (1987) onwards.

2 The following are a fairly random sample: Bohman (1995), Cohen (1993), Larmore (1990), and Nagel (1987). A similar point is made, albeit in a non-Rawlsian way, by Berlin. See the discussion in Gray (1995), and also Walzer (1995).

3 See, among many others, Gray (1986) and Manent (1987).

4 Originally, toleration was purely legal and political rather than doctrinal or intellectual. As Locke's *Letter concerning Toleration* (1689) shows, it was precisely as erroneous or even abhorrent that, within strict politically defined limits, beliefs were to be tolerated. For a more general discussion, see King (1976), Hampsher-Monk (1995), and McClure (1990).

5 An exemplary summary of the characteristic nineteenth-century liberal view is John Stuart Mill's *On Liberty*, especially chapter 2.

6 Hayek provides a rare explicit development of this idea: see Hayek (1982), chapter 17 of which is entitled 'A model constitution' (III, pp. 105–27). Formally, Hayek keeps the basic democratic principle of election as a privileged mechanism for selection, but his overriding concern to insulate the legislature from political pressure (by a 'career structure' modeled on the judiciary) is clearly (and designedly) the negation rather than the expression of popular sovereignty.

7 The classic exposition is Dunn (1969).

8 See Howard (1993). Howard regards this necessarily immanent structure as definitive of modernity.

9 The point is not that all nineteenth-century liberals sincerely believed in democratization in the sense of being immune from snobbery. But at least a distinction, now largely lost, was still possible between contempt for ignorance and contempt for the ignorant.

10 Conversely, the intellectual weakness of contemporary French liberalism corresponds to the prevalence of more or less explicitly Hegelian themes, which are seen as justifying state-centered political thought. Relevant examples are Lavau and Duhamel (1985), Schnapper (1994), and Tenzer (1994).

11 Incidentally, this underlines, as Foucault suggests, the close family relationship between liberalism and Marxism, running far deeper than their fierce local quarrels (see Foucault [1966], pp. 265–75; appropriately enough, this section ends with a reference to Nietzsche and to the 'last man').

12 None of the writers mentioned was a vapid optimist. In all, the deep underlying tensions of liberalism are already at work. The basic confidence, however, is not yet undermined.

13 See Bellamy (1992), pp. 157–216, who largely discharges Max Weber, at least, on this count.

14 See most explicitly Rawls (1993b).

15 It is notable that, for the first time, the United States contributed decisively to this new configuration. The common sense of the 'Age of Reform', across the whole political spectrum, was that suffrage restrictions were necessary to produce good government—that, in other words, liberalism and democracy are ultimately incompatible. See further Crowley (1993a).

16 This is not intended to suggest that liberals are the only people worried about the way the world is going—simply that they are peculiarly threatened. Conservatives or communitarian democrats (say), while they may share the worries, are conceptually better equipped to make sense of them. Representative analyses are, respectively, Bloom (1987) and Barber (1996).

17 See *Also Sprach Zarathustra*, I, U5.

18 The scientific or technological connotations of 'invention' are apparently to be taken seriously. The last men take 'a little poison', now and then, for sweet dreams, and in the end a large dose, for a pleasant death. A brave new world indeed!

19 There is no compelling reason to regard this as a Nietzschean reference—but who knows? There are just two references to Friedrich 'von' Nietzsche (as the index bizarrely has it) in the *Collected Essays, Journalism and Letters*, both cryptic, and neither relevant to the 'last man' theme. What is Nietzschean in Orwell is the critique of hedonism, both as a basis for domination ("because of his own streak of savagery London could grasp something that Wells apparently could not, and that is that hedonistic societies do not endure ... A ruling class has got to have a strict morality, a quasi-religious belief in itself, a mystique" ['Prophecies of fascism' (1940) in *CEJL*, II, p. 46]), and, more ambivalently, as an acceptable philosophy in itself (see his review of *Mein Kampf*, ibid., pp. 27–29).

20 See Rorty (1991). Francis Fukuyama's *The End of History and the Last Man* (New York: Free Press, 1992), on the other hand, the best-known recent attempt to tackle this theme, takes a fairly sanguine view (in these terms), based on the anthropological axiom that the human desire for recognition is too powerful for the 'last men' to remain last men for long.

21 An untypical dissenting liberal view is Barry (1991a).

22 But see Barry (1991c): "We do not act as if we thought [that life has infinite value], and, although this is more difficult to prove, I do not believe that we think it either. I am inclined to think that the idea is a piece of sentimentality that will not stand up to scrutiny" (p. 128).

23 Jon Elster has extensively developed this theme, for which he provides a very apt metaphor. The precautions of Odysseus, in plugging his companions' ears and having himself tied to the mast in order to listen safely to the song of the Sirens, are precisely analogous to the essence of constitutionalism (see *Ulysses and the Sirens—Studies in Rationality and Irrationality* [Paris: Maison des Sciences de l'Homme/Cambridge: Cambridge University Press, 1979]).

24 To the point, in Rawls (especially in *Political Liberalism*), of hostility to politics per se (as involving messy compromises and non-moral forms of argument), and not simply to the possibly illiberal outcomes of political debate. That distaste for politics actually fits poorly in the structure of Rawls's argument only makes the feature more striking.

25 See Crowley (1993b). Such mechanisms obviously work only if there is actually a cohesive and self-conscious elite, which probably requires both commonality of background and strong incentives for cross-party cooperation. Arguably, neither condition is satisfied in the US, which may explain some of the peculiar features of its liberalism.

26 Strong (1996), p. xxvi. Strong presents this as "one of the deepest premises of liberalism".

27 In addition to the references already quoted, see Rorty (1985), and Walzer (1987 and 1988).

28 A clear statement of what is currently an unfashionable view is Barry (1991a).

Liberalism, Value, and Social Cohesion

ROBERT GRANT

It is usual to begin inquiries such as this with an attempt to define liberalism and to distinguish its varieties. I propose, however, to start from the other direction, beginning with social cohesion. From there I shall work back to value generally, and conclude by asking what liberalism understands by value, and whether—or how far—liberalism is compatible with social cohesion.

To see why social cohesion—or order—is to be valued we need look no further than Hobbes's *Leviathan*. Imagine, says Hobbes, a world without government. Here, since there is no single center of power to contain it, force alone rules, both locally and overall. This is Hobbes's so-called state of nature, the war of all against all. Hobbes believed that men were born egoists, but whether or not he was correct does not affect the obvious truth, that in the state of nature, if they wish to survive, people have no choice but to be egoistic. (And, one might add, can hardly be blamed for being so, unless self-defense is a sin).

In the state of nature fear and misery are universal. No man has any protection except his own puny powers. Furthermore, and (perhaps more importantly than anything else) everything is so unpredictable that no long-term project is worth undertaking. Any kind of worthwhile life depends upon cooperation. Cooperation is essential to both trade and the spontaneous division of labor which creates the commodities to be traded. It is also essential to the more formal division of labor found in joint productive enterprises.

Cooperation is impossible without some external guarantee that the terms on which it is undertaken shall be adhered to.[1] This takes the form of power, and a power which is not merely discretionary (since discretionary power is unpredictable). It must rather be legal, that is, take the form of fixed and familiar rules the outcomes of whose operations are generally predictable. Life without order is a mere hand-to-mouth existence, and that not for long. In the state of nature, says Hobbes in a famous phrase, man's life is "solitary, poor, nasty, brutish and short".

Let me add what Hobbes omits. When we speak of social order we are not talking merely about the persistence through time of a certain more or less constant framework of formal procedures. It is, of course, a precondition of the efficient dispatch of business and similar activities that there be regular, normal, prescribed, and—sometimes—enforceable ways of doing things. But the principle applies also to morals, customs, and culture. The object here is to foster not production, but solidarity. By solidarity I mean the sentiment which underlies true social cohesion.

Solidarity consists of social feelings and allegiances such as honesty, trust, national and community loyalty, law-abidingness, a presumption of strangers' fair intent, and the like. Temporally speaking, it must be posterior to such things as law and compulsion, in that, without the security which those things guarantee, the sympathy and openness towards other people and their designs which solidarity involves cannot be afforded. Otherwise, however, solidarity is logically prior to law and compulsion, and essential to their proper working. Law and compulsion alone are insufficient to create solidarity. Indeed, by themselves, and indiscriminately applied, they can do much to destroy it.

Here it becomes obvious that the expression 'social order' can mean two quite different things. It is possible, by the use of arbitrary power, physical coercion, threats, and so on, to create something that looks like order, as those who lived under communism well know. But such an order is merely what the English Romantic poet Shelley, in criticizing the anti-revolutionary measures taken by a repressive Tory government, called "The Mask of Anarchy".[2] Here is something which, because of its smooth, stable, regimented exterior, *looks* like order, but is in fact merely anarchy in disguise.

Where force alone rules, the result is not really order. It may be centralized, and thus meet one condition of a genuinely civil order—since, as Max Weber pointed out, that always requires a monopoly of force—but as far as its subjects are concerned, they are little better off than they would be in the state of nature. (They might even be worse off, since in the state of nature they were at least able to defend themselves.)

A society faced with an external enemy is characteristically drawn together by the common threat, as Machiavelli and others have noted. If it is a society in good moral health it will have a high solidarity quotient. But where the enemy is internal and controls domestic politics—the dictatorship of an individual or a party, say—such a tyranny will naturally maintain itself by the atomization of society and the breaking down of solidarity, so that no common focus of opposition to it can be formed. It will deliberately sow distrust between its subjects by inserting informers into every nook and cranny of social life. In addition, either by deliberately creating scarcity, or because its economic system is likely to be extremely inefficient, it will force its subjects into naked competition even for the bare necessities of life. They will be kept so busy just trying to survive, and to fulfill their immediate duties to family and friends, as to have neither the time nor the energy to combine, either in shared enjoyments or in political opposition to their oppressors.[3]

Here, then, is a society which appears to be orderly only because its members are forced to act either in a collective unison unsupported by any substantive underlying unity, or, when they act individually, according to a single, unvaryingly self-interested principle. This is evidently no order that any normal person could in fact desire to be a part of; indeed, even the rulers do not enjoy it very much, since they fear each other as much as their subjects, if not more. It is, in effect, merely a formalized version of Hobbes's state of nature. At the very most, in that there actually is a single center of power, it is something that is only just beginning or moving away from pure anarchy in the direction of genuine order.

Social order proper is something quite different. It is a fact of nature, almost a tautology, that people would rather do a thing voluntarily than be compelled to do it. (This simple fact is actually liberalism's trump card, and if life—or liberalism—were equally simple, liberalism would long ago have swept everything before it.) A civilized social order—which in historical terms might actually be quite early—is one which is held together by sentiment, voluntarily.

This is not to say that such a society can dispense with social and legal rules, norms, sanctions, and so on. It cannot do so simply because any society contains a small number of criminally inclined people who can be controlled only by punishment or the fear of it. But if most of us obey the law, and treat our fellows with justice and consideration, it is not out of fear, but because we want to do so, and think it right. It follows that, having voluntarily identified ourselves with our society's norms, we do not for the most part experience them as constraints. (And therefore, for us, they are not, since the objection to constraints is only to the *feeling* of being constrained.)

A society of this kind will be virtually self-policing. Its members will regard it as a free society, since they are doing mostly what they want to do. It may not always look free to outsiders (and especially not to certain liberals), but whose opinion of a society should we trust, if not that of those who have to live in it?[4]

What are the conditions under which we feel most impelled spontaneously to obey the law and treat our fellows with justice and consideration? First, we have to recognize the law as just. The law is not just (as the so-called legal positivists think) simply because it *is* the law. Justice is moral before it is legal, and legality is nothing, in the sense that no one will be spontaneously impelled to observe it, if it is not perceived to be in accordance with morality.

I do not mean by this that every moral judgment should be backed by legal sanctions. That, if it were not impossible, would seem exceedingly oppressive, at least in modern Western societies. What I mean is that legal judgments cannot consistently fly in the face of morality, as they now frequently do, without eventually bringing law itself—and thus the entire social order which rests on it—into contempt. The consequences of this are serious, and I shall return to them.

All this is merely to repeat the point that custom, the moral order, and the moral law are prior to law and politics, in the sense that the social order, like power itself, derives its legitimacy from them and must uphold them if it is to survive. Indeed, it must do so if *they* are to survive unimpaired. The social order and the moral order require each other.

Secondly (it seems to me), we are most likely to treat our fellows with justice and consideration if we have a reasonable expectation that our concern for them is likely to be both understood as such and subsequently reciprocated. At least, if we knew that our care for others would not be understood or reciprocated, it would seem a quixotic, futile, and even sentimental gesture to extend it to them.[5] I do not mean that goodwill is necessarily a *quid pro quo*. All benevolence must involve a certain element of risk if it is not to seem purely calculating. But be that as it may, the chance of understanding and reciprocation is enormously increased by a shared culture.

A Kantian would say that we owe a certain minimum of consideration to all rational beings, independent of any shared political or cultural membership. Indeed we do. But such a minimum is so basic as to be barely interesting. It is as much as individuals in the state of nature might feel obliged to extend to others, so long as it was safe to do so (as it mostly would not be). Even in society, this Kantian minimum involves merely observing the constraints imposed by natural justice, that is, doing as one would, in similar circumstances, hope to be done by.

I do not mean to underrate such things. I am merely saying, contrary to Kant, that they are not enough. For Kant the principles of morality were derived from reason itself, and being so (he thought), supplied their own motive for obedience. This might be plausible if all human beings were rational. But there is, moreover, something emotionally desiccated about a purely rational morality. In reality, rationality needs to be supplemented, as the philosopher Roger Scruton pointed out in a first-rate pamphlet called *Animal Rights and Wrongs* (1996), by three other vital components of morality: sympathy, virtue, and piety.

All of these provide us with a much more powerful motive to obey the moral law than merely its own rationality. And there are times, Scruton rightly says, when these other sources of moral behavior justifiably override the strict rational impartiality demanded by Kant. For the fact is that we do not have the same duties to all people equally; or, if we do, it is only in respect of that minimum already mentioned. It is surely clear that I have a greater obligation than you have to see that my child gets an education and my sick father his medicine. It is clear also that I must not be blamed if, in keeping with my greater obligation, I extend to them a greater degree of sympathy and piety—call it emotional favoritism—than I extend to you and yours, whom I do not know. Neither is it unfair or unreasonable that I should, since I extend to you the same right to favor your own as I claim for myself.

There is in fact a kind of Kantian reciprocity even here, but it is between groups of 'significant others' rather than between individuals. It is not difficult to imagine the same principle being broadened to apply to societies as a whole. On this basis, patriotism would be justified as a kind of analogue of family loyalty. It is just 'natural' to put your own country's interests first. Of course, that does not for one minute mean that the interests of other countries are not to be considered, or their own patriotism not respected. Nor does it mean that we are to put our country's interests above our obligation to respect other countries' basic rights. It means merely that, as in the market place, and so long as we observe the rules of equity, we are justified in primarily consulting our interests rather than theirs, exactly as they are justified vice versa. Whatever violates their rights, so considered, rather than what merely conflicts with their interests, may well be in our interest, but it is not an interest which we ought to promote. Here, I believe, is a defense of a kind of limited nationalism which would be structurally similar to Mill's defense of individual liberty. It would also be a good deal more realistic, since the individual of whom Mill speaks is not to be found outside the philosopher's study, either in nature or in society.

For the fact is that, if considered apart from the Wittgensteinian 'forms of life'—that is, social and linguistic communities—in which all of us are embedded (and in which we gladly participate), the individual is a chimera. Almost all of us seek and find our individual identities more or less unselfconsciously, in our various common projects, institutions, values, and ways of life. Even those who repudiate the common life affirm their identity by repudiating it, so that they too are no less existentially dependent on it. It is because our identity, our sense of self, is so dependent on our membership of various social groups, and because we have a reason to wish to preserve that identity, that we have a habit of loyalty towards them.

I am not concerned here to rank these groups in any order, but it should be observed that our identity is so deeply rooted in them that in many cases they actually constitute our life and its meaning. This means that we may be prepared to risk, or even sacrifice, our physical lives for them. Few people, I imagine, would ever willingly lay down their lives for their golf club or the street where they live. But nobody except a very enlightened person regards it as irrational to defend one's country, family, or friends with one's own life or even to risk one's life for a stranger in distress. (One might well, however, regard it as irrational to risk one's life for the said enlightened person, if obligations are intelligible only when underpinned by the possibility of reciprocity.)[6]

Whatever the normal person is instinctively prepared to risk or sacrifice his life for may justly be called a genuine value. At any rate, it will be something more than a mere preference, for which one could in principle accept a substitute (as on an economist's indifference curve). Values pertain to what is loved, rather than to what is merely (and self-centeredly) desired. And love alone can exact death-defying allegiance, because loving—and being loved—is the only thing which confers permanent meaning on our lives.[7] No society hitherto has survived without, in extremity, being able to count on its subjects' willingness to risk their lives for it.[8] I refer the reader to Machiavelli's observations on those societies rich and soft enough to rely entirely on mercenaries for their defense (*The Prince*, chapter 12). Mercenaries' allegiance is and must be primarily to themselves. If that leaves their paymasters in the lurch in their hour of need, that is doubtless as it should be.

What I am suggesting is that a society in which hedonism is the nearest thing to an ultimate value is likely to prove unviable in the long run. I say 'the nearest thing to a value' because if an ultimate value is defined as that for which people are prepared to die, then it seems as though hedonism could not be one. It is probable also that a largely hedonistic society—and what I am describing is surely something like the way the liberal societies of the Western tradition seem to be going—will not be resolute enough to exclude from its territory, or to prevent from developing within it, cultural groups who give less than a fig for its values, since they will not—and perhaps rightly—think that it has any, or any worthy of respect. (Such groups, let me add, need not be immigrants or in any way ethnically or visibly distinct from the majority: witness the various dissident religious cults, militias, and so on, in the USA.)

The fact is that indiscriminate toleration engages nobody's respect, or indeed allegiance, since it seems to demonstrate that whoever practices it has no values, and thus has nothing to defend. Is it possible that freedom and toleration themselves are absolute values, and that we should stake everything, even our lives, on them?

The question here is neither ethical nor theoretical, but empirical. On what kind of freedom *are* people in general really prepared to stake their lives? Would anyone seriously go to the gallows to defend, say, the right to abort an unwanted fetus? Or to exhibit indecent works of art in public spaces? Or to insult others' religions by blasphemy? If liberals really cared about such things, they would be prepared to suffer for them, just as the anti-communist dissidents of Eastern Europe suffered—as their counterparts in China today still do—for defending the humane decencies. Most of that really amounted to defending the right to do one's duty. (Not even a liberal would say that we have a *duty* to display obscenities, outrage pious feelings, and so on.[9] In fact liberals are generally not keen on duty, which to them smacks of God, unfreedom, compulsion, authority, and so on.)

Instead, as we all know, the reverse is the case. It is so-called liberals who make others suffer, not merely the things objected to, but also the penalties for objecting to them.

Among those penalties are a sneering contempt, widespread media vilification, and, in a profession such as mine, a perceptible reduction in career prospects. There are and have been many kinds of liberal, some of them wholly admirable. But the dominant kind today is the one who airily tolerates virtually any kind of licentiousness but will not tolerate—in fact will actively persecute—what he calls 'judgmental' attitudes. Actually, the intolerance which such attitudes are supposed to exemplify usually amounts to no more than calling immorality and vice by their proper names and disapproving of them as they ought to be disapproved of.

All this is, of course, more complex than I have assumed, and deserves further discussion. All that needs to be said here and now, however, is this. It is a purely practical point, and as such, I believe, uncontentious. A liberal society in which the authorities and the establishment generally not only decline to underwrite the moral and other values to which most of their subjects subscribe, but actually persecute, or allow to be persecuted, those who defend those values, will lose its legitimacy. It will find that its subjects are no longer prepared to defend it, or even to obey its laws.

Some of them, as we already see from various fundamentalist groups, may feel justified in breaking its laws and even in taking up arms against it. And that will lead to a crisis of authority which will hardly be resolved in liberalism's favor. In all probability, everything which liberals of every stripe have ever cared about, the good and the bad, the valuable and the worthless alike, will be swept away. Nothing is more arduously won than freedom, nothing is more easily abused, and nothing is more easily lost once it has been abused. I refer you only to Weimar Germany, whose outward appearance of decadence, no matter how undeserved, made it all the more vulnerable to the rise of National Socialism, since not enough people could be found to defend it.

To head off such dangers, I think, liberals had better decide just what things they want us all to be free from and why, and whether we too want to be free from them, before we find that none of us has any further choice in the matter. There are some things—love, friendship, duty, loyalty—for whose expression we seek freedom, but from which the normal conscience seeks never to be free. The normal conscience accordingly deserves our, and the liberals', respect. If liberalism withholds that respect, it is certain to find itself despised, its enactments disobeyed, the political order it has created crumbling to dust, and the door opened to tyranny. It is thus of the utmost importance for those of us who value liberalism's positive aspects to ensure that the liberal elites who rule us learn to recognize, to fear, and to inhibit its opposite tendencies towards social dissolution.

Bibliography

Grant, Robert. 1992. 'The Politics of Equilibrium', *Inquiry* 35. n. p.
Havel, Václav. 1986. *Living in Truth*, ed. J. Vladislav. London: Faber.
Scruton, Roger. 1996. *Animal Rights and Wrongs*. Pamphlet published by the independent 'think-tank' Demos. London.

Notes

1 A fact sometimes thought to be illustrated by the game-theoretic construct known as the Prisoner's Dilemma. See Grant (1992), especially pp. 425–27.

2 See 'The Mask of Anarchy' (1819). The title involves a pun on 'masque', since the poem describes an imaginary allegorical procession of contemporary political figures. (Something similar is found in Shelley's later, unfinished poem 'The Triumph of Life', in which 'triumph' signifies both the literal victory of the life-process over the things of the spirit, and a Roman-style 'triumph', that is, triumphal procession.)

3 A point made more than once in Havel (1986).

4 "If any ask me, what a free government is, I answer that for any practical purpose, it is what the people think so; and that they, not I, are the natural, lawful and competent judges of this matter" (Burke, *Letter to the Sheriffs of Bristol*, 1777).

5 The agitation for so-called animal rights (as opposed to merely securing decent treatment for animals) is a case in point. No animal is capable of understanding either human rights, or other animals' alleged rights, or those bestowed on it by animal sentimentalists. Nor, since animals are not moral beings, can it have any duties correlative to such 'rights'. If animal rights mean anything at all, the term is merely a kind of shorthand for our intuition that animals are not to be treated as creatures of no consequence and that we do have duties towards them, or in respect of them, in this regard.

6 The novelist E. M. Forster once notoriously observed that if he had to choose between betraying his friend and betraying his country, he hoped he would have the courage to betray his country. If we assume that the said country is one worthy of allegiance (and not, say, a superimposed, inauthentic political order like that of Nazi Germany, which the conspirators of July 1944 sought to overthrow precisely in the name of what they saw as the 'true' Germany), Forster's reasoning becomes almost unintelligible. For in the absence of a decent political order, such as the one to which Forster was subject, friendship is scarcely possible, since (as already observed) egoism is the only rational attitude to adopt. Friendship cannot trump its own indispensable condition. And the only case in which Forster's conflict could occur under a decent political order would be one in which the supposed friend was, in fact, a traitor. One who thus betrayed the very condition of friendship could hardly expect to benefit from others' loyalty, or any longer to count as a friend.

7 Nobody would be prepared, except in pathological cases, to risk or sacrifice his life for a mere object of desire. But in the otherwise anomalous case of the stranger in distress it is obviously not the stranger who is loved (since only what is known can be loved, and he might not in any case be very lovable), but the virtuous act of saving him. There is in such deeds a kind of superb poetic nonchalance which even those otherwise without a scrap of poetry in their make-up are capable of displaying, and without which, indeed, human life would be a poor thing. There are also, of course, certain professions, such as the police or fire services, whose ethic positively requires their members to risk their lives for strangers. In this there is something like what William James called "the moral equivalent of war", meaning the heroism without the killing. A nineteenth-century French writer, indeed, called the fireman the "*soldat pacifique*".

8 It once seemed possible, in the light of the so-called Star Wars project, that technological advance might alter this situation, but as the Tokyo subway gassings show, we still are—and are likely to remain—vulnerable to manually delivered chemical and biological weapons. To that extent our defense will still depend on the courage and virtue of significant numbers of citizens, be they soldiers or civilians.

9 "Les trois quarts de l'Europe attachent des idées très religieuses à cette hostie ... à ce crucifis, et voilà, d'où vient que j'aime à les profaner; je fronde l'opinion publique, cela m'amuse; je foule aux pieds les préjugés de mon enfance, je les anéantis; cela m'échauffe la tête" (Sade, *Justine*, quoted in Mario Praz, *The Romantic Agony* [Fontana, 1960], p. 126). Not even Sade, I imagine, supposed he was somehow *obliged* to think this way, let alone that any existence was possible in which everybody did. Compare the following:

> The pleasure which the Camp took in regarding itself as scandalous was actually the chief source of its inspiration ... the idea that they were sufficient unto themselves was very necessary to them; but it was nothing else than the truth, that they depended basically upon a solid, shockable world of decorum and common sense. They had to believe that a great ox-like eye was fixed upon them in horror. Without this their lives lost their point.
> (L. H. Myers, *The Root and the Flower* [Secker and Warburg, 1984 (1935)], 351)

The Value of Liberalism

SANDRA PRALONG

In this paper I shall argue that the 'value' of liberalism is precisely that it lacks any claim to substantive values, both for the individual and collectively. Thus liberalism's greatest value is ... the absence of values! This leaves the individual free to choose his or her values and to express them in individual and/or collective projects, thus asserting an identity based on them. But how can any order emerge out of the chaos of such conflicting values and projects? Can society be entirely permissive and tolerant of a diversity of value judgments without falling into anarchy?

The liberal paradox, then, is as follows: since individuals differ so much in their conceptions of 'good' and 'bad', of 'dos' and 'don'ts', is there any single, binding, 'liberal' value that all can agree about, an 'ethical code' common to all liberals that does not preclude individual freedom and value pluralism?

In their introduction to the 1996 Prague Colloquium on Liberalism, Jiří Musil and Zdeněk Suda asked if, in the wake of the totalitarian collapse, "liberalism is merely a reluctant heir" to a once powerful ideology, or does it still have the potential to assert itself strongly as a political choice, and, if so, how? I will not discuss here liberalism's status as an ideology, but wish merely to highlight its value, and to translate that value—if one can—into a possible ethical stance, applicable by individuals in their private as well as their public, political lives. This may seem overly pretentious, but my ambition is quite modest: I merely wish to show that, opinions to the contrary notwithstanding, an 'ethics of liberalism' is possible.

'Freedom for What?'[1]

To all the specific definitions of liberalism one can find, I would like to add a more generic thought: liberalism is about relationships. It is about how to handle them, and about which institutions can mediate them (and how). Our relationship to the world around us runs the gamut from metaphysics to politics to interpersonal exchanges. And so does the spirit of liberalism, which can be found in theology and politics, as well as in individual relations. I will leave aside metaphysics and theology—although much can be said about the correspondence between the Reformation and the subsequent development of political liberalism—and I will focus only on the political dimension and the corresponding collective and individual relationships it involves.

In politics, liberalism deals with the relationship between the individual and society, and establishes ways in which this relationship is mediated by the state and its institutions. Since liberalism is keen on preserving the sanctity of the private sphere it addresses individuals only in their public roles—there is no 'liberal ethics' to speak of, other than the necessity for toleration.

Before I delve into discussing liberalism's conception of 'relationships', I would first like to make a more general point about liberty. As it has often been remarked, liberty is the core concept of liberalism, although it is a loaded, elusive one. Let me say bluntly that I do not subscribe to the restrictive reading of Isaiah Berlin's dichotomy of "negative" and "positive" liberty. The two forms of freedom are not just compatible, but they share an indispensable complementarity. I agree with Berlin that "negative liberty"—that is, liberty *from* something—is indeed the key and the most critical concept (as it is the one most in need of defending when freedom is threatened). But negative liberty in itself is not sufficient, although it is indeed necessary. One does not assert one's 'space' for freedom in order to create a vacuum. Thus, negative freedom alone is, well, vacuous!

The space created by negative liberty is essential indeed, but it is important primarily because it makes room for us to assert a will. (The idea of asserting a will, of having a project, applies to individuals as well as to communities, to groups— in short, to 'society' at large). So, in my opinion, freedom in and by itself (that is, in Berlin's conception, 'negative freedom') is a necessary but not sufficient condition for human endeavor. If we merely stop at the boundaries of negative liberty, freedom becomes useless or empty.

To go back to Berlin's typology of two (different) types of liberty: only when they are considered from separate perspectives are these two forms of freedom indeed dichotomous. Negative liberty is incompatible with positive freedom only when we look at them from two different angles. Your assertion of positive freedom may, under certain circumstances, infringe upon my negative liberty. The two perspectives, yours and mine, may indeed be potentially incompatible. However, the two are very much related and continuous if we look at them from the consistent perspective of only one vantage point (that is, of one actor): my negative liberty is a precondition for my asserting my positive freedom, my will.

To borrow from Rawls's preference ordering: the two— negative and positive—freedoms are thus lexicographically ordered. In the binary world we have created for ourselves, a world of 'us' versus 'them' (and especially in the world of political science), this point is often lost. We rarely account for events from a 'clinical' perspective: tracing their continuous evolution; we most often focus on discreet and occasional conflicts among actors.[2]

But, regardless of our view of the world, the fact remains that 'others', alterity—or, more generally, the environment in which we exist—is primarily a catalyst to our own evolution, and not merely a hindrance or an opportunity to create conflict. I have no intention of descending into solipsism, or of creating an 'autistic' argument, so I shall leave it at that. But my point here is to plead for us to abandon, albeit for a moment, the binary paradigm when we consider liberty, and to focus instead on how positive freedom can be an extension of negative liberty when we look at both in a single, continuous perspective.[3] Thus the absolute, indispensable corollary to freedom is not, as is widely asserted, 'responsibility' (although responsibility is essential, of course). In my opinion, the indispensable partner to liberty, the other side of the coin, the necessary twin to freedom, is will.

Values and the Self: Deriving Identity from 'Belonging', 'Being', or 'Becoming'

In politics, as in the rest of life, nature abhors a vacuum: collectively, we either struggle to defend our (negative) freedom from its enemies, or, once that is secure, we consume our energies to assert our (positive) will.

Historically, the West, during the Second World War and the Cold War, was busy with the former (defending freedom), while communism, like Nazism before it, focused on the latter (creating a new man, a new race, or a new society). History has shown that, while the defense of negative liberty could—indeed had to—be a collective endeavor, the assertion of positive freedom (that is, the assertion of will), when undertaken collectively, was the surest way to tyranny and dictatorship. In its mildest form, it is, if nothing else, the "tyranny of the majority" discussed by Tocqueville. It follows that the only way to pursue positive liberty is not collective but individual. Bar those unique and often utopian instances where group cohesion is such that the will of one is the will of all (and where the commonality of values is so perfect that the common good is consensual and irrefutable), more often than not value pluralism precludes collective pursuits because they encroach on individual freedom. In other words, a 'thick' conception of the common good leaves little room for value pluralism, while a 'thin' conception (with no, or only a few, common projects), makes possible the individual assertion of positive freedom. As liberalism offers a thin conception of the good and encourages value pluralism, by the same token it also creates the necessary 'space' (negative liberty) for the individual to assert his or her values and will (positive freedom).

One of the most original insights of liberalism is the idea that individuals are not only autonomous agents but also self-originating sources of value. In other words, individuals have the ability—indeed the right—to make up their own mind about what matters to them. This idea has potency, especially if we consider negative and positive liberty in a continuous rather than a dichotomous perspective. Indeed, it is only if I can (and want) to fill the vacuum protected by my negative liberty—and only if I have a will to assert—that I can actualize my potential for being a self-originating source of value. This idea, too, has two immediate implications: one is its impact on the way in which we define our identity; the other is the issue of choice and the relationship between individual and collective values.

Let me start with the issue of identity. Ackeel Bilgrami defines identity as that which remains of our values after we have changed our mind. (His actual formulation may have been closer to: "Identity is defined by those values we are still willing to defend even though we may not believe in them any more".)[4] Therefore, if identity is given by one's values, two ideas follow:

(i) Since human beings are self-originating sources of value, the locus of identity—that is, that which generates the values one espouses—is the individual (by definition). This may seem obvious, but in light of so much current debate about group identity and communitarianism, it is not.

(ii) Even though there is a sense of the permanence of values in Bilgrami's definition of identity, it nevertheless also implicitly acknowledges that, over time, values may change. Thus our identity, as defined by the values we strongly believe in, may also evolve with time (albeit slowly in some cases).

Contrary to Bilgrami's assertion, the idea of values possibly being altered over time—even marginally—makes us want to define identity not according to the strength of the belief, or its duration, but according to the locus of change, which, again, is the individual. To use a tautology, the important element in determining our identity is that it is ours, and given by us! How much control we have over our changing values (which define us), is that which will determine the identity we choose for ourselves. We generally seem to choose those values we have most control over and define ourselves by them.[5]

Thus, regardless of how long we have held our values and beliefs, or whether anyone else shares them or not, we define ourselves by those values we choose as our own. This may seem like what the French call *"enfoncer des portes ouvertes"* (to break through open doors). But the debate about minority and ethnic rights,[6] or about life-style options, makes it seem that the current trend is towards group assertion of identity—towards an identity derived from 'belonging'—and towards legitimation of values by virtue of their being shared among group members, rather than by virtue of their being what each individual has identified as valuable for him- or herself.

I am neither an anti-communitarian nor an anarchist in disguise. But the problem with an identity derived from allegiance to a group—identity derived from 'belonging'—is that it requires the individual to delegate part of his or her power of decision over values to other people.[7] Yet we have accepted that identity, by being an assertion of one's values, ought, by definition, to be (as much as possible) under one's control. Thus the idea of 'belonging', no matter how important in other areas, cannot alone determine one's identity, just as individual values are not legitimated by their being shared. Moreover, an identity based on anything other than the self and self-generated values, negates the very liberal creed of the individual as an autonomous agent.

If the locus of identity is the self and not the group, it follows that no relationship we enter into will define us in the absence of a self-generated definition of ourselves. It also follows that, since we are going to be changing over time (and our relationships will change too), we need to redefine and re-evaluate those relationships as we redefine and re-evaluate our own identity. Thus, all relationships we enter into are negotiable—some tacitly, others explicitly—and none is static; all are changing, evolving, constantly deepening, or pulling apart.

This means that relationships based on a 'thick' conception of the good (on a substantive set of strong common values and projects) are less likely to facilitate the assertion of individual identity than are those based on thinner conceptions.

So while we have concluded that our identity cannot be derived from our group allegiance, it also appears that it cannot be derived from the current state of our relationships either, for two reasons:

(i) In order to allow our identities to blossom, relationships have to be based on very thin conceptions of the good (that is, on very little of substance), and this is contrary to the very idea of a relationship, which, when it is not procedural and merely formal, is usually based on shared values.

(ii) Relationships, like everything else, are also subject to change. More importantly, such change is not entirely under our control as autonomous agents, since it results from the interaction of all parties in relationships with us. Such lack of control negates our agent-status and is therefore not fully compatible with a liberal definition of the self.

Thus, in essence, our identity cannot be derived from 'being' in a current relationship any more than it can be derived from 'belonging' (to a group). Both being and belonging are subject to change dictated by factors not entirely in our control. They are not fully the result of a change of our will, but rather they are dictated by changes in circumstances (and we, as agents, have little say over them.) Consequently, we cannot be autonomous agents and self-generating sources of value (according to the liberal definition), if our identities are derived from circumstances outside the realm of our will.

Two ideas then follow:

(i) Since our values change, our relationships change with them and so do our identities. What this really means is that as our identities change, our needs change as well and, therefore, so do our life-projects.

(ii) As our needs change, the life-projects we design in order to fulfill these needs represent our innermost aspirations. Thus life-projects are a shorthand for our 'becoming'.

Since we are self-originating sources of value, it is our aspirations which most accurately translate our values. And even though these aspirations may be influenced by our environment,[8] they are not subject to change other than that decided on by us as autonomous agents. Thus life-projects—that is, our 'becoming'—represent the measure of identity most compatible with the view of the individual as an autonomous self-originating source of value. Given our definition of identity based on values, and given that only those values one has mastery over qualify as 'legitimate' criteria for determining the identity of an autonomous agent, one can sum-up one's identity as being defined by one's life-projects (embodied by one's aspirations) rather than being reflected by one's group allegiance or current status. In short, our identity is not determined by our 'belonging' and not even by our 'being', but is most visible in our 'becoming'.

Thus others—other people, families, groups, institutions, and so on: that is, our environment at large—are the catalysts, the facilitators, and the 'midwives' of our becoming, just as we are of theirs. This is not an 'instrumental' view of the world, in that I do not mean to say that we merely 'use' others for our own purposes. Quite the contrary: following Kant, by treating other human beings as ends rather than means, we increase the chances that they too will treat us as such, and thus will help contribute to our transformation just as we do to theirs. It is not a utilitarian view in the political-philosophical sense either, in that I do not think that—as creatures—we necessarily always pursue pleasure rather than pain, although pleasure is probably an important by-product of our 'becoming', of our projects being fulfilled.

To continue with this train of thought for a moment, I do not think that as humans we can be defined by our sentience any more than we can be defined by our rationality. We are never fully rational, as we are never seeking pleasure alone in the face of duty or obligation. I believe, however, that what makes us human is precisely our ability to conceive of projects and pursue them in a variety of ways.[9] Thus, if I can be allowed a rather elusive formula, I believe that human beings can be defined as 'beings in becoming'. Our becoming can be conscious and explicit, or it can be subconscious and implicit, but the important thing is that we are defined by our projects, our plans. In plain speech, these projects are what 'keep us going'. Without projects, large or small, we are lost, prey to depression, drug abuse, crime, violence—in short, to in-humanity.

In this context, the value of liberalism is precisely the freedom it affords us to become whatever we choose to be—

for liberalism leaves individuals free to give meaning to their lives. So, 'beings in becoming' that we are, we are defined by our projects, which dictate our identity. But how can we become whatever we choose without hindering others? What rule of thumb can we follow to make sure that the assertion of our will (our positive freedom) does not encroach on anyone's private space (their negative liberty), or hinder others' ability to pursue their own life-projects?

'Liberal Values': Substantive or Procedural?

Jiří Musil, in his introduction to the 1996 Prague Colloquium, discussed the idea of liberalism as a precondition of modern society. But once society has become modern, what then? In Musil's example, Eastern Europe offers an enlightening illustration: "Under communism, we were all liberals", says Musil. "But now, we don't know anymore", he laments.

To go back to the original discussion about liberty, it seems that there are two kinds of freedom, although this dichotomy is different from that of Berlin:

(i) One is freedom as *an end in itself*—the freedom for which, for instance, those who fought communism yearned.

(ii) The other is freedom as *a means to an end*—the freedom most of the world enjoys now (and does not quite know what to do with).

Freedom-as-an-end-in-itself is self-contained. But freedom-as-a-means requires (by logical extension) the assertion of will: 'freedom for what'? Thus freedom as 'a means to something' requires a plan, a project.

Back to the perspective of Berlin's negative and positive liberties: freedom-as-an-end is a close parallel to Berlin's 'negative liberty' (freedom from something, freedom for its own sake), while freedom-as-a-means runs hand-in-hand with Berlin's 'positive freedom' (freedom to/for something).

We noted at the beginning that this idea of the two freedoms as complementary rather than dichotomous should be understood conceptually, as it applies both to individuals and to groups and communities. Let me discuss here the 'value' of liberalism, going from the individual to the collective conception of freedom. As determined earlier, the value of liberalism derives precisely from its lack of attachment to specific substantive values—liberalism is notorious for its lack of ideological pretensions. Yet Zdeněk Suda accurately observed that while liberalism as a collective project lacked the makings of an ideology (Suda and Musil, 1996),[10] as a descriptive tool it could be matched only by religion in its conception and its breadth of explanation of the way things are. So, then, how exactly are things when groups share liberal values?

From empirical observation (or in historical perspective) we determined that, while the pursuit of negative liberty can be a collective endeavor and still be compatible with value pluralism, the assertion of will (that is, positive freedom), if collective, is likely to be tyrannical.[11] Thus liberalism shines in the absence of a collective goal; there is no 'liberal project' to speak of, other than the commitment to an order which shuns any substantive, collective project. However, we customarily grant liberalism a few substantive values, which eventually play a normative role. These are:

(i) liberty;
(ii) the right to property;
(iii) what is called in the USA the right to "the pursuit of happiness", or the right to choose one's own path in life. (This is a poetical stance for the liberal view of the individual as the ultimate decision-maker about what is of value to him or her, which grants him or her the status of a 'self-originating source of value'.)

All these elements, although in and by themselves substantive, considered collectively amount to very little of substance. Yet, in order to make them applicable at the individual level, they need to be collectively considered in a procedural (rather than a substantive) perspective. In other words, while the recognition of value pluralism precludes that any of the values mentioned above should acquire substantive status as 'common conceptions of the good' (that is, taken collectively they are merely procedural norms), they nevertheless remain substantive at the individual level, where they accommodate varying values and individual conceptions of the good.

In short, collectively, 'liberal values' merely set the stage for the procedural architecture that enables individuals to pursue these and other substantive projects of their own. We therefore deal at the collective level with a formal process, while at the individual level we engage in a substantive search (for meaning, values, and projects).

Considered at the political level, for instance, democracy is a collective (political) *process*, while liberalism itself engages primarily in an individual *search*. The collective process we call 'democracy' is merely one procedure (among many) for allocating claims in society—the worst possible one, bar all the others, said Churchill. As mentioned above, just like any other relationship, the political arrangement it represents is negotiable, either via elections or through changes in legislation. But can democracy be defined by procedures and institutional arrangements alone, in the absence of any collectively shared, substantive values? Liberal democracy focuses on the defense of negative freedom as a common conception of the good. It is a thin conception but it is nonetheless a substantive value.

However, pushed to its logical conclusion, the defense of negative freedom eventually results in an institutional vacuum and social anarchy. Following the lexicographic ordering discussed above, the defense of negative freedom alone is necessary but not sufficient. Protecting freedom alone is not a viable social project, because once freedom-as-an-end has been reached society runs the risk of institutional collapse. (Parenthetically, this is what seems to be happening in most Western democracies now that the Cold War is over.)[12]

Thus, the conquest of negative liberty has to be supplemented by an assertion of will, by positive freedom, which then becomes a means to an end (a means to a project). This means that once freedom is achieved, negative liberty *per se* cannot determine the collective agenda anymore. In politics, this translates into the need for a new common project. But the catch is this: short of a perfect consensus, how can a collective project respect individual freedom and value pluralism? We have seen that the project cannot be substantive. It cannot offer a 'thick conception' of the good (that is, it cannot set common values for the group as a whole) since that would exclude those group members whose values are different (and imposing common values would amount to despotism and tyranny).

Thus if the collective project cannot be substantive it ought to be procedural. The social contract is one such procedural collective project. A social contract defines and establishes the relationship between the parties to the social arrangement. It spells out which substantive goods (or values) are to be exchanged, and establishes the procedure to be followed by the parties during the transaction. For instance, the procedural means to allocate scarce goods in society will depend on the choice of regime, which helps establish and enforce the criteria for allocation.

I see the social contract—like all social relationships—as constantly being renewed, either formally (via elections), or informally, via enactment of legislation, changes in public attitudes, and so on. For me, this contract is not a one-off metaphorical construction, but an overall commitment society agrees upon with every generation, even though the agreement may only be implicit. Thus the contract can be partially modified (by institutional adjustment) or completely transformed (in revolutions). Like all human relationships, it lives, therefore it changes.

With the end of the Cold War, the social contract, both East and West, seems to have come up for a (formal) renewal. The old terms have expired—the parties in the West have acquired the necessary guarantees that principles of liberty and human rights will not be challenged, while the East has abandoned its will to create a new world order according to communist values. A new social contract is therefore needed to reflect the changed realities, the transformed identities, and the new expectations and values both East and West. But a new social contract requires commitments of both principle and substance, and cannot be limited to considerations about procedure alone. So how can a liberal society respond to the challenge of establishing collective commitments about substantive values when it shies away from proclaiming any 'common goods'?

The answer is: it probably cannot, and certainly should not, since declaring any substantive values to be collectively desirable would contradict liberalism's commitment to protect value pluralism. Yet a common denominator in the value sphere among individuals is needed in order to establish a new social contract—or are we to accept that the idea of 'common liberal values' is an oxymoron, and move on?

Is There an 'Ethics' of Liberty?

In a liberal perspective it seems that the idea of 'common *substantive* values' is indeed a contradiction in terms. However, establishing universally valid *procedural* methods can lead to a consensus without hindering the freedom of autonomous agents to choose their own substantive ends (that is, without hindering value pluralism). Therefore, to design a new social contract, we need to find those procedural values that are acceptable to all parties, and can apply both individually and on the collective level. As already discussed, in a liberal democracy, while the defense of negative liberty can—indeed should—be an object of collective endeavor, the assertion of positive freedom, if collective, may turn despotic.[13] That means that the collective '*Minima Moralia*' cannot be substantive, it can only be procedural.

Leaving aside a complex discussion about procedural issues, such as the rule of law and obedience to the law, how can ethics (that is, ideas about 'good' and 'bad') be 'procedural' without falling into utter moral relativism? And if we cannot design a substantive, explicit morality, with clear 'dos and don'ts', what are ethics to be made of? Even the mild—and seemingly reasonable—varieties of moral precept, such as, for instance, the 'ethics of responsibility' everyone now wants to embrace, are ruled out since they are substantive and thus can, in practice, become despotic too.

So where does this leave us? What can we do? We want, indeed we need, a common denominator to bind society together, and the libertarian ethos is not enough.

We need to build into the architecture of our social contract not just procedural means to protect our liberty (so that we can choose our own values), we also need to designate a shared value, a common ethical standard, which, as we have seen, cannot be substantive. Can this shared value—an ethical stance—be merely procedural, and if so, how? In ethics, the narrowest common ground requires toleration of diversity and respect for others as equals, as ends in themselves, rather than as means. The lowest common denominator in this realm is Kant's categorical imperative, which, one could argue, elaborates on Jesus of Nazareth's Golden Rule: 'Do unto others as you would like them to do unto you'. But one can easily see why, in a liberal perspective, this can be a 'road to hell paved with good intentions'. The expectation of reciprocity can lead to imposition: if I want to be treated in a certain way, I may treat others in ways they disapprove of, or dislike. Examples abound.

Criticism of the Kantian categorical imperative has focused mostly on its lack of substantive content. The injunction to act only in such a way that you can also will that your maxim should become a universal law has been considered too 'procedural', for it does not spell out exactly how one should act, but merely what effect our actions ought to have (that is, create 'universal law', and to treat others as ends, not as means). I disagree with this criticism.[14] First, charges brought against the categorical imperative as being merely 'procedural' are wrong since the categorical imperative does have an overriding, ultimate substantive value—that of 'achieving a kingdom of ends'. But my second disagreement is even more basic. It applies both to Kant and to the Golden Rule, and it is this: as we set about choosing ways to treat others (or as we design the 'laws' we want to see become universal), we are engaged not in procedural matters but in making substantive choices. We are putting forth some very particular values—ours—for others to follow.

Given the way in which the two ethical stances are formulated (that is, in the affirmative, by enjoining one to 'do unto others', or to 'act as if ...'), both the Golden Rule and the categorical imperative err, if anything, by being too substantive and not procedural enough, although the norm is given by the individual. Therefore, the categorical imperative and the Golden Rule are not the right common ethic, since, being substantive, they may become despotic. In its worst incarnation, a version of the Golden Rule (that is, wanting for others what we think best for ourselves) led, for instance, to the totalitarian experience under communism.

Yet because both ethical stances are not merely ego-centered and substantive, but also encompass a procedural aspect, both the categorical imperative and the Golden Rule should be 'salvaged', as they seem the only ethical principles versatile enough to gain consensus. Kant's injunction to us to treat others as if we were designing universal laws of behavior, like Jesus' Golden Rule, easily transcends cultural and religious boundaries since it does not explicitly specify any particular behavior. On the other hand, as we have seen, both rules can also lead to an imposition of (one's own values, over others') values.

So, can anything be done to preserve the categorical imperative and the Golden Rule in some form, and 'save' them from the charge that they hold the seeds of despotism? In other words, is there an ethical principle fully compatible with both negative liberty and positive freedom, that dutifully preserves value pluralism?

My answer is 'yes', provided that we look at the categorical imperative and the Golden Rule in a different perspective—or rather, provided we enunciate them differently. For this, let us first go back to the lexicographic ordering of the two types of liberty, where negative liberty necessarily precedes positive freedom. If the categorical imperative is a substantive assertion of (positive) will—that is, if it reveals my preference for how I would like to be treated—then the necessary precondition is to secure a sufficient space of negative liberty for myself, so that I will not be treated as others may want to treat me (and I will be left alone to decide for myself what I want). In other words, I need to secure sufficient liberty in order to assert myself as a self-originating source of value(s).

However, in order to secure for ourselves that space of negative liberty, we need to reciprocate by also securing it for others. Thus, it follows that the only meaningful way in which I can treat others is to preserve their negative freedom and never do unto them that which I do not want them to do unto me. This negative formulation (a sort of 'negative Golden Rule') respects our lexicographic ordering: I must first preserve for myself (and for others) that which enables us all to fill our life with meaning (and value)—that is, our negative liberty—which then allows us to assert a positive will. The negative formulation liberates us from the potential tyranny which would prevail if we imposed substantive values on each other and leaves ethical precepts in the realm of procedure alone.

In short, the 'negative Golden Rule' ('do not do unto others what you would not want them to do unto you'), as well as a possible negative formulation of Kant's imperative ('never act in ways in which you would not want others to act'), best respect the individual's freedom and guarantee value pluralism.

However, while the negative formulation strips the ethical rule of any potential substantive content (rendering it purely procedural), it nevertheless has important substantive implications. For instance, it precludes violence from the liberal repertory of means: as I would not want to be treated violently by others, I will abstain from violence myself. Or, regarding income distribution: as I want to avoid starvation while I pursue my meaningful life-project, I need to prevent others from starving while I have plenty to eat. Thus, since the ethical norm is to never do unto others that which I would not want others to do unto me, if I fear hunger for myself, I cannot accept a system that would allow others to go hungry.

To be secure, freedom does not need—indeed is incompatible with—a strong moral order (either based on religion or enforced by the state). True liberty accommodates only the thinnest conception of the good, and leaves only a very narrow basis for common ethics (that is, those that preserve negative freedom). In addition, as we have seen, these ethics work to preserve freedom only if they are procedural, not substantive. Inside the 'space' thus kept free (negative liberty), we can then each develop our own individual conception of the good, apply our will, and try to shape our destinies (positive freedom). This procedural ethic, which collectively preserves individual freedom yet provides a shared value for all individuals, seems to me to represent a possible common 'value' of liberalism.

The Burdens of Liberalism

I would like to conclude by going back to what I believe has changed since 1989, when the social contract came up for renewal. Since we can freely claim our identity from our 'becoming' (and liberalism helps us set up social arrangements in which we may become whatever we wish to be), we face several interrelated burdens that we might call the 'burdens of freedom'. All of these will eventually force us to rethink our social and economic arrangements, and our (political) relationship to the state (that is, to renew our social contract).

More deeply, these burdens will completely alter our relationship to our general environment (and since they deal with our relationship to the world, they are within the realm of liberalism). Let me outline each separately, and link them to what I believe to be the common value of liberalism.

(i) As Jiří Musil's observation indicated, freedom-as-an-end—especially in the West—has been replaced by freedom-as-a-means. But the immediate corollary to this is that we must now figure out to *what* it is a means. We are faced, therefore, with what I would call the 'burden of choice'—and liberty is, indeed, having to make choices. What will we fill our freedom with? What will we choose as our life-project, both individually and as a group or society? These are the hard questions we now have to face as we acknowledge our full and unmitigated responsibility for the choices we make.

(ii) Since, from the liberal point of view, we are self-generating sources of value, we alone can find value and meaning in the projects we undertake. We do not derive our identity from belonging but from becoming, and even though we rely on each other and interact constantly, no one else can dictate to us what to value—indeed, that would be an unacceptable imposition in the liberal perspective. This means also that we are alone in making choices. Therefore I will call the second burden we bear the 'burden of loneliness', or of aloneness (even though we feel alone in an increasingly large crowd, as the world seems to become smaller and smaller). The burden of loneliness means that we cannot rely on ready-made answers or on the stale solutions of defunct ideologies—from Left or Right. It also means that we cannot hide our individual responsibility in the midst of traditional families, kin groups, or nations. We alone are responsible for the choices we make, and our responsibility extends not just to ourselves but to all those around us, to those far away, and even to the as yet unborn.

(iii) Since the terms of our old social contract have expired (rendered obsolete by the collapse of totalitarianism) and we need to design a new one, there is one thing to remember: under the old contract social cohesion was given by shared enemies (in the West), or by shared ideological goals (in the East). Now, with the Cold War over, social cohesion must be found without any common substantive values to bind us to one another—neither mutual hatred nor idealistic hope (nor, until recently, religion). Yet, even without relying on common values, a common outside threat, or a common aspiration, we must realize that bound together we are, if only by procedural rules. We must therefore create our community on the thinnest of premises: toleration (of each other's differences) and respect (for each other's freedom).

Since we now live just about everywhere in (relatively) open societies, and as open systems are not just open but open-ended, I will call this third burden the 'burden of conscience'.[15] Our hard-won freedom to choose our own values, and our struggle to be identified by those choices, has a cost: responsibility. We now discover that individual responsibility is not only towards ourselves, and our own well being, but, directly or indirectly, towards all others. Released from the fear of nuclear destruction and from the constraints of ideology, we must realize that each and every one of us is now responsible for every turn society takes, as well as for the environment (physical, cultural, and so on) in which we live. And although we cannot spell out any one substantive value to guide us all, we can revert to one common liberal

value: we can pledge to respect others as we would like ourselves to be respected, and 'not do unto them that which we
do not want them to do unto us'.

Notes

1 Title of an essay by Robert Grant, 'Freedom for What?', in *Morality and
Religion in Liberal Democratic Societies* (New York: Paragon House, 1991).

2 As we pursue our way, our relation to others can indeed be antagonistic,
or, as Robert Grant stresses in his contribution to the present volume,
'Liberalism, Value, and Social Cohesion', it can be based on love. Hence exchanges can be harmonious rather than conflictual.

3 If we look at negative and positive liberty in a binary perspective, not
only do we see them as antagonistic, but we also get a closer insight into how
the two main ideologies of the last half-century have concurred to create
monsters: the pursuit of 'negative liberty' alone led to the current 'blah' in the
West, where individuals and societies seem now adrift, devoid of hope or
moral goals. On the other hand, under communism, the assertion of positive
freedom with no regard for the preservation of 'negative' individual liberty,
turned a potentially valuable collective project into a despotic, tyrannical
prison sentence for millions.

4 Professor Ackeel Bilgrami, class notes, Columbia University, 1995.

5 Ethnic strife may seem to belie this thesis, but nevertheless, people
choose to uphold their ethnic allegiance and become politically involved in
nationalist arguments.

6 See the issue of 'collective rights' in Europe.

7 This is the issue faced by hundreds of 'dissidents' the world over: one
can get trapped into being identified with a group whose values one does not
fully endorse anymore. How does one mark one's identity? By belonging and
sharing the group's values or by rejecting those one does not agree with?

8 See Marx's discussion of 'false consciousness'.

9 I am indebted to Professor David Johnston, of Columbia University, for
this insight.

10 Z. Suda and J. Musil, 'Reluctant Heir—Liberalism in Central
Europe', paper delivered at the 1996 Prague Colloquium.

11 See the ideological struggle during the Cold War, and the idea that the
assertion of collective will is potentially tyrannical.

12 The purpose of the Cold War, in the West, was to 'defend freedom'.

13 A substantive will can be exerted only at the individual (actor's) level.
Collectively, only the pursuit of negative freedom can represent a common
goal. 'Actors' can be individuals, groups, or—in the international arena—even
states. The key way of avoiding getting confused about this idea is to maintain
the consistency of the level of analysis. For instance, in a universe of individuals, the defense of (negative) liberty can be proclaimed by all as a collec-

tive goal without loss of freedom to any of them. A society—or a group of individuals—that chooses the defense of liberty as its common goal is still compatible with individual value pluralism. On the other hand, the same society that chooses to assert a 'positive freedom', a particular substantive end, cannot do that without loss to the individual's ability to make his or her own choice of values. The same holds true if the actors are groups in a universe of groups: no common goal for all groups is compatible with their freedom to choose their own scope, unless there is a predetermined consensus over ends. Likewise, in the international arena: a universe of states (collective actors) can be brought together to defend peace on Earth (in case of, say, alien attack) without hindering their respective abilities to pursue their own ends, yet this very same group cannot be brought to agree to peace on Earth as a substantive collective end (and make it enforceable), and still be compatible with the ends of individual states that may, for instance, wish to make territorial gains from their neighbors. Another example, showing the incompatibility of positive freedom (assertion of will) with value pluralism, is the WTO and the difficulty the organization has in maintaining its scope while accommodating the conflicting economic systems of its members.

14 Professor D. Johnston, class notes, Columbia University.

15 I borrow the term 'burden of conscience' from an unpublished manuscript by George Soros. Although I have not read it—and therefore I ignore its premiss—nevertheless I find the title most appropriate to underscore the underlying mechanisms of the Open Society.

Communitarianism in Practice: The Threat to Individual Rights from the Institutionalist Interpretation of the German Basic Law

Thomas Scheffer

About ten years ago, the modern Anglo-Saxon social philosophy of communitarianism became popular in continental Europe. As far as its real influence on the public political debate is concerned, it seems that it has remained a somewhat romantic basis for a number of conservative political programs without its goals being realized in political practice.

In this chapter I want to show that this impression is only partially correct. Although the attacks of Sandel, MacIntyre, and Taylor on the Enlightenment and on negative freedom are rarely used as arguments, their collectivist and traditionalist view of social life is shared at least in Germany by many theorists of public law who have great influence on the criteria of political decisions, namely, the interpretation of the basic rights of the German constitution. Although as a philosopher I am no expert in public law or the history of constitutions, I find it alarming that there are close analogies between a certain unpopular but influential theory of public law and the general principles of the popular but seemingly unsuccessful communitarianism.

The fundamental right to act according to one's own will as long as nobody else is hindered thereby can be interpreted in two different perspectives: one is concerned with the extent and the other with the strength of the right. In respect to its extent we can ask whether it implies prima facie—that means, given that nobody else is inhibited—the permissibility of any action, or whether it only contains the permissibility of particular kinds of actions that are, for example, of special relevance to the personal development of the actor. The classical liberal view here is that this permissibility should, prima facie, be universal. Communitarianism, on the contrary, holds that only actions that agree with the tradition or cultural identity of a nation or any other well-defined community can be permitted prima facie.

In the second case, we can ask whether the fundamental right to act freely only equals the guarantee of non-interference with one's actions or whether it establishes a claim to the material support needed to realize a multitude of actions, as for example the claim to a subsistence level of income. Most liberals here argue for a basic right to some material support, but waver between mere protection against destitution on the one hand—as for example Hayek (Hayek, 1981, 122) or Buchanan (Buchanan, 1984, 58n)—and, on the other hand, social-liberal conceptions like Rawls's that demand everybody's participation in the profits of the successful sectors of society. Communitarians urge the right of individuals to comprehensive life-long support, but in most cases legitimate this right as a requirement of moral duty or social solidarity (Sandel, 1982, 179).

There is no need to explain that the social-liberal interpretation of the basic right to act often stood freely, and recently has again come under pressure for economic reasons. But it is interesting to see that in Germany even the purely legal and negative liberal interpretation is being attacked for reasons that sound quite communitarian.

The constitutional court of the Federal Republic of Germany always interpreted article 2 paragraph 1 of the Basic Law ("Everyone has the right to the free development of his person insofar as he does not interfere with the rights of others and does not violate the legal order or the moral law") as a guarantee of the universal freedom to act. According to this interpretation the article protects "not only the limited realm of personal development", but prima facie "any kind of human action" (BVerfG [*Bundesverfassungsgericht*: Federal Constitutional Court]—decision of 6 June 1989; BVerfGE [Decision of the Federal Constitutional Court] 80, 137 [152], with hints at previous decisions).

Despite wide acceptance of this interpretation it has been increasingly criticized since about 1970. One of the most influential objections to it was expressed in a dissenting opinion by Dieter Grimm, a judge of the constitutional court itself. In his view, article 2 paragraph 1 does not protect the freedom to act according to one's will; the protected behavior rather has to be as important to personal development as similar forms of behavior protected by the special basic rights (BVerfGE 80, 137 [165]). Grimm sees clearly that universal freedom of action could be restricted by ordinary law. So his objections are in fact directed less against the extent than against the intensity of the protection of individual freedom. In its practical interpretation, according to Grimm, this basic right gives the competence to anybody to demand with legal force that any restriction of his freedom be based on valid law, and by this, he argues, the objective principle of the rule of law is changed into a subjective right (BVerfGE 80, 137 [167]). In his opinion, this is intolerable because now everybody who is affected by any action of the state can force the constitutional court to adjudicate the constitutional correctness of any law (BVerfGE 80, 137 [168]). That means that Grimm wants to reduce the intensity of the protection of the freedom to act in favor of the state's capacity to act.

The general view of the function and meaning of basic rights that forms the background of Grimm's objections is the so-called institutionalist theory of basic rights. The jurisdiction of the Federal Constitutional Court is only partially influenced by it, but even today many theorists of public law share this view. The term itself contains its key concept—institution—whether merely juridical or, more importantly, social. According to this view, for example, the basic right to marriage and to have a family not only signifies the permissibility and juridical possibility of marriage, but also ensures the continuous existence of the juridical and social institutions of marriage and the family (Starck, 1979, 45). Institutionalists also interpret the basic right to religious freedom primarily as the objective obligation of the state to protect the traditional religious confessions and not as the guarantee of the choice to accept or reject a religious confession at will. According to the institutionalist view, the individual with his subjective right only participates in this objective obligation. In the same way, the guarantee of a free choice of one's profession and of the freedom of scholarship are, on this view, primarily objective and restricted to traditional kinds of professions and scholarly investigation or to those that are of public interest (Häberle, 1983, 103).

The reason usually given by institutionalists for these restrictions is that social stability and well ordered prospects are to be expected from social institutions. One of the most prominent institutionalists, Peter Häberle, speaks of a "corporate side" of all basic rights. This corporate side, according to him, is dominant in respect of freedom of opinion, freedom of worship, and freedom of profession; but in general he holds every basic right to be the "basis for participation in political, economic, and cultural processes"; and so the common function of all basic rights is to integrate the individual into the community (Häberle, 1983, 344).

The basic rights as subjective public rights not only characterize the status of the individual within the state; they also refer to his or her status in the diverse relations of his or her life. "The basic rights not only determine the relation of the citizen to his state, but also the life of the citizen within the objective constitutional order. In both cases the subjective public right of the individual is assigned to an institution and thus to a juridical institution, namely, to the institution of all institutions, to the state, and to its juridically regulated life relations, that is, to the objective order ... The objective institution and the subjective status form a whole, the whole of each basic right" (Häberle, 1983, 112n).

According to the institutionalist view, all basic rights protect traditional ways of life for all citizens in order to give their individual freedom "direction and measure, safety and security, meaning and a sense of purpose" (Häberle, 1983, 98). The original guarantee of individual freedom in this conception is narrowed down to the secondary function of securing a minimal private life.

As far as I know, neither the German nor any other institutionalist theory of basic rights has been adopted by communitarian theorists. Nevertheless, their theories and demands show many analogies and can be seen as parallel doctrines, with similar intentions. The common and principal end of all basic rights in their institutionalist interpretation—the integration of the individual into the community—is also the main purpose of public law and social justice for most communitarians. But the concept of 'integration' also leads back to the 'doctrine of integration' (*Integrationslehre*), developed by Rudolf Smend in the final years of the Weimar Republic (1928–33). The similarities between the institutionalist and communitarian theories and this doctrine make it clear that any institutionalist interpretation of a basic right should be given very careful thought. Like the institutionalists and the communitarians of our day, Smend lamented that the liberal basic rights of the Weimar constitution secured the citizen in his role as a "cunning and selfish individualist", who was "incapable of love and adventure, of beauty and inner liveliness", and of whom "nothing can be expected by way of a contribution to the creative building of an exciting new world" (Smend, 1955, 311–13). The same objection is raised by the communitarian Michael Sandel against the liberal theory of John Rawls. The egoistic individualist whom Rawls puts behind the 'veil of ignorance' when selecting the principles of social justice, according to Sandel never seems prepared to share his profits with the worst-off, as the second principle requires. Social altruism could be expected only in someone who sees himself less as an individual than as a participant primarily in the collective identity of his family, community, class, or nation (Sandel, 1982, 43, 80).

In contrast to the liberal individualist picture of man Smend in 1933 proposed to go back to the ethics of the ancient Greek citizen, that is, to understand him as a 'member of a national community that gives his life substance and sense' (Smend, 1955, 312). In the same way, Alasdair MacIntyre chooses Aristotelian ethics as the basis for his communitarian theory. In his opinion, the common fundamental moral convictions of the Western world can be grounded only in a common Christian history: the classical Christian moral doctrine of Thomas Aquinas is just an elaboration of Aristotelian ethics (MacIntyre, 1987, 75n).

From the same ground Smend draws the consequence that any basic right has to serve the 'integration' of the individual into the national community. In every basic right a 'political good' has to be anchored, in the commitment to which the nation—in this case the German nation—wants to be united (Smend, 1928, 91). Thus, the basic rights, according to him, 'proclaim' a certain cultural and normative system as the essence of public life, especially of a particular nation (Smend, 1928, 264n).

In the same way, MacIntyre explains the origin and function of social morals. Many ways of life that are characteristic of a given community are, in his opinion, ends in themselves, which means moral ends that can only be realized by the interaction of many; which again implies that the individual, in order to act morally, has to integrate himself into the community (MacIntyre, 1987, 274n). Moral standards are formed by the obligations and duties which a person takes over from the past of his family, city, tribe, or nation (MacIntyre, 1987, 294n).

In direct reference to constitutional law the communitarian Charles Taylor declares basic individual rights to be of secondary importance, if the survival of the culture of a nation is in danger. In favor of this collective good, in his opinion even the right to equality can be neglected, for example, in order to create a single national language (Taylor, 1993, 56n). Taylor sees very well that this priority of collective goods over individual rights endangers plurality within a society, but pluralism itself in his eyes is just one collective good among others that a nation may adopt (Taylor, 1993, 56n). However, Smend in 1933 took his arguments a little further, totally rejecting parliamentary democracy because it only means an "anarchistic conglomerate of political groups in an armistice of class struggle" (Smend, 1955, 323). He opposed it with the demand that the basic rights of any constitution have to serve the interests of the state as a whole (Smend, 1928, 91).

In fact, the German constitutional court has given an institutionalist interpretation to many of the basic rights. Some of them are in themselves formulated objectively—so, for example, the guarantee of the freedom of the press (art. 5, par. 1, sent. 2), the protection of marriage and family (art. 6, par. 1), and the rights to ownership and inheritance (art. 14, par. 1). As a limit to the subjective right to ownership the collective good of common welfare is quoted in article 14 paragraph 2:

"Property carries obligations. Its use must also serve the common welfare." Beyond that, the court itself adopts the institutionalist interpretation when it finds that freedom of the press is not only a subjective right of those who work in that field, but also guaranteed as the "institution of a free press". Freedom of the press, it says, "is more than a mere subcase of freedom of opinion, because beyond this the institutional independence of the press is guaranteed—from investigation to the dissemination of the message and the opinion". "This institutionalist protection of the press as an instrument and disseminator of public opinion in the interest of free democracy *entails* the subjective public right of those who work in this field" (BVerfGE 10, 1 [121]; my emphasis). Similarly, the article about freedom of union activities (art. 9), according to the court, contains an institutional guarantee, namely, that of the system of wage agreements. Not only the right to freely create coalitions, "but also the coalition as such" and its right to pursue its aims are guaranteed (BVerfGE 19, 303 [312]).

But this does not mean that the constitutional court primarily interprets the German constitution in an institutionalist and thus communitarian sense. From the beginning of its jurisdiction it repeatedly stressed that basic rights "in the first place are individual rights, human or civil rights, which have as their object the protection of concrete, particularly endangered spheres of human freedom"; if they, beyond this, have an objective—ultimately institutionalist—meaning, "this only serves to strengthen their validity" (BVerfGE 7, 198 [205]; 50, 290 [337]). Further theoretical explanations or abstract criteria that say what kinds of collective goods are compatible with the dominance of subjective rights are not given by the constitutional court. The formulation that any objective meaning of a basic guarantee only "serves to strengthen its validity as a subjective right" seems to restrict collective goods to the role of mere means to the realization or fulfillment of subjective rights. At first sight, this does not seem convincing. If, for instance, private property is nationalized for the purpose of building a motorway, the common welfare for which this is done is neither the object of any basic subjective right nor is it sure that those who pay for the motorway or give their land for it will profit in the same degree. Here, obviously, some differentiation is necessary. First, a certain reduction of a basic freedom or competence in a given degree is to be distinguished from its total displacement. An expropriation is acceptable—and thereby legal—only if the dispossessed person receives compensation. Common welfare is to this extent not a collective good that could obliterate the subjective right to ownership totally. Second, we have to distinguish between two different kinds of possible collectives: (i) the collective of all involved or really existing bearers of subjective rights, and (ii) the collective of the numerous potential bearers of these subjective rights. In respect of many public institutions, the collective in favor of which they are established can only be the collective of the potential and future citizens of the state.

The constitutional court takes this universalistic perspective on basic rights by interpreting them as containing 'values' or even an "objective order of values which as a fundamental decision of the constitution is binding in all fields of law" and gives "guidelines and impulses for legislation, administration and jurisdiction" (BVerfGE 39, 1 [41]).

In respect of philosophical moral theories one normally distinguishes between theories of values and deontological theories which may make use of the criterion of universalization. Philosophical theories of value—such as the 'Wertlehre' of Max Scheler—mostly hold that we grasp values by intuition. Deontological theories in their most prominent version—that of Kant—see a basic rule at the bottom of all moral obligations, which we know through our rational dispositions. But leaving aside these material differences between value theories and rule theories we can treat the difference between values and normative rules as a mere difference in formulation (Alexy, 1986, 126n). Leaving aside questions of justification and epistemic status, the claim that freedom is a value means nothing else than that the rule 'realize freedom!' is valid.

Seen from the deontological point of view, the positive basic rights of a constitution can be understood as rules of thumb, each of which has to be applied in ordinary situations. With respect to extraordinary situations, however, these rules of thumb may conflict and have to be weighted correctly by referring to their common purpose as expressed in the underlying fundamental principle. The common function and purpose—and consequently the underlying principle—may be read off the structure of the given guarantees. Thus, in relation to the German constitution Günter Dürig in 1956 found that the two aspects of the dominating principle—that is, obligation and the corresponding universal subjective claim to the dignity of man in article 1—are laid down in the following two articles, namely the two general aspects of freedom and equality. The latter are specified for certain standard situations or aspects of life in the subsequent, more concrete basic rights. If we see them—from the axiological point of view—as guarantees of values, then a '*Wertordnung*', a system of values, corresponds to this system of principles. From the special systematic order of the basic rights it follows that they are basically individualistic in their meaning. But from their objective meaning as general obligations of the state—that is, from their value content—it follows that they refer not only to actual citizens or living men, but also to those to come.

From these differentiations in the systematic order and the range and scope of the validity of the basic rights of the German constitution it follows for their relation to collective goods that such goods can limit individual rights only if other rights or interests of at least potential citizens of the state are thereby proportionately improved. The criterion of the maximization of individual rights plays a pragmatic role, like the basic rights, understood as rules of thumb themselves. Essentially, the constitution aims at the same real and prima facie unrestricted freedom for any potential citizen or person, and therefore is of a deontological kind.

But still the question remains whether there are collective goods which have the power wholly to outweigh individual rights in a special case. As such 'outstanding collective goods' up to now the German constitutional court has qualified only goods that can be considered to be necessary conditions for the free development of all individuals, as for instance 'public health' (BVerfGE 7, 377 [414]), or the existence of parliamentary democracy (BVerfGE 2, 1n; 5, 85n). In these terms, it remains true that individual rights can be outweighed by collective goods only if the gain for the free development of at least potential citizens or persons is greater than the loss.

Finally, it remains to ask what should happen if particular means for the free development of future citizens can be achieved only by ruling out basic rights of the members of living generations. The answer of the constitutional court here surely would be that the end does not justify the means. In its arguments for its ban on the former KPD the court declared that the deprivation of elementary freedoms in favor of the free lives of future generations is not concordant with the constitution, because every individual has the same right to these freedoms (BVerfGE 5, 85 [205]). According to the court, the realization of any "utopian ideal" that demands "sacrifices of generations to which neither freedom nor equality can be granted" is to be rejected (BVerfGE 5, 85 [206]). Even if it were possible to create a perfect world by treating men as mere means to collective goods, in a liberal state this could not be achieved legally. Let us hope that the court will also be circumspect in the acknowledgment of collective goods in the future.

Bibliography

Alexy, Robert. 1968. *Theorie der Grundrechte*. Baden-Baden: Nomos Verlag.

Buchanan, James M. 1986. 'The Political Economy of the Welfare State', in J.M.Buchanan and Robert D. Tollison, *Public Choice* II. Ann Arbor, Michigan: University of Michigan Press.

BVerfGE. 1950. *Bundesverfassungsgerichterlass* (Ruling of the German Federal Constitutional Court) nos. 2, 7, 10, 19, 39, 50 and 80. Karlsruhe, Germany.

Hayek, Friedrich A. 1981. *Studies in Philosophy, Politics and Economics*. Chicago: University of Chicago Press.

Häberle, Peter. 1983. *Die Wesensgehaltgarantie des Artikel 19 Absatz 2 Grundgesetz*. Heidelberg: Müller, Juristischer Verlag.

MacIntyre, Alasdair. 1984. *After Virtue*. South Bend, Indiana: Notre Dame University Press.

Rawls, John. 1971. *A Theory of Justice*. Cambridge, Massachusetts: Harvard University Press

Sandel, Michael. 1982. *Liberalism and the Limits of Justice*. Cambridge: Cambridge University Press.

Smend, Rudolf. 1955. 'Das Recht der freien Meinungsäusserung', in Rudolf Smend, *Staatsrechtliche Abhandlungen*. Berlin: Duncker & Humblot.

————. 1955. 'Verfassung und Verfassungsrecht', in Rudolf Smend, *Staatsrechtliche Abhandlungen*. Berlin: Duncker & Humblot.

————. 1955. 'Bürger und Bourgeois im deutschen Staatsrecht', in Rudolf Smend, *Staatsrechtliche Abhandlungen*. Berlin: Duncker & Humblot.

Starck, Christian. 1979. *Vom Grund des Grundgesetzes*. Zürich-Osnabrück: Edition Interfrom.

Taylor, Charles. 1993. *Reconciling the Solitudes: Essays on Canadian Federation and Nationalism*. Montreal: McGill University Press.

Liberalism in the West

The Limits and the Crisis of Liberal Polities

Marion Gräfin Dönhoff

It all started off so well: the Enlightenment paved the way for liberalism. And the efforts of liberalism, in turn, gave us the rule of law: that is, civil rights and release from subordination to the Church and to the absolute control of state authorities.

How is it, then, that liberalism of all things now poses a threat to social solidarity? The answer is that people are unable to resist the temptations of affluence and power. Most of them do not realize that true freedom calls for self-restraint, because freedom unchecked inevitably leads to its antithesis: an authoritarian state.

But first I would like to share with you some thoughts about the nature of today's liberalism and today's liberals. Liberals are concerned about making government control bearable and do not believe ideologists who hail their own system as the key to happiness and justice. Liberals must, to my mind, see their permanent function as that of acting as a counterpoint within the political sphere. This means reminding us of ethical principles, when pragmatism degenerates into opportunism; and pointing to reality, when daydreams are offered as concrete remedies or when private interests are passed off as ideals. One could also define the liberals' function as urging restraint when the atmosphere is emotionally charged; and conversely, as finding arguments to inspire people when they appear to be on the verge of succumbing to resignation.

To liberals there is no system that can guarantee a satisfactory final state of things. They do not believe in messages of salvation of any sort, and they are, at the same time, obliged to question their own position continually, in order to keep society open to change, because a rigid balance of power and ownership obstructs freedom.

The liberal newspaper *Die Zeit* has a great deal of experience in this connection. During the 1968 rebellion we tried to generate some understanding for the revolutionary students among their professors, and were charged by the Right with being anarchists; later, when we spoke out against the violence used by the students, the Left called us reactionary. What I learned from all this was that the legitimate place for a liberal is between all positions.

What is the principal aim of liberalism? Its most important goal is to secure tolerance, meaning that:

(i) unorthodox ideas must not be branded as heretical; criticism of the status quo must not result in persecution;

(ii) the rights of the majority must not mean disregard for the protection of minorities;

(iii) the claim that the choice of means is irrelevant if the ends are noble must be exposed as a sinful mistake whenever it is raised.

And now to liberalism after 1989. In the early 1990s, I heard that the Harvard professor Jeffrey Sachs, an absolute and enthusiastic proponent of the free market economy, was to go to Poland in order to help implement economic reforms. I had serious reservations because it seemed conceivable to me that, as an American, he might know very little about Eastern Europe. So I suggested that *Die Zeit* invite Jeffrey Sachs to Hamburg to take part in a discussion. He came, and there were about ten of us, including Helmut Schmidt and some colleagues from the economic affairs editorial staff. As I had suggested the idea, I was asked to open the discussion. I said that I found it hard to imagine that one could dive head first from a planned economy into a market economy, and from an authoritarian society into a permissive society, without establishing certain structures first. To which Jeffrey Sachs replied: "You are completely wrong. All it takes is two things: the creation of private property and the lifting of controls on prices—the market will take care of the rest."

Well, the Polish are clever people; they carried out their own economic reform and advised Jeffrey Sachs to go to Russia, where his theories were to give the Mafia there an un-dreamed-of impetus. It should be clear that the opportunities afforded by such a hasty change will always be exploited, par-ticularly by the ruthless and by potential criminals.

Can we really leave everything up to the market? Can the market engender social justice and equal opportunities? Can it find a balance between citizens' contributions on the one hand and their needs on the other? In certain areas the state is essential: education, research, unemployment, care for the homeless. A market economy, which corresponds to the po-litical maxims of the democratic system as applied to the economic sector, is certainly the most efficient economic system possible. But if you do not try to contain it within a particular framework—for example, Ludwig Erhard's social market system—then the society that develops will be one in which the rich become richer and richer, while the poor be-come ever poorer. We owe the rule of law—and with it civil rights—to liberalism; but in line with its intrinsic nature, lib-eralism places far greater emphasis on individualism than on the community, and on rights rather than on responsibilities. This is precisely why structures need to be established to institutionalize the community spirit that is lacking. In a market economy, based as it is on the system of competition, everything depends on one's being better, earning more than one's competitors. In other words: the driving force behind this system is self-interest. This self-interest that does not shy away from brutality, which instigates corruption, in many places even up to cabinet level. Nobody considers himself responsible, everyone thinks of his own interest first, and feels that the state is obliged to attend to the public good.

An ethic of responsibility is more necessary today than ever before. The philosopher Hans Jonas once said: "In times gone by, the Ten Commandments may have been ade-quate as a guideline, but in the age of globalism, in view of the destructive potential to which mankind now has access, and considering the technological progress that makes it possible for us to alter genes, maybe even create a new hu-man being, we need to develop an ethic that will make us ap-preciate how great is our responsibility." Every society needs bonds; without rules, without traditions, without a consensus regarding standards of conduct, there can be no community. A society which does not agree upon a minimal ethical consensus is not sustainable. And a market economy which does not recognize very specific moral maxims will inevitably degenerate into a free-for-all and may ultimately collapse, as did the socialist system not long ago. The solution cannot be to reverse secularization—that is impossible. It must, however, be possible (i) to reach a minimal ethical consensus, and (ii) to induce citizens to take on more responsibility. Only if these two premises are fulfilled is there a hope that liberalism will not merely survive, but will shape society to become more human than it is today, where everyone concentrates only on earning money, while every intellectual and every artistic enterprise is pushed aside.

Some years ago, a movement began in America whose members call themselves communitarians. These members are mainly intellectuals: academics, social scientists, philosophers. They hold the view that the citizen's sense of responsibility for the community should be revived by getting the public involved; the market, which has lost its 'ethical substructure', should once again be put in a moral and social context; in other words consumer capitalism should be countered by a system of values. In addition to this they advocate the principle of subsidiarity: that is, no longer to delegate to the state things that can be accomplished on a family or local level. In this way, they hope, citizens will come to look upon the community as 'their' state—one might also say to identify with it. The communitarians have already set up a network of such organizations in the United States. In Europe, too, we will have to do something, both in the West and the East, to control errant developments—such as corruption, brutality, and the lack of a sense of responsibility. Perhaps the American example can be a model for us.

Social and Cultural Problems in Contemporary Europe: On Recent Challenges to Liberal Ideas

KARL ACHAM

Introduction

The twentieth century is ending with problems for which no-body claims to have clear and convincing solutions in contemporary Europe. The very fact that, after 1989 and the breakdown of the USSR in 1991, dozens of new territorial states appeared, without any objective criteria making it possible to determine their borders, speaks for itself. All this was accompanied by severe socio-economic problems and a rebirth of nationalist mass movements seeking to compensate to some extent for the lack of moral orientations and social virtues in Eastern Europe, where the moral foundations of the class struggle have become obsolete. There is, however, a crisis of cultural identity also in the European West, paralleled by specific shortcomings on the socio-political level. Let me quote in this connection someone who can certainly not be accused of having a predilection for European decadence, *fin de siècle* moods, or German-type *Kulturpessimismus*. In a lecture given at Georgetown University in late 1990 Zbigniew Brzezinski, expressing "a gnawing philosophical anxiety", stated: "Democracy has won. The free market system has won. But what in the wake of this great ideological victory is today the substance of our beliefs? To what is the human being in the democratic West now truly committed? ... [To] hedonistic relativism? ... I think this emptiness, this potential emptiness, if not yet the reality, is dangerous" (Brzezinski, 1990, 3, 7).

I agree with those who argue that there is no reason to lament or panic. European civilization, in the course of its history, has overcome a number of profound social and cultural crises, and there is no reason to doubt that it will be able to cope with the present one, too. On the other hand, it would certainly be foolish not to listen to the warnings of those who feel that Western liberalism has reached a critical stage.

In this chapter I shall deal with only two dimensions of the current societal problems: economic and cultural change. In view of recent economic developments, in the first part Hayek's economic theory will be reconsidered from a social-liberal perspective, while in the second part, cultural libertarianism will be shown to erode exactly those values of liberty which are supposedly favored by the proponents of libertarianism.

I will not be concerned with the situation in East Central Europe and that of the European parts of the former USSR. Instead, I will refer to Western Europe and, in the first part of my discussion, to a special topic of the socio-economic debate, which was opened in the USA and then spread quickly among the majority of the capitalist countries in the West. This debate may, nevertheless, also be quite important for East Central Europe, since Western intellectual modes and knowledge may spill over rather quickly into the former Eastern bloc.

Economic Change and Economic Policy in Contemporary Western Europe

Within the last fifty years Europe has been under the influence of three types of economic policy (and the corresponding economic theories): (i) a centrally planned socialist, (ii) a moderate *laissez-faire*, and (iii) a mixed or intermediate one.

One worrisome development in the economies and economic policies of Western Europe can be seen in the loss of a sense of direction concerning what might be called the intermediate or mixed programs and policies which had presided over the impressive economic miracles of Sweden and Germany, to name only two. These had pragmatically combined the public and the private, the market and planning, the state and business, as the occasion and local ideology warranted. The problems here lay not in the application of some intellectually attractive or impressive theory—whether or not it was defensible in the abstract—for the strength of these programs was practical success rather than intellectual coherence. They were caused rather by the erosion of that practical success determined by the limitations of the welfare state. There are several concrete examples in support of the forecast effects of this lasting tendency in Western Europe. Some Western European countries (Sweden, France, Italy) seem to have evolved social policies incompatible with economic development, particularly job creation. The main problem they have encountered is the excessive level of social transfers, caused mainly by overblown pay-as-you-go pension systems. Another problem is that of institutional barriers to employment. Only a few Western European countries have been able to start reforming their welfare states on time, that is, before a profound crisis emerged. Criticism of the crippling consequences of expansionist welfare programs which impede economic growth, and of the patronizing attitudes of the authorities which threaten individual freedom, are now receiving increasing attention.

Hayek was always a proponent of Western capitalism, combined with the British-born model of liberal democracy, and he incessantly emphasized the inescapable connection of freedom in both the economic and the political spheres. As a consequence, he was one of the harshest critics of the welfare state, which he considered a dangerous phenomenon threatening individual liberties in a free society. It may be that the revision of a few of Hayek's arguments will lead us to a model which retains his fundamental aim of preserving an innovative and dynamic society, but which arrives at different conclusions, namely, a more favorable assessment of welfare policy.

Hayek's Stance

According to Hayek, who preferred to call himself an "Old Whig", Cartesian rationalism and a Hegelian philosophy of history deepened the fundamental intellectual error which holds that men consciously choose institutions because of the expected advantages which they will provide for them. In fact, according to Hayek, institutions come into being as a result of trial and error, and they withstand evolutionary pressure because they are useful. Thus, the most relevant institutions are ordered and structured, but essentially they are elements of a 'spontaneous order', that is, they are rooted in particular patterns of human behavior—however, they are not the products of human design. Like language, customs, and morality, institutions are unplanned phenomena which we cannot claim to have been constructed by conscious human will. In the intricate realm of modern societies the complexity of structures and networks exceeds by far our capacity to plan and control social institutions and their interrelations. On the contrary, evolutionary success is the only proof of their superiority. Thus, constructivist or voluntaristic illusions about the possibility of planning the whole of society must fail.[1]

So, in his theory of the origin and evolution of institutions, Hayek makes three general assumptions which have to be emphasized if one wants to apply this theory to social policy issues:

– the historical process secures the selection and survival of efficient institutions;
– societies, especially modern ones, cannot be planned and controlled on a large scale;
– the self-stabilization of a spontaneous order is dependent on freedom: since society needs to adapt to social change, there must be room for a perpetual revision of all ideas to secure progress in the future.

The application of Hayek's ideas of institutional change and social evolution to the main issues of social policy requires several basic considerations:[2]

(i) Even a moderate degree of interventionism favoring a planned economy is dangerous; a 'third way' in the area of economic process—that is, between freedom and regulation—is impossible. A free society declines when the government is no longer viewed as an instrument for protecting property rights, but as an institution for redistributing wealth. According to Hayek, a welfare state which redistributes income and strives to realize 'social justice' will gradually transform its structures into socialist ones and finally use violent measures characteristic of a socialist system. Therefore, Hayek aims to destroy any hope of a 'mixed system'.

(ii) An odd interpretation of democracy—the unrestricted application of majority rule—threatens individual freedom. The majoritarian principle of modern democracy enhances the departure from classical liberalism. If the majority of the representatives in the Parliament, according to doctrinaire 'democratism', may decide whatever they want, the idea of democracy will be perverted to the justification of arbitrary power.

(iii) Public subsidies have to be strictly limited to the minimal level, so that the state is kept at the periphery of social and economic activities. According to Hayek, the state may provide social security at the subsistence level, that is, a minimal social net: "There is no reason why in a free society government should not assure to all protection against severe deprivation in the form of an assured minimum income, or a floor below which nobody needs to descend" (Hayek, 1982, vol. II, 87; cf. also vol. III, 54–55).

(iv) The egalitarian elimination of prosperous classes threatens future economic growth, since inequality must be recognized as having a very positive function in the social system. So, for instance, the rich are able to take risks, to promote art and research, to resist repressive government measures, and to stimulate others to upward mobility.

(v) Creeping welfare interventionism corrupts people. Thus, a curious type of social policy destroys the consciousness of what the principles mean that are fundamental for a free and dynamic society. General irreverence towards universal rules grows, and, as a consequence, every social group tries to profit from public programs. Ultimately, the distribution of resources merely depends on the political power of various groups, and the political sphere becomes a battleground where everybody tries to obtain better access to the public trough.

In sum, Hayek's arguments against the allegedly illusory ideas of 'social justice', unlimited majority rule, and egalitarian social policy, rest on the assumption that fatal consequences must be expected for the political and economic system if politicians attempt to realize these ideas. And indeed, a dynamic society is in constant need of inventions and innovations, and it is obvious that the given institutional framework may either promote or prevent them. Thus, we may agree with Hayek's basic assumption that it is only a free society that can provide the opportunity for social change in the process of social evolution. But what are the relevant characteristics of a free society?

Hayek's Position Revisited

Cultural changes, which could generate human beings with attitudes conducive to a sufficient rate of innovation under other circumstances than those of a free market economy, are not considered in Hayek's work dealing with social freedom. Taking into consideration the model of the rational economic man, one may, nonetheless, ask which mix of options and risks men may choose, so that a high rate of innovation is obtained. Here I will attempt, mostly endorsing the arguments stated by Manfred Prisching (forthcoming, section 6), to formulate four counter-theses to Hayek's blank condemnation of the welfare state.

(i) For many individuals competition is only attractive if particular risks are eliminated. An extremely liberal model may discourage innovation, when the unlucky loser is threatened by being reduced to a subsistence level of income. Thus, individuals may optimize their welfare by staying at modest, but secure income levels. "A higher rate of innovation may be obtained, when the loser falls down, but only to a lower level which allows him to live decently, while the winner does not get the whole amount, but sufficient high rewards for his risk. Many people start experiments if there is a social net" (Prisching, forthcoming, 13). Correspondingly, the principles of the market order are accepted by the majority of people when the risks of pauperization are excluded by public programs.

(ii) Social policy can be of economic value. Thus, it may be an expedient solution to pay unemployment compensation above the minimum subsistence level in order to maintain human capital which otherwise would be wasted too quickly. It may, to give another example, be an appropriate solution to provide a public school system for most of the population in order to tap the abilities of those who can contribute to an innovative and dynamic society. There seems to be no justification for arguing that it is, in every case, the minimum level that produces optimal dynamics and efficiency.

(iii) Social policy may secure the consensus of the people and thus stabilize the system of political freedom. It may be reasonable to provide a sufficient degree of old-age security which minimizes social conflicts and satisfies the expectations of employees. Social peace in society is a fundamental precondition of economic stability and growth. Thus, public satisfaction is a public good.

(iv) The welfare state may be a good example of a trial and error process in which social institutions are generated, and not merely a manifestation of social constructivism. Social policy institutions have come into existence, and have been abolished and reformed, often in a random way. The system of social security was not invented at a stroke. On the contrary, the welfare state encompasses the experience of decades, or even centuries, and reflects the experience of past generations. If historically transmitted institutions embody the wisdom of historical selection, as Hayek teaches us, the welfare state may be a good example. Recent experiences, however, will lead us to admit that the welfare state of the industrialized countries urgently needs reform of some of its features—otherwise it will not remain an innovative system.

Summing up the central points of our discussion, we can recognize, in Manfred Prisching's words, "that the highest rate of innovation is not necessarily obtained when markets dominate all areas of life, only slightly constrained by programs securing subsistence levels; but that the highest rate of innovation will be obtained by an appropriate level and structure of social programs which, according to the specific psychological dispositions of individuals, supply a portfolio of opportunities with a 'just' distribution of risks and chances" (Prisching, forthcoming, 14). Thus, the model of the innovative welfare state need not be a constructivist, but rather a constructive model, as long as the suitability of a 'social market system' to optimize the rate of sustained innovation is not empirically disproved.

On Libertarian Culture

If the programmatic ideologies born of the Age of Revolution and the nineteenth century find themselves at a loss at the end of the twentieth century, the most ancient guides to the perplexed of this world, the traditional religions, provide no plausible alternative. The Western ones are in disarray in Europe, even in the few countries—headed by Ireland and Poland—where church affiliation and frequent attendance at religious rituals are still habitual. Nonetheless, Europe may be confronted in the near future with a rebirth of religious fundamentalism under the auspices of—and as a counter-movement against—the pluralistic spirit of the post-industrial age. In several Islamic countries, which provide many immigrants to Europe, the appeal of politicized religion is all the greater because the old religions are, almost by definition, enemies of the Western civilization which has been the agent of social disruption, and of the rich and god-less countries that look, more than ever, like the exploiters of the Third World's poverty.

Not only the various Third World resentments against the Western way of life are worth mentioning in this context. Every philosopher and social scientist has to take special note of the widespread conviction that the very cause of the cultural crisis in the Western world in general—and in Western Europe in particular—is an exaggerated individualism.

The Dual Nature of Liberalism

According to many observers of Western mores, various forms of excessive individualism were initiated by libertarian ideas. From an historical point of view, however, there are two penchants in the liberal mind. One has to do with the idea of negative freedom, that is, with the limitation of force and coercion by means of the rule of law and a constitutional order; the other concerns a specific idea of positive freedom, permitting one to do what one wants to do, even if one thereby reaches the boundaries of license. To explain these different ideas requires going back to the origins of liberalism in the eighteenth and nineteenth centuries, primarily in Great Britain and France (Nisbet, 1982, 210–17).

Liberalism has a dual origin. On the one hand, there is the liberalism that became best known in the writings of the Scottish moral philosophers and economists, the Founding Fathers in America, and John Stuart Mill. The emphasis of this wing of liberal thought was on the individual's freedom from all kinds of tyranny or potential tyranny, including, when necessary, the state, public opinion, and business enterprises. On the other hand, there is the liberalism of the French Enlightenment, reaching its height in the second half of the eighteenth century in the writings of Jean Jacques Rousseau, Abbé Mably, Morelly, and Gracchus Babeuf. These authors and their successors did not necessarily like what they saw in the French government. But they were able to make a clear distinction between the *ancien régime*, which they disliked, and the intrinsic power of the political state, which they liked very much. According to them, a new type of state should be created in order to destroy the traditional social authorities: the patriarchal family, the aristocracy, the guild, the ancient commune, and, above all, the church in its many forms. This centralized state, designed by the *philosophes* and brought about in part by the Jacobins, found its realization in the bureaucratized and militarized government of Napoleon.

A small group of thinkers in France, the most celebrated of whom was Alexis de Tocqueville, recognized that what was being created was an omnipotent state of the masses. According to Tocqueville, liberty in a democracy can exist only on the basis of a strong moral and social order, an order replete with natural authorities. The same holds of a true intellectual and artistic culture: only if pre-democratic and pre-liberal standards and canons survive will the culture of democracy remain healthy. But as Tocqueville also repeatedly stressed (and Robert Nisbet admonishes us not to forget), "the very nature of democratic political power is to become ever more centralized and bureaucratized and, in so becoming, to erode the pre-democratic social and cultural strata, leaving in consequence the plebiscitary, absolute, infinitely penetrating state and below its government, a vast horde of atomized individuals rendered egocentric, selfish, grasping, and hedonistic" (Nisbet, 1982, 212–13).

There is every reason to call Tocqueville a liberal—freedom and human diversity were his obsessions—nonetheless, there is a great distance not only between Tocqueville and the 'liberation movement' of the Jacobins, but also between Tocqueville and the proponents of an egotistic *laissez-faire*.

Cultural Laissez-Faire

Throughout the nineteenth and early twentieth centuries in the United States and Great Britain, the libertarian ethos was largely dominant. According to its main proponent, John Stuart Mill, the government is justified in interfering with an individual's thought and behavior only when that thought and behavior can be shown to jeopardize the existence of others in society. But what does that mean? Is there any limit to a conditioning practice generating human beings who, although objectively threatened and shocked, will not feel themselves subjectively jeopardized? According to Nisbet, the great deficiency of this classical liberalism was its inability to recognize the indispensable importance of the social contexts of individual freedom, *laissez-faire*, and the non-interventionist state. "So consuming", Nisbet concludes, "was the emphasis upon the individual that the social sources of individuality tended to get neglected" (Nisbet, 1982, 213).

In the period after the First World War two powerful currents of heterogeneous liberal ideas came on the scene: one, a legacy of the French Enlightenment and Revolution, the other, a product of Mill's radical individualism. Completely purged of any moral attitude—which was, for instance, highly significant for the eminently cultured and self-disciplined Mill—these ideas together make up contemporary cultural liberalism. The culture of the 'Roaring Twenties' long remained the perfect symbol of this drive towards individual liberation from the traditional moral and social authorities, followed by particular tendencies of the movement of 1968 in Western Europe. At that time (and up to the present), the societies of various European countries—in some ways similar to the situation of East Central Europe nowadays—were shot through with permissiveness, starting with the family, the natural authority of which has been usurped in large part by the bureaucratic state, thus leaving the individual members of the family uncertain about their roles. Similar events and phenomena have been seen in the school, the university, the law court, and the local community.

Liberalism is misconceived by those who attempt to use it as an 'all-terrain vehicle'. Liberalism presupposes particular conditions which are not produced by liberalism itself: authority (on which freedom is, in a sense, based); a moral order of solidarity and fairness; the ability to generalize or universalize moral norms and criteria; a power structure which guarantees a longer time-horizon so that the meaningfulness of individual effort is not put at risk.

Any implementation of these values, however, though logically prior to any empirical value research, is at odds with an assumption of recent cultural relativism according to which all values are ultimately determined by the individual's socialization. This sociologistic malady is closely connected with the insidious apothegm "To understand all is to pardon all". Various schools of psychology, virtually the whole of *milieu*-oriented sociology, and the 'progressive' education of the past few decades have all laid strong emphasis upon the non-responsibility of the individual and the full responsibility of either an unmanageable Id or a harsh and exploitative society.

This kind of popular philosophy is not, of course, directly responsible for the urgent cultural and social problems facing us today. It gives, nonetheless, some support to the tendency to 'explain them away' by stressing the allegedly determining forces acting upon the social actors. However, what is the nature of the social problems which are sometimes dedramatized in terms of societal determinism? Instead of repeating a list that anyone might compile from a single reading of such newspapers as *Le Monde* or *The Guardian*—drugs, dropouts, vandalism, crime, violence, the breakup of the family, child abuse, racial tension, and so on—instead of elaborating that litany of human misery, let me make only one general point. I see the real threat, not in revolutions and street fighting, but in a growing deterioration, already taking place, in human relations, in the way people treat each other, which is the substance behind the abstract term 'society'. I have in mind both the private world of the family, personal relations between men and women, the treatment of children and the old, and the public world of politics, local and national—even international relations— the school, and the community, including relations in the workplace. If I had to describe the situation I fear I would use a term coined by Alan Bullock, namely, "the autistic society". This signifies a world in which men and women shut themselves up in their own private worlds and become so afraid of communicating with each other that they lose the habit of it.

In light of all this one inevitably feels tempted to ask the following questions: How can we recreate values in the modern world? How can we extend older traditions, among them that of liberalism, which we are associated with in several respects? I suspect that this can be done by a direct transfer. A recreation may be successfully pursued by encouraging young people to discover, or rediscover, values for themselves, out of their own experience and insights, often in discussion with their peers, not accepting authoritarianism in the vulgar sense but being deeply influenced by the sympathy, and above all the example (practice, not precept), of older people.

Final Remarks

It remains unclear whether and how Western Europe can solve the problems it is facing at the end of the millennium. At present, the European Union is about to continue integration based on the free market economy—which should eventually encompass more than the current fifteen member states—and to round it off by means of political and military integration. Integration based on the free market economy implies, in and of itself, far-reaching political and social consequences, as the example of the European agricultural market testifies. Its achievement consists in providing the population with cheap agricultural goods the growing of which is in an ever-increasing measure subject to the dynamics of the capitalist mode of production; the drawback of this subjection is the so-called creative destruction of tradition, of the rustic way of life, and—due to large-scale migration to the cities—a corresponding change in the demographic structure. In principle, it will be necessary to question the limits of the efficiency of the European Union's functional integration. Probably the most momentous consequence of this process will be the creation of an area characterized by a *pure* market economy which will lead to its detachment from the *social* market economy. The latter sets legal limits to the unbridled application of the pure principle of power and seeks to establish a balance between labor and capital by locking the profit interest of capital onto the system of social relations and compensatory obligations. Nation-states lack the authority to impose such limitations within the framework of the European Union, as Ernst Wolfgang Böckenförde has recently explained. Yet nation-states continue to be responsible for economic, job-market, and redistributive social policies.

However, this evidences a thorough transformation of the traditional European principle of statehood. According to this principle, collective competence and collective responsibility for the commonweal of the people forming the given political unit constitute two indispensable elements of statehood. Due to the new political and economic structures of the West European transnational state organization, however, the idea of the collective responsibility of the nation-state is gradually becoming obsolete, since the necessary responsibility is legally vested neither in the European Union nor in its member countries. The Union does not possess any authority outside the economic sphere, while the member states have no competence to intervene in the area of economic regulations aiming at the implementation of the four basic freedoms. Actually, Western Europe is being confronted with a kind of 'cultural lag': European citizens as electors expect their governments to bear the responsibility for the common good, as in the past, although the national unity of political, economic, and social space—achieved at the cost of arduous struggle—as the foundation of the functioning of the modern welfare state and the social market economy, has already been *de facto* abandoned as a consequence of the new European Union's regulations.

No doubt in the future difficulties will arise related to this central problem of a new Europe. European citizens will certainly stand up to one phenomenon which has been characteristic of recent developments: the use of the process of integration, based on the institution of the market economy, as a means of applying indirect pressure towards greater political union, without an explicit political decision having been taken. Another key problem of the European Union is that, although the Union is ready to strive for greater solidarity, it cannot cope with the financial problems likely to result from the far-reaching integration of the former socialist countries. The accession of the four Visegrád states now designated as aspirants to EU membership would, within the framework of the current rules, double the agricultural component of the EU budget. This could lead to either a substantial departure from the agricultural market as it now stands, or to the emergence of a split market.

A third fundamental problem is the Europe-wide crisis affecting welfare systems, further exacerbated by recent demographic developments. An ever larger number of elderly people have to be provided for by an ever smaller number of people of working age, despite the fact that many of the latter are unemployed. Unemployment, however, is likely to persist, even increase, as long as the principle of the virtually unlimited power of the market prevails. One way out of the possible disaster could consist in reaching broad agreement on a substantial decrease of general welfare expenditure—for the sake of argument, of about 20 per cent. This, however, would lead to other problems, due to the resulting lack of the means necessary to continue the already mandated transfer payments.

If we are not mistaken, the application of the market principle as the vehicle and motor of integration may not unite, but rather split Europe. What seems to be urgently needed is an extensive political debate about the basic aims of European unity: where is Europe supposed to go, and on what basis could these aims be reached without using means that in themselves contradict the basic intention of unification? Especially when considering the expansion of the European Union towards the East, Europe can no longer be seen as a mere technical pragmatic construct, dictated by economic rationality, but rather as an organizing idea. It would be foolish to reassure ourselves that, as far as this issue is concerned, we can indulge in a kind of *laissez-faire* optimism and that the clear self-image which Europe so badly needs—notably as regards the goals of the integration process, the scope and degree of integration in the various European regions, and the territorial extent of the desired united Europe—may come about spontaneously.

Bibliography

Brzezinski, Zbigniew. 1990. 'Post-Victory Blues.' Lecture at the Academy of World Inquiry (25 October). Washington, DC: Georgetown University, School of Foreign Service.

Hayek, Friedrich A. 1937. 'Economics and Knowledge', *Economica* 4.

———. 1945. 'The Use of Knowledge in Society', *American Economic Review* 35.

———. 1960. *The Constitution of Liberty*. London.

———. 1970. *Die Irrtümer des Konstruktivismus und die Grundlagen legitimer Kritik gesellschaftlicher Gebilde*. München-Salzburg.

———. 1982. *Law, Legislation and Liberty. A New Statement of the Liberal Principles of Justice and Political Economy*. 3 vols. London–Melbourne–Henley. First published in one volume in 1982.

Nisbet, Robert. 1982. *Prejudices. A Philosophical Dictionary*. Cambridge, Massachusetts and London.

Prisching, Manfred. Forthcoming. 'A Model of the Dynamic Welfare State—Friedrich von Hayek Revisited.' *Geschichte und Gegenwart* 19. (2000).

Notes

1 See, for instance, Hayek (1937), pp. 33–54; Hayek (1945), pp. 519–30; Hayek (1960); and Hayek (1970).

2 For the following, see Prisching (forthcoming), section 3. In the following passage I do not cite all the considerations mentioned by the author.

Two Dilemmas of Liberalism: Historical Exhaustion and Internal Division in a World of Globalization

MICHEL GIRARD

Having participated very actively in the extension and globalization of the market economy and the recent world-wide triumph of models of democracy, liberalism has carried home a considerable but ambiguous prize, one which might result in difficulties in the future. The uncertainty of liberalism's future seems to stem from two fundamental causes. The first is that by becoming—however late in the day—political reality, liberalism appears to have partly exhausted its historical virtues. For a long time, liberalism was a utopian enterprise whose purpose was to engage in a decomposing and modernizing critique of old-fashioned institutions and traditions. Now, owing to its very victory, it is experiencing a loss of momentum due to the weakening of the enormous tension between ideal and reality from which it used to draw its impetus. As a result, this important source of its influence could dry up.

Today, more than ever, liberalism is confronted with a perennial and well-known dilemma, common to all major systems of thought which inspire high hopes: to find a way of becoming thoroughly integrated in the real world while running the risk of disenchantment and exhaustion, or to remain partly confined to the world of incompletely achieved ideals, thereby maintaining its reign over human minds and hearts.

The second reason for concern, as far as the future of the liberal enterprise is concerned, has to do with an internal division which currently appears to threaten the stability of the whole fabric of liberalism. In this era of globalization of technology, finance, production, and trade, the tension or contradictions between the twin forms of liberalism—economic liberalism and political liberalism—seem to have reached a hitherto unknown level. For a long time the intimate homology and the profound affinity which have united the two faces of liberalism since the Enlightenment, produced a degree of harmony or synergy which facilitated their coexistence. The current situation testifies to an increasing dissociation between the imperatives of the globalization of the liberal economy and the prerequisite conditions of political liberalism in a world still divided into separate nation-states. At present, liberalism appears to be confronted with a second dilemma, altogether novel, which from now on could make it face a choice between its economic and its political requirements.

It is true that, during the past century, liberalism managed to outsmart the socialist challenge in becoming itself concerned about social issues and by accepting, against its original principles, some innovatory compromises which have become constituent parts of the welfare state. In the future, will liberalism manage, without negating itself, to carry out the necessary adjustments in order to overcome the danger of historical exhaustion as well as the threat of a further dissociation between its goals in economics and politics—a dissociation which eventually would make any liberal design void of sense?

The Principal Parameters of Liberalism

Without entering too far into the ritualized debates about its definition, let us note that liberalism is above all a system of thought which puts at the center of its preoccupations an individual motivated mainly by the conscious and logical pursuit of his own interests. Thus, any liberal system of thought necessarily contains elements of individualism, rationalism, and 'economism'. In order to expand, liberalism assumed a level of individualist behavior, attitudes, and ideas which was already quite advanced. This was only possible in societies which had already reached a high level of individuation. The society of individuals, which drew the attention of Norbert Elias towards the end of his life (Elias, 1987), is the product of a long historical evolution, in the beginning limited to Europe and, later, to the Western world. It is only in more recent times that individualism seems to have made global headway against widespread resistance. The theme of the natural rights of the individual (liberty, property, security) which has taken up a large part of liberal thought since its origins, both in Europe and in the United States, did not develop into a universal theme of human rights until after the Second World War. More recently, the triumphant freedom of modern man and its disturbing other side, the anguished solitude of the postmodern individual, appear indeed to characterize not only the societies represented in the OECD, but can actually be found almost everywhere, from the suburbs of Pretoria to the center of Singapore.

A liberal person is a being who is free to determine his preferences and his goals, but who nevertheless remains subject to the laws of mathematics and reason. Whatever his position in society, whether humble or distinguished, whatever social utility he may have, immense or minute, he is to be seen as a consistent entrepreneur with a clear idea of his own interests and able to act rationally in order to defend or promote them. He may well be blind in many respects; his understanding and his culture may well be wanting; but he is at least supposed to have the intelligence to recognize his own interests, and this is seen as sufficient. The various passions which drive him still remain subordinate to this one specific and 'compensating' passion, that is, the speculative pursuit of his own interests (Hirschman, 1977). Underneath its different aspects, the paradigm of the rational agent which stems from economic analysis and which has gradually invaded the political and social sciences since the 1960s, is in fact no more than a somewhat formalized recomposition of a fundamental assumption of liberalism which is more than two hundred years old. The concept of man which has been put forward by liberalism is most certainly utopian. It has, however, a strong and logical coherence which has been an essential condition of its long duration and its firm grip on the world.

In a way, by origin liberalism is an 'economism' insofar as it bases its interpretation of social phenomena on the behavior of individuals who always act according to their economic interests. From its very first formulation onwards, from John Locke to Adam Smith, liberalism has turned out to be at least as economic as political, even though the economy which it promoted was a 'political economy'. The liberal agent, the 'owner animal' (*"Animal propriétaire"*: see Manent, 1986, 315; 1994), is the constituent element of a system of pure exchange, that is, a market within which the domination of man by man can be abolished and superseded by a superior mode of regulation that is much more efficient, as it is abstract. Indeed, the more people barter, buy, sell, and speculate, the more they contribute—partly without their knowledge—to promoting a new order in which the sovereign and menacing hand which commands is replaced by the gentle and invisible hand which disposes.

In the liberal vision of things, partially realized today, the ideal schema of the market as a place of regulation by optimal yet gentle alchemy is poised to become the organizing figure of the world of exchanges between individuals. And this not only in the economic sphere, where the logic of trade is cut out to exert its universal grasp, but also in the political or social domains where elections, opinion polls, and market surveys are becoming recognized instruments of the legitimization of the ruling power. The giant figure of the market-place even casts its shadow onto the cultural and artistic sectors, where it influences both their functioning and their products.[1] This systematic preference for economics is reflected in the symbols which the liberal world attributes to itself: yesterday, the trader, the bank manager, or the industrialist; today, the financier, the executive, or the smart consumer.

The Exhaustion of Liberal Utopianism

This economic, rational, and individualist being that liberalism invented and then contributed to its realization, ought to be seen less as a conservative and tranquil bourgeois than as a genuinely revolutionary agent, who has come to turn the traditional fabric of human relations inside out and upside down, without remorse. Liberalism has always found its strength in its ability to act as the enemy of tradition and the speaker for modernity. It took decades of effort, during the nineteenth century, for socialism to succeed, albeit partially and temporarily, in stealing this comfortable role and relegating liberalism to side with social conservatism and the narrow-minded bourgeoisie. Yet, by a tremendous sleight of hand of history, in less than a century liberalism managed to rebound and turn against its 'revolutionary' adversary. Moreover, it participated in socialism's final defeat by exposing the economic irrationality, the political despotism, and the immense social and intellectual conservatism which reigned in most of the countries claiming to be true followers of socialism. At present, the belated victory of liberalism is sufficiently widespread to look definitive. However, this seemingly final victory places liberalism in a unique historical situation, where—since there are few real enemies left— it is at risk of finding itself without a cause and without a plan, thus expiring little by little through sheer exhaustion. We just might witness, if not the 'End of History', then the end of the history of liberalism.

If it is true that every man who commands is, within the limits of his power, "a whimsical and opinionated despot" (Manent, 1994, 19), the enterprise of the liberal construction of the world is indeed liberating in its very principle. In opposing the absolute principle of the natural rights of the individual to the previous forms of submission and allegiance, liberalism pretends to substitute a liberal polity for the existing institutions of authority. By promoting a society which supposedly is the true aggregation of these rights in accordance with the fairly equivalent models of the social contract or the market, liberalism cancels or delegitimizes any other power system than its own. Even in its most conservative versions—like that of Edmund Burke, who believed that it is possible to see the truth of the natural rights of man in the lessons of experience and the dictates of tradition—the liberal position is basically a way of resisting domination and oppression; a systematic limitation of any kind of authoritative system, whatever it may be. Thus, whether it is progressive, moderate, or conservative, liberalism is always to a certain degree a subversive enterprise threatening virtually any form of political or religious power which maintains domination by the few over the rest.

In the liberal political alchemy where everyone decides for him- or herself and in relation to everybody else, so that the general interest is but a result of compound particular interests—of variable complexity according to the different versions of liberalism—the distinction between rulers and ruled tends to disappear. When contemplating the liberal project, the previous systems of allegiances and dependencies of the feudal, colonial, aristocratic, or monarchical-despotic type, could see their forthcoming dissolution very early on. For Alexis de Tocqueville, this discovery was not a conclusion but a point of departure. During the first half of the nineteenth century in Europe, as during the French and American revolutions, liberalism represented a new and still incredible world, for the political, economic, and social realities were still very remote from the liberal model. At the time, liberalism had all the colors and flavors of a real-life Utopia. The distance between the ideal which it promoted and the historical universe in which it unfolded enabled it to capture worlds of aspirations that allowed powerful and efficient processes of intellectual and emotional mobilization to develop. Liberalism is never more elating than in times of oppression; especially when the oppression, though still powerful, is beginning to yield and crumble. How do you convey to someone who has never felt it the wonderful magic of the moment when the utopian project, on the verge of triumph, still fragile but already almost victorious, is yet untainted by the shady compromises implied in its embodiment?

However, liberalism does more than oppose *anciens régimes*, which was the belief for more than a century, when liberalism appeared to merge with modernity and when history seemed to obey the relentless law of political and social progress: indeed, it can just as well be a threat to despotic enterprises posing as 'new' or 'revolutionary', from the moment they attempt to establish some form of domination by man over man, whether overtly or covertly.[2] This point was only fully revealed in the course of this century. Indeed, at the end of the nineteenth century and at the beginning of the twentieth, the different forms of socialism which emerged, whether of utopian, anarchical, or Marxist inspiration, succeeded overwhelmingly in making liberalism seem an outdated and conservative ideology, no longer embodying a project for the future but on the contrary representing a defense of established interests. Pushed back into the contemptible camp of capitalism, with which it obviously maintains an elective and intimate relationship, liberalism went through some hard and yet happy times during which it at least knew which adversary it had to defeat, although it could not be sure of victory. Under the most authoritative of dictatorships, as well as under the most totalitarian of despotisms, the liberal principle never ceased to generate its critical and beneficial effects by offering a frame of reference and defense to all of those who refused to submit, and usually paid a high price. It looks as if liberalism can only be true to itself in adversity and in the dialectics of struggle. Indeed, how is it possible not to see that a society which wants to be 'open', in the sense of Karl Popper, must inevitably define or delimit itself by the boundaries provided by its enemies? The idea of a liberal society without an enemy is, to say the least, problematic.[3]

Now that liberalism seems to be prevailing almost everywhere in the world, and most countries claim to have explicitly identified formally with its ideas and principles in one way or another, liberalism no longer appears to be so critical and utopian. The risk of historical exhaustion is threatening, at least morally and politically. Liberalism probably still has a few important and declared opponents; something which holds the promise of yet more glorious wars to wage. Above all, however, it has a lot of false friends who only pay lip-service to its premises and learn only what suits them from its lessons. Yet, bearing in mind that at present the liberal way of thinking has achieved universal acceptance to a degree hitherto unknown in history, there is reason to fear a certain erosion of its ability to critically project its values and ideas, and to shape the human relations of the future. The danger of a loss of moral and political vitality seems all the greater because in the societies where liberalism seems to rule undisputedly—that is, in the rich, postmodern, liberal societies—the new phenomenon of massive indifference prevents people from exercising the rights and obligations of citizenship. At the same time, these phenomena are turning the public sphere, which is supposed to be a place of dialogue or transversal communication, into a field which is, to a great extent, dominated by those who master the techniques of communication and know how to match them with the bad inclinations of the tyranny of the majority. How indeed do we prevent the normative dream from becoming damaged or disenchanted in the ungrateful mirror of empirical reality? How do we continue to conquer or mobilize hearts and minds in a world which is commonly believed—perhaps wrongly so—to have been conquered already? Too much success may well be harmful, but it is not unlikely that liberalism will face a couple of severe defeats in the future and thus hopefully find a new source of inspiration. After all, a Utopia cannot contemplate absolute triumph without actually repudiating or negating itself.

The Dissociation of Economic Liberalism and Political Liberalism

For a long time, political liberalism and economic liberalism have been considered to be two complementary sides of one and the same theme, or two twins considered—perhaps too quickly—to be homozygous. As freedom was held to be indivisible, one thought that the freedom of the citizen conditioned that of the economic agent, and vice versa. The liberal history of Europe or North America never really seemed to teach anything else. Yet, an examination of today's world reveals a different and more disturbing reality. Numerous societies that were converted to liberalism from the outside, through economic globalization, convey the impression of having remained deaf to the calls for political liberalism.

This is of course the case of a country such as China, where the economic opening up to the liberal world economy has not yet been translated into the transformation of a power structure that is particularly anti-liberal. Those who bet their money on politics lagging behind economics and thus wish to wait, speculating on a possible catching-up in the future, may well be wrong. The case of China is not isolated, besides, since in a number of societies in Asia and in the Middle East the spread of the global economy, sometimes at an advanced stage, has introduced market forces which have not exactly upset the existing relations of domination and allegiance. Therefore, the classical relationship of interdependence which traditionally united the two faces of liberalism often seems not to be working these days.[4]

True enough, almost everywhere the introduction of the law of the market seems to go hand in hand with the principle of elections, but the former often has much more content than the latter: in many societies, relatively open to the world economy, elections are staged simply in order to underpin oppressive structures which shamefacedly or brazenly ignore the most fundamental human rights and the basic principle of allowing opposition. The most frequent interpretations of this paradoxical dissociation stem from the culturalists. They point out that liberal economic reasoning has been imposed from the outside, rather than having developed naturally after a long period of ripening in the cultural, political, and social domains. Due to the fact that it has been imported by economic necessity into cultures which were not ready for it, liberalism has not been able to develop the roots which are vital for it to acquire its full political dimensions. Many even believe that it is the fate of a system of ideas having appeared in a Protestant—or at the very least Judaeo-Christian—universe, not to be suitable for grafting onto other religious and cultural stocks. This kind of analysis may not be totally implausible, but it is no doubt seriously wanting insofar as it ignores the immense faculty of compromise, adaptation, and acclimatization which liberalism has already shown several times in the past.

Furthermore, the dissociation between liberal economics and politics is not only a particularity of developing countries which have only recently converted to the laws of the global market. Indeed, it is possible to perceive subtle symptoms of it even in the most advanced societies, with a long historical development behind them; the very ones that cradled liberalism. So if liberalism appears to be limping everywhere, although to different extents, it is because a general and universal discord has taken a firm hold within it. As long as the scales of the economic system and political society were on the same level, however approximately,[5] the two sides of the liberal enterprise maintained a clearly synergetic relation. But today's economy is a global phenomenon, whereas the political communities remain limited by the borders of the state. Economics and politics are no longer on the same level, and they are no longer concentric. As a consequence, the former may very well be of quite a liberal inspiration without the latter necessarily being so. The globalization of the economy has revealed that the apparent twin harmony mentioned above in fact concealed fundamental differences which had not really been perceived previously. Political liberalism is not and cannot be simply the homologue of economic liberalism. In fact, political liberalism is never entirely reducible to the rational behavior of free individuals, moved only by their relentless pursuit of the maximization of utility. Liberal political man has, just like anyone else, a crucial need for identity, and in order to explain his political activity accurately, it is necessary, if not to "substitute a reasoning in terms of identification for a reasoning in terms of utility", as Alessandro Pizzorno suggests, then at least to try and combine the two (Birnbaum and Leca, 1990).

A careful examination of the recent evolution reveals that where liberalism, too dominated by its economic motivation, has chosen to favor without restraint the global dimension of its preoccupations, it has been weakened politically and exposed to severe competition from quite illiberal formulas. These formulas, which are often of nationalist, populist, or traditionalist inspiration, have clearly been much more successful in the identification references which they have offered to citizens disoriented by the alienating effects of economic globalization. Far from always weakening the powers of the state, which had been the prediction of a rather outdated transnationalist creed, economic globalization thus seems to have favored the political opponents of liberalism by reinforcing the illiberal power structures from which these opponents drew their strength. Unless it awaits the rather unlikely advent of a world-wide political community, the liberal enterprise will have to choose, within itself, between the imperatives of economic globalization and the necessity of political identification which is vital to any polity, even a liberal one, if it is to avoid utter ruin.

Until now, historical necessity has forced the liberal system of thought to show an enormous ability to adapt and rebound, in compelling it to absorb schemas originating in unfamiliar and sometimes contradictory frameworks. Thus, accepting the compromise of the welfare state, currently in difficulty, liberal inspiration has had to be associated with principles of socialist or Keynesian origin. It is within this dialectical relation with other systems of thought that liberalism, always partially thwarted and therefore always utopian, has been able to pick up new energy. Nothing prevents us from believing that liberalism could avoid the threat of historical exhaustion by striking a hitherto unknown and sustainable compromise with its populist and nationalist adversaries, which, at the same time, would enable it to escape the announcement of the final divorce between its economic ambitions and its moral and political pursuits.

Bibliography

Birnbaum, Pierre, and Jean Leca, eds. 1990. *Individualism: Theories and Methods*, chapter 12. Oxford: Clarendon.

Elias, Norbert. 1987. *Die Gesellschaft der Individuen*. Frankfurt am Main: Suhrkamp Verlag.

Hirschman, Albert O. 1977. *The Passions and the Interests, Political Arguments for Capitalism before Its Triumph*. Princeton: Princeton University Press.

Manent, Pierre. 1986. *Les libéraux*. Vol. 1. Paris: Hachette Pluriel.

———. 1994. *An Intellectual History of Liberalism*. Princeton: Princeton University Press.

Russett, Bruce. 1993. *Grasping the Democratic Peace*. Princeton: Princeton University Press.

Notes

1 Thus, in the social sciences other than economics, a great many concepts or recent systems of thought should be analyzed as variations, often subtle and sometimes contradictory, on the economic theme of the market. This is the case, for instance, with concepts such as 'field', 'international regime', and 'network'.

2 With the notable exception of this particular and gentle form constituted by the majoritarian domination within democratic tyranny which, as Tocqueville pointed out with lucidity, is the Achilles heel of political liberalism.

3 Besides, the examination of the data on armed conflicts shows that, if liberal democracies rarely go to war with one another, it does not necessarily mean that they are particularly pacific or pacifist. See Russett (1993).

4 For the time being, the examples given by Russia and the East European countries offer quite an uncertain teaching as far as the relations between the two dimensions of liberalism are concerned, because they both seem to have comparable difficulty in becoming established there.

5 In fact, during the phase of globalization which characterized the period of industrialization in the last century, the economic sphere, although only partially dominated by liberal reasoning, was often far more encompassing than the political one. However, as the British experience has shown, the imperialist system underpinned the concentric character of both the economic sphere and the political one.

German Difficulties with Liberalism. A Historical Outline

BEDŘICH LÖWENSTEIN

Early Liberalism: Basic Positions and First Crisis

At the beginning of the nineteenth century stood an omen: Napoleon's empire (Th. Nipperdey). At first, its fall seemed a demonstration of hubris and the vengeance of the gods, but in the long run, the neighbor states were not able to escape the tempting example of a national power state, national glory, and unscrupulous success. Of course, this development was not inevitable, and the German Confederation, resulting from the Congress of Vienna, had a real opportunity to develop as a Central European league of peace, as well as a potential economic area. But that opportunity was not seized because the leading conservatives were afraid of revolution and nationalism, and the public was not sufficiently aware. The structures created in 1815 were brought under crossfire from the side of a gradually rising and frustrated middle class, or rather their liberal representatives. The leading idea of early German liberalism was the constitutional *Rechtsstaat*, which was not simply due to the civil service mentality of its bearers, seeking to exclude arbitrariness from above and below. Quite the reverse: the liberals were no longer satisfied with happiness bestowed from above à la Joseph II, or with the enlightened bureaucratic benevolence associated with the reforms of Stein and Hardenberg. They demanded constitutional guarantees and elected chambers of deputies, which had indeed been in operation in some southern and central German states since 1817. These chambers should be, ac-

cording to the principle of the separation of powers, an insti-
tutionalized organ of control and a counterbalance to the
monarchal executive, not a possible alternative. This idea
corresponded to the prevailing power relations, but also to
the view of the German liberals that the chambers represented a guarantee of society, order, and culture against anarchy and chaos.

This law-and-order philosophy, which was also present at
a later date, was by no means typically German, but corresponded to the attitude of all members of the well-off middle
classes. For many, it served rather as a warning related to the
negative consequences of industrialization, mass poverty, and
laissez-faire. Early German liberalism was directed mainly
towards the lower middle classes and had communitarian
traits: it tried to avoid both the moneyed aristocracy and
proletarization. Unrestricted freedom of trade was, particularly in southwestern Germany, regarded as something of a
'war of all against all' (Rotteck). It was characteristic that free
trade had basically been the business of governments until
1878, but not the creed of the majority of the liberals. In
their opinion, the state had a positive role to play on top of
maintaining order, namely, maintaining social equilibrium.
Thus, not only did the privileged aristocrat have a negative
image, but also the figure of the parvenu, with his imputed
'private arbitrariness'. By contrast, the gradual spread of
middle-class values and life-styles among the different social
classes was expected, as well as their integration into an expanding civil society.

Consequently, up to the late nineteenth century the civil
notables regarded themselves as the mouthpieces of the
whole nation. Moreover, they tried—with initial success—to
channel social protests in order to promote their constitutional demands.

For that reason, the broad basis—consisting of reading-
and educational clubs, religious reform movements, singing-
and sports associations, even associations concerned with
church buildings and monuments—formed a dense civil
network, which could be politicized in a liberal direction. At
the same time, they all regarded themselves as *nationalist*,
particularly because of their negative view of political parties.

This social and national identification of liberalism turned out to be unexpectedly problematic in its first great crisis of 1848–49. At first, this West and Central European crisis of transformation had resulted everywhere in the seemingly total victory of the liberals. In their own view, they had spared the dynasties and, unlike the democratic Left, the liberals had hoped to gain the princes' support for the creation of a liberal and national German Federation. Between the 'anarchy of the street' on the one hand, and the preservation of the dynastic order on the other, they believed—remembering the frightening momentum released by the French Revolution—that they had to pursue a path of moderation, reason, and compromise. This meant containing extra-parliamentary revolutionary movements and sharing power with the monarch. The compromise revolutionary Constitution of 1848, in many respects remarkable, did not fail due to liberal doctrinairism: the final vote was pushed through *against* liberal principles. The decisive factors in the failure of the constitution were particularistic, monarchist interests—especially those of Austria and Prussia—which proved to be much more capable of action than had seemed possible in March 1848.

This attempt at a balancing act between the dynastic establishment and the radical people's movement ended in disappointment and bitterness. The liberal claim to speak for *all* Germans had proved an illusion, as well as the idea that heterogeneous geo-political components of the German Confederation could continuously and without violence be transformed into a national federal state inspired by liberalism. Neither the European powers nor the non-German peoples in Central Europe wanted this solution. But, above all, the old dynastic forces had no intention of allowing their sovereignty and power to be restricted by parliamentary rules. With that, a first chapter in the history of liberal politics in Germany, induced by enlightenment, idealism, and the Biedermeiers' need for social harmony, seemed to have come to an end.

'Realpolitik'

The feeling of helplessness which marked the years 1848 to 1850 had been a lesson to the German liberals. They based their hopes increasingly on (Prussian) *power*, not because they were masochists, but because of their aversion to weak particularism, the unpredictable masses, and obscurantist Catholicism. Another reason was their fear of the new, autocratic French empire and the conviction that history would force the ruling powers to form a coalition with the liberal middle classes. All this caused the liberals to put up with concessions and compromises concerning their own political creed; moreover, the liberalized economy saw an enormous upturn from the 1850s.

The governments, including the Austrian neo-absolutist member states of the German Confederation, had hoped to use society's newly released acquisitive drive as a means of depoliticizing society. Initially, this did not work out. On the contrary: the civil middle class became more self-confident, and its political spokesmen gained economic independence from the state apparatus. The revival of the economy also met with opposition from parts of the deserting liberal clientele, particularly from the craftsmen and the rural population. For similar reasons, the German countryside communities resisted moral permissiveness and free marriage until the 1860s.

At this point, political and social freedom drifted apart and could be played off against each other. In general, however, modernization, industrialization, and secularization brought about new political thinking, more closely linked to the practicable and the concrete than to doctrines and ideas.

The creation of a German national state was one of the aims of *Realpolitik*, now pursued by the liberals, although they had to pay a price for it. After some years of difficult confrontation with Bismarck, the majority of the liberals came to terms with him. Again, this was due not only to opportunism, but also to the obsessive belief that a modern economy and politics could only be pursued within a great state, and to the expectation that an all-German reform movement would have effects on the semi-authoritarian Prussia. Condensed into a simple—but fatal—formula, every step towards *unity* would also mark a progress towards *freedom*.

This expectation proved to be illusory, at least in part. Bismarck had no intention of creating ministers of the *Reich* endowed with real authority, or of subordinating the armed forces and foreign policy to the *Reichstag*. Trade, economics, transport, and the legal system, however, could be separated from the patronage of the state, and in this respect, the achievement of the liberals, especially in the field of legislation, was remarkable.

They did not dare to raise the question of power because they were afraid of putting their accomplishments at risk. Thus, they became more and more caught up in the rhetoric about the nation, which certainly represented an authentic value for them, but which was also a rather questionable means of integrating all the social classes. A strong, prosperous, liberal national state should also give modest wealth, civic rights, and support for self-help programs to the working classes (the Schulze/Delitzsch initiative). But few had faith in this process, and the early foundation of an independent workers' party (1863, 1875) took those 'troops' away from the liberals which would have been needed to make an assault on the authoritarian positions of central government. Their Marxist rhetoric, last but not least, cooled the liberal enthusiasm for democratization. Thus the new empire remained a provisional creation and it was not only the liberals who doubted its stability and permanence. They had difficulties not only with the socialists, but also with the Catholics, Poles, and Alsatians. A different, pluralistic and secular formula would have seemed unacceptable to them, and therefore the marriage of reason with the military state continued. (On the other hand, one might wonder whether the policy of condemnation, exclusion, and confrontation did not in fact strengthen the radical, 'fundamentalist' traits of the enemies of the *Reich*.)

In view of the dramatic problems created by industrialization, urbanization, and mobility, not to mention the rising politicization—'fundamental democratization'—the elites counted on two pre-democratic curbs: (i) the fiction of a strong state 'above political parties', and (ii) the notion of a pre-political national community. Both were seen as sheet anchors, emergency means in view of real or supposed dangers. In retrospect, however, both proved to be serious obstacles in the way of an open civil society.

The mooring of the political parties in terms of an ideologically based social background was another obstacle. In particular, the Catholic Centrum party and the social democrats, but also the rural, Protestant voters, had pre-political identities of this kind. The German liberals lacked such a mooring in determinate social backgrounds and in regional strongholds, although they were able to survive for a long time, particularly because of the tax-linked voter census.

The liberal notables believed the *Reich* to be the completion of Luther's Reformation, and therefore they opposed the Catholic Church, which barricaded itself behind dogma and *syllabi errorum* against the onslaughts of modernity.

Liberal cultural Protestantism thought itself obliged to fight this ultramontanism in the name of a free conscience and cultural freedom. The liberals, who were dropped by the government in cold blood after 1878, tried to counteract their gradual decline (from an absolute majority to one-fifth of the vote) by means of a new concept of mobilization.

Moreover, liberals of all persuasions were forced by populist pressure groups—such as the *Bund der Landwirte* or League of Farmers—to organize themselves more tightly and to seek a more solid social basis. This did not fail completely—for example, the *Hansa-Bund*, a liberal trade union founded in 1909—but the economization of politics (Langewiesche, 1988, 177) threatened the liberal program, which had subordinated economic interests to politics until that time. In their opinion, to the national idea belonged a sort of solidarity pact and the balance of interests within the framework of middle-class society. Therefore, social-liberal initiatives were not mere tactics to dilute the class struggle. The liberals, as the party of economics, would otherwise come off worse and lose their ability to integrate, being perceived as mere representatives of class interests. This danger was real, but the development could not be stopped. Many significant initiatives—for example, the *Verein für Sozialpolitik*—directed towards social reform met with little response from wide sections of society; the same goes for liberal educational clubs, popular libraries, and so on. Others were more successful in creating their own clientele, particularly Bismarck, who had again swung in the direction of conservatism with his protection of workers and special social legislation in the 1880s, aiming to isolate the liberals and to make the authoritarian state's interventionism attractive to the lower middle—and agrarian—classes. In this way, the liberal principles of self-help and association were set aside. The cities, administered by liberals, could not pursue a policy oriented towards communitarian interests, on top of the management of local schools, theaters, museums, power plants, and gas production. This resulted in mutual reproaches being made, one accusing the other of practicing 'state socialism' or 'municipal socialism'. This was in fact social liberalism at the local level in an attempt to ameliorate the worst aspects of *laissez-faire* administration and urban decay. Characteristically, this happened on the basis of a restricted suffrage, which remained in force in most places until the end of imperial rule.

'Weltpolitik'

After 1890 attempts were made at national liberal cooperation with the conservatives; on the other side, there were local interludes of solidarity between left-wing liberalism and social democracy. In this way, liberalism tried to regain the ability to act in an age of organized interests. Given its own, pan-class approach, this could be achieved only on a nationwide basis.

Unfortunately for the liberals, Bismarck had repeatedly been able to win domestic support by profiting from foreign policy crises and successes. In this respect, the national liberals in particular were able to learn much from Bismarck. In the idea of a German *Weltmachtpolitik*—in other words, of a German colonial empire—non-liberal politicians too believed they had found an all-national goal with which to bridge the gap between the parties. Therefore, it was not the acquisition of territories where the surplus population could be settled, and raw materials and new markets won, which had priority, but the domestic impact of this 'social imperialistic' policy. The liberals also hoped that their world power policy would have modernizing effects, weakening the agrarians and giving the Parliament greater influence. In any case, the mouthpieces of colonial and navy propaganda were mostly liberals or former advocates of liberal programs.

For them, it is often said, the building of a navy and the quest for colonial and imperial splendor was a kind of substitute for their lack of political power. It would, however, be one-sided to maintain that the perverted German policy of prestige, pursued as a consequence of failed democratization, was the cause of the First World War. The irresponsibility of the emperor and the relatively strong position of the agrarian–military elites were undoubtedly a bar to rational policy making, but chauvinism and the pursuit of prestige were then widespread also in the rest of Europe, and not limited to one form of political regime.

Although it was not the German desire to annex foreign territories which caused the war, after its outbreak exaggerated territorial aspirations were stirred up (G. Mann). The most radical promoters of the demands for annexation were the national liberals, a policy seemingly in contradiction with their objective of increasing the responsibilities of the *Reichstag*.

The parliamentarization of the *Reich*—which was carried through in October 1918, the last month of the war—took place under very different auspices, namely, the approaching defeat. This defeat, which had been concealed from the public, and the first chaotic years following the war created a negative image of parliaments and democracy, which were seen as responsible for the surrender: "liberalism means the death of the people", wrote A. Moeller van den Bruck in his widely read book of 1922.

The 'German Ideology'
and the Decline of Liberalism

These discouraging experiences with liberalism made the German past appear in an anti-liberal light, too. An anti-enlightened and anti-modernistic current, which had existed since the Romantic age all over Europe, was re-evaluated in the twentieth century and became the main tendency of the German intellectual and political identity. Its purpose was to reunite and stabilize a society which had been split into different parties, denominations, and interest groups; simultaneously, non-historical and rationalistic individualism and allegedly superficial utilitarianism were countered by an organic value orientation which sought to take account of the whole.

One outstanding point of reference was the authoritarian *state* which was considered to stand high above the egoism of a contractual society. The Prussian state in particular was stylized as a model for the German nation—and not just after 1871—and was regarded as superior to the allegedly shallow liberal concept of the state. German spirituality and sensitivity, anchored in devotion and duty, were now attributed to the Prussian state. It was, in the words of K. Voßler, a "metaphysical, speculative, fanatic, abstract and mystical politicizing" which took up these intellectual weapons against the liberal democratic constitution of Weimar and, perhaps even more so, against the emerging peaceful civil society based on acquisition, often the breeding ground of corruption and viewed as a force for social disintegration. On this view, a strong will and determination, the authentic elements of 'true' politics, ought not to be destroyed by parliamentary nonsense, the merely mechanical addition of single egos, and the economic and international balancing of interests.

These views, which were neither new nor specifically German, had a ready audience in post–First World War Germany. The conduct of the war and the refusal to accept defeat—an eventuality which was not recognized as a suitable occasion for a general settling of accounts with imperial rule because most people feared a Bolshevik-style revolution and, of course, rejected the allied thesis of Germany's war guilt—as well as the intransigent policies of the victors, all these factors created an atmosphere of bitterness and self-righteousness in which the opportunity to create an open civil society was lost.

The principal causes of the failure of the Weimar Constitution were not the weak president, the parties' mutual distrust, and the incoherent coexistence of social and democratic constitutional promises, but rather the fatal tendency to mythologize both the state and national considerations in a crisis situation. Attempted coups, hyperinflation, and the French occupation of the Ruhr made it difficult to believe in rational, democratic decision making, provoked an irrational image of the 'enemy', and alienated the middle classes, who in 1919 had still voted for the liberals. The Weimar Constitution emerged from a compromise between social democracy, left-wing liberalism, and the Catholic Centrum party.

The function of the liberals shrunk to that of the 'party of business'. They gave up the unstable consensus which had been adhered to only half-heartedly by all concerned. In the best case, it would have demanded a longer period of economic growth in order to consolidate it, but when, after a few years of progress and remarkable social improvement, a deep economic depression got under way, self-restraint and moderation turned into panic and anger. The German political tradition's positive view of the strong, non-party state, on the one hand, and the large measure of government intervention which society was accustomed to, on the other, now had fatal consequences for the republic, which was blamed for the disastrous economic situation (Langewiesche, 1988, 238).

The urban middle class, which had helped both liberal parties (DDO, DVP) to obtain more than 20 per cent of the votes as recently as 1919–20, changed its allegiance to the right-wing parties and demanded the reduction of what it called the 'social command economy'. The middle classes had not only been affected by economic problems and loss of social status, but also by a cultural upheaval which was hard to harmonize with their value system. On the other hand, the term 'liberal', which was used rather pejoratively, seemed to many people to be synonymous with the supposed general decline. A growing part of the German population believed that remedies were needed which were quite different to those offered by worn-out liberalism. With a slow death lasting some twenty-five years, the liberals, reduced to representing economic and class interests, had become almost non-existent even before they fell apart in 1933.

A New Beginning and Outlook

The totalitarian rule of National Socialism was followed by the total breakdown and rejection of everything that had contributed to its existence. Nevertheless, 1945 did not mark a completely new beginning. The plans for a loose German confederation were quickly forgotten and a single federal state was founded with a constitution which followed on from that of Weimar, with some amendments. But the structure of the population had changed radically and had been worn down by war, degradation, refugees, and so on, so that the impression of a relatively class-homogenous society arose, which could be called neither proletarian nor bourgeois. Gradually, social differences and pre-democratic attitudes developed again, but social dynamics and mobility, and a more demanding public were the decisive factors.

The old socio-cultural backgrounds which had influenced mentality and politics before 1933 had clearly broken down. As a consequence, the new parties sought to appeal to all social classes, regions, and religions. No single social or interest group was able to influence decision making fundamentally in post-war Germany. This reflects an important aspect of modernity which Gellner termed "modularity", meaning functional compatibility in contrast to predetermined roles and sacralized status. Furthermore, the value of the economic liberalization connected with the figure of Ludwig Erhard was not at all self-evident in 1945; a more logical solution would have been a planned economy, together with corporate and government regulation. This was supported not only by the SPD—even some within the CDU were in favor of it.

So-called 'Manchesterism' had a bad reputation after the experiences of the early 1930s. Thomas Mann was a typical representative of his time, with his war speech condemning unrestrained individual freedom, which he contrasted to social democracy. Concessions to equality and economic justice were inevitable.

The result was the 'social market economy' which was the brainchild of the CDU, but also fitted in well with the middle-class ideas of early German liberalism. This was a solution in terms of which, for the first time in German history, the state, rather than standing *above* society, was to serve as an institution whose aim was to meet individual and social needs (K. Sontheimer), a model not too far away from the classical political ideas of Locke.

The belief in Europe, the overcoming of nationalist provincialism, was a third important change of paradigm. Initially, it was perhaps only a declamatory statement, occasioned by the circumstances. But the exclusion of the German question (reunification, the former Eastern territories) from practical politics, the complete dependence on the West, and the gradual coming together with it in almost every field, reduced the idea of a united German nation to insignificance.

In the 1950s, it was the liberal FDP which took up the idea again, but in the long run it was not successful. In this way, liberalism gained widespread acceptance in the Western part of Germany without the help of a liberal party, strictly speaking, although the FDP played a not unimportant role as 'king-maker' in the political life of the Federal Republic. For the first time, liberal values have fully permeated society, politics, economy, and culture. Of course, this pluralistic society benefited from the American model, economic growth, and social and foreign security, accompanied by a change of mentality, oriented towards materialistic consumerism and individualistic hedonism.

All these things—not unproblematic themselves—favored a critical analysis of the totalitarian and authoritarian German past. This analysis, lasting five decades, has, in turn, contributed to the reinforcement of the new values and identities.

This liberal and European Germany has withstood all the critical situations it has faced up to now, including the overthrow of the Yalta and Potsdam order. The future is always open, but it is likely that Germany will withstand all future tests, not just the timidly begun restructuring of the economy and the associated austerity policies.

Last but not least, there is a reasonable hope that Germany will use its relative strength not to pursue antiquated national politics, but to continue the drive towards solid European unity.

Note

This chapter is particularly indebted to Dieter Langewiesche's *Liberalismus in Deutschland* (Frankfurt am Main, 1988).

Liberalism in the East

The Burdens of the Past

Jiří Musil

As so often in Europe's modern history, since 1989 there have arisen a number of misunderstandings and disappointments in the communication and interaction between the politicians and intellectuals of East Central Europe on the one hand, and their Western counterparts on the other. The seminar organized by the Central European University in Prague in 1996 constituted an important step towards remedying this. Its purpose was to do something to repair the damage caused by these mutual misapprehensions and misinterpretations. The primary task is to point out explicitly the areas in which these mutual misunderstandings have emerged. One important source is no doubt the two partners' disagreement concerning how to classify and define the various terms and concepts. However, a still deeper cause is the transfer or transplantation of particular political and economic conceptions into different social and cultural environments which may significantly change their anticipated effects, even when they are semantically correctly interpreted. There are many cases of such distortion, as we now know. In this chapter I shall try to present the most important of them. The clearest instances are to be found in the application of some of the standard principles of market economic theory. The different groups of actors in the market simply do not seem to have reacted in the manner assumed in economics textbooks.

The Importance of Context and History

There exist, however, other, more subtle forms of the failure of market mechanisms. What is important in this context is the circumstance that this failure is not caused by the misapprehension or misapplication of given ideas. The level of misunderstanding in this case is of a distinct sociological, rather than semantic nature. An example can best illustrate this. Contemporary mature capitalism is made up of a system of very complex institutions and rules. These are very well defined and known in the West. It was assumed that if they were transferred to the former communist region, and properly underpinned by the law, their beneficial effects would soon become manifest. Other implicit assumptions were that, first, all participants in the economic process could understand these rules, and, second, they would be willing to observe them. Unfortunately, this has very often not been the case. For a modern capitalist economy to function, it is not enough to carry out institutional and legal reforms; it is equally necessary to have people who both understand the rules and, above all, are willing to abide by them. It is not possible to operate a well functioning, robust modern capitalist system without a particular kind of actor, who has not only internalized the legal forms of market behavior, but also accepted the ethics of market relations. Ethics, mutual trust, respect for the law, contractual obligations, and the rules of the game: all these are conditions of a working market economy.

The legal and moral context in which the market operates has been underestimated by a number of avowedly liberal politicians in the former communist countries. Their counterparts in the West err in their failure to make explicit what they take for granted in the societies in which they live—in their analyses they sometimes even assume that the same sociological and cultural conditions prevail also in the nations which are currently attempting to renew—or in a number of cases to introduce for the first time—a market economy. Although both these mistaken approaches necessarily derive from different perspectives, they both lack what I would call 'contextual sociological thinking', the viewpoint which attempts to look at the economy as deeply embedded in the entire multilevel and complex social system. To put it another way, many scholars and experts, particularly if they are economists without a sense of context or for the role of institutions, do not sufficiently grasp that in the course of the communist experiment not only were the institutions and mechanisms of a market economy lost, but the functioning of the so-called command economy changed human mentalities and erased—or prevented from developing—the patterns of behavior which are the sine qua non of market operations. The political and economic elites in the East, in their turn, succumbed to the temptation of a technocratic vision of the world.

In explaining the causes of the difficulties impeding application of liberal principles in the political and economic life of East Central Europe since 1989, analysts tend to emphasize the immediate past. Countless studies point to the survival of institutions and legal norms, but also of social networks, mentalities, values, and attitudes which came into existence during the decades of communism. There can be no doubt that the seventy-odd years of dictatorship in the former Soviet Union and the forty years during which the rest of the Soviet bloc suffered under totalitarian regimes left a deep political and economic imprint. However, it is equally evident that the roots of many of their political traditions and of what we could call their 'political mentalities' go back to a more distant past. We could even argue that the most serious obstacles in the way of development towards liberally oriented democracy stem from a peculiar amalgam of social and ideological elements, consisting of, on the one hand, the familiar legacy of Marxist socialism and, on the other, previously existing agrarian and corporative social structures.

This remarkable—and so far little investigated—combination of agrarian, communitarian, and semi-feudal traditions with Marxism-Leninism or Stalinism was 'blended' in a different way in each country: the Czech Lands, Slovenia, and Estonia, for example, show a pattern distinct from those of Bulgaria, Russia, or Ukraine. These differences are undoubtedly connected with the specific economic, political, and cultural evolution of the various countries of the former

Soviet bloc in the nineteenth and twentieth centuries, and even earlier. A number of available historical and sociological studies call attention to the fact that the differences in political culture and mentality of the individual East Central European countries are the consequence of differences in their political and economic histories. These dissimilar histories also shaped dissimilar social structures and, later, dissimilar political orientations. Often we must take account of historical processes which ran their course as long ago as the sixteenth and seventeenth centuries, or earlier. From this point of view, the differences between the political and economic histories of the Balkan countries, and those of Hungary, Poland, and the Czech Lands are especially important. To an often surprising degree, the distinct political mentalities of these nations mirror, to this day, the pattern in which, at the dawn of modern European history, the power relations of the various social classes and strata crystallized in this region.

Although we can find many common characteristics which clearly resulted from the effort invested by the Soviet Union to homogenize the whole region, economically, politically, and socially, older and—in the consciousness of the social actors—deeper-seated historical social memories have preserved specific socio-cultural mentalities. These have partly gained strength over time, as the post-communist transformation process advances. In the cultural—and intellectual—vacuum created since 1989, the political elites have often turned to the past to seek models for the present. Of course, it would be a mistake to overestimate the influence of these past 'codes'. The morphogenetic forces of the recent past, as well as the forces represented by the contemporary transformation processes, are indisputably very strong and must not be underestimated. Nevertheless, to overlook the power of the more remote past would be equally wrong. This is valid especially of the structure of what I, together with Edward Shils, define as the "core values of societies".[1]

The degree to which the past has influenced the present consciousness of the former communist societies varies from country to country. It depends for example, on the strength of the already mentioned 'past code', that is, on whether it was suppressed under communist rule, as well as on whether it fits, or at least is similar to, what is happening there at present. In this respect, for instance, the countries which, as early as the nineteenth and at the turn of the twentieth century, had relatively strong democratic institutions and political traditions can fall back upon past experience. Conversely, the countries that between the two world wars experienced authoritarian or fascist regimes will find it hard to draw upon their traditions.

All this—and, of course, the differences in economic and social development—reminds us not to forget, while trying to understand the difficulties connected with the implementation of liberalism in East Central Europe after 1989, that we are moving in a terrain marked both by *common* and by *specific* traits. In practice, this means that we have to take into account the given political and socio-cultural subdivisions of the space we are studying. Any generalization of the characteristics of this region has always to be balanced in terms of the specific aspects.

All economic and social historians who have systematically dealt with East Central Europe have been aware of this fact. Daniel Chirot (1989) in the introduction to his *Origins of Backwardness of Eastern Europe* emphasized that at the beginning of the modern era there existed at least four distinct parts of Eastern Europe: "To a considerable extent [they] still exist. Contact with the West, absorption into the world economy, the rise of nationalism, even socialism, have failed to eliminate such deep historical differences. The great transformations that have taken place since 1500 have been channeled into streams whose banks were partially formed before that time" (Chirot, 1989, 6).

Therefore, it is indispensable, when we seek the causes of the weakness of liberalism in contemporary East Central Europe, to combine the following two approaches: (i) to examine this phenomenon as it appeared in the more remote past, the more recent past, and even the present time; and (ii) to analyze the difficulties encountered by liberalism separately for each of the principal regions of post-communist Europe.

The Heritage of the More Remote Past

It follows that the explanation of the different political and economic development of Western and Eastern Europe—that is, the interpretation of the causes of the rise of the former and of the backwardness of the latter—should provide the general framework for an understanding of the nature of the obstacles to liberalism's progress in post-communist East Central Europe. We have no space here even to superficially touch upon all the theories which purport to explicate the distinct evolutionary trajectories of these two parts of the continent.[2] What we must do, however, in order to grasp the political situation in contemporary Eastern Europe, is to describe the conditions which opened the way for the West to create a dynamic, liberal capitalist society, and the absence of which blocked for Eastern Europe development in the same direction.

A list of the conditions that made possible the escape from relatively closed, stable, and illiberal agrarian societies can serve also as a catalogue of criteria which must be met by a liberal society. Where such conditions were not given, robust capitalism, the rule of law, and liberal politics did not develop. At best, only some aspects of the West European model were accepted, by way of compromise. If we compare such a catalogue of criteria with the actual historical development of the various parts of East Central Europe, we will arrive at a relatively reliable picture of their situation vis-à-vis Western Europe.

For purposes of comparison, Ernest Gellner's catalogue of the "conditions of existence" of agrarian societies in his seminal work *Plough, Sword and Book* (1988) is extremely useful. In his view, these conditions were also the premises of the rise and formation of modern industrial societies. They include: (i) feudalism as a matrix of capitalism; (ii) church–state dualism; (iii) a restrained state; (iv) restrained burghers; (v) a permeable aristocracy; (vi) availability of an expanding 'bribery' fund; (vii) a rising ceiling of discovery; (viii) free peasants; (ix) the clerical origins of individualism; (x) the Protestant ethic; (xi) the plural European state system; and (xii) a national rather than a civic bourgeoisie.

Not all conditions enumerated by Gellner are relevant to the problem we are studying here; therefore in our comparison we will disregard some of them. The results of the comparison can be recapitulated in the following conclusions:

– In the countries of Eastern Europe that belonged to the sphere of the Russian Orthodox Church, no dualism of church and state existed: the head of the state was at the same time the head of the church. This caesaro-papism was undoubtedly a significant factor determining the specific development of these countries. In the Central European countries that had accepted Western Christianity—for example, in the predominantly Catholic Habsburg Empire—the interdependence of state and church was also exceptionally close until their final demise. The separation of church and state, as it came to exist in the West, did not exist in this region. It would be difficult to claim of the states of East Central Europe, which included three multinational empires—the Austro-Hungarian, the Russian, and the Ottoman—that they exercised power with restraint, as required by point (iii) in Gellner's list. These states wielded strong and insufficiently controlled power based on the interconnected centers of the court, the aristocracy, and the army.

– The bourgeoisie and the middle classes in general in this region were weak, both numerically and as far as their power position was concerned, and consequently there could be no question of a revolutionary role in most of these empires. An exception is Austria–Hungary, which was profoundly shaken by the liberal revolution of 1848.

– Upward mobility in the form of the passage from the status of burgher to that of aristocrat did exist in this region, for example, in the Habsburg Empire. The openness of the Austrian aristocracy, nonetheless, was notably less than that of, for instance, the English nobility.

– The opportunities of the state to corrupt various strata of society by means of 'ransom payments' (what Gellner calls 'Danegeld') were more limited in the countries of East Central Europe than in the West. The cause of this was a lesser amount of resources available for distribution. Forced to maintain strong armies within weak economies, the state corrupted the aristocracy by giving it a free hand in exploiting the peasants. This, of course, led to the familiar phenomenon known as 'second bondage', that is, to the creation of a dependent and powerless peasant mass which could defend itself only by sporadic outbursts of rebellion. This situation, understandably, was a formidable barrier to the development of capitalism in agriculture.

– The fewer resources available for 'redistribution', whether up or down the social scale, was due also to poor technological development in the countries of East Central Europe. It was precisely technological progress that helped create sufficient reserves for the necessary redistribution carried out in West European states. To put it simply, any redistribution presupposes a relatively strong and efficient economy based upon well-functioning technology.

– In contrast to some parts of northwestern Europe where the farmers have always been free to a significant degree and lived in nuclear, separate families, the farmers of East Central Europe have usually been tied to the aristocracy which decided on their living standards and other private matters. Apart from this vertical dependency, they were subject to a form of lateral dependency relative to extended families and communities. Society in the East Central European countryside was thus oriented in a strong communitarian sense. This circumstance, combined with the weakness of the cities, helped create a very hierarchical and paternalistic social structure that was not apt to stimulate the development of liberalism and capitalism.

– The individualism observed in some parts of northwestern Europe has deep historical roots, as has been stated, for example, by Alan McFarlane (1978). According to McFarlane, the English version of individualism goes far back into the history of its agricultural families. A number of studies of Norwegian families point to a similar origin. Traditions of this kind either did not exist at all or were very weak in East Central Europe. Traces of them could perhaps be found among Calvinist farmers in Hungary or in the small islands of Protestantism in Bohemia and Moravia.

– A substantial portion of East Central Europe lacked the Protestant religious sources of individualism. The East—

with the exception of parts of Hungary, Bohemia, and southern Poland—was not influenced by the Protestant ethic, either, an indispensable condition of the growth of capitalism. By contrast, the role of the parish, extended kinship, and the community—the village—has always been stronger in Eastern Europe. Conformity instilled by *Gemeinschaft*-like relations guaranteed a more peaceful and stable, but also a more limited, social life.

– East Central Europe has also not known a developed plural state system in international relations; on the contrary, political power was concentrated in a few empires with various degrees of centralization, and with a relatively well-developed tradition of bureaucratism. Mobility among the states of East Central Europe—and for a considerable time also in the interior of these states—was not easy. On the whole, geographical mobility here has always been more restricted than in the West.

It should be evident from this historico-sociological comparison that the conditions in East Central Europe during the whole of the New Age were less favorable to modernization than those in Western Europe. That is why Eastern—and partly also Central—Europe perpetually lagged behind the economic, social, and political developments of Western Europe. It is probable, however, that in the Middle Ages these differences were not so great. They began to show as early as the sixteenth century, but increased considerably with the advance of modernization in Western Europe, as it appears from records documenting the processes of industrialization, urbanization, and growth, but also the demographic revolution and democratization. These differences, with a few exceptions, lasted until the first half of the twentieth century, as is stressed by Ivan T. Berend who calls this part of the continent "the crisis zone of Europe" (Berend, 1986).

It is equally evident that this lag has been manifest also in respect of human rights, legislation, education, and—especially—in the political sphere. It was reflected in the participation of the various components of society in political decision making, in the articulation of problems in the ideological sphere, and in the structure and orientation of political parties. After the French Revolution, as a consequence of expanding contacts with Western Europe, the influence of liberal ideas grew all over East Central Europe. This influence, however, remained weak in the strictly political sense, even in the countries where industrial development and modernization processes seemed to create more favorable conditions, as for example in the German nation-state after 1871, in Austria, and in the Czech Lands. Classical political liberalism, which the Czech philosopher and statesman T. G. Masaryk identified as "moral individualism", as well as the economic liberalism of Franco-British provenance, have never had an easy position in East Central Europe. It would be possible to claim that the most severe criticisms of the liberal doctrine, especially in its later version, combined with economic liberalism and classical economic theory, have come from Central Europe. This has, no doubt, political and sociological, but also intellectual reasons, connected with the delay of modernization processes in this part of Europe. It is not possible to overlook the fact that, at the turn of the nineteenth century, the conglomerate of German states had for a long time been considered as a kind of 'Second World' of Europe, and that much of the intellectual energy produced in this region during the nineteenth century was spent either on 'catching up' with Western Europe or in resisting its ideological influence by means of its own ideas. Thus, for example, the political resistance against the French Revolution and the Enlightenment which was traditionally linked to it has been one of the propelling forces of German historicism. It would be difficult to explain the origin of German subjective idealism without reference to these connections. The emergence of critiques of rationalism, the Enlightenment, classical liberal economic theory, and democracy—as well as the mobilization of conservative traditions on the one hand and the shaping of socialist programs and radical communism on the other—in the geographical and cultural space east of the Rhine was not accidental. It grew from a soil which had been made ready for this kind of intellectual response by a long economic, political, and social development. The same could be said of Russia, and partly also of a number of Central European countries. Austria–Hungary was continually being shaken by confrontations of the mutually opposed *Gemeinschaft* and *Gesellschaft* ideologies, involving the 'communitarians' of the age and the liberals, throughout the last seventy years of the Habsburg Empire.

The nationalist messianic current of thought in Poland, Serbia, Croatia, Russia, and, to a certain degree, also in the Czech Lands, was actually a regional reaction to the pressure of the modernization trends coming from the West. The outcome was a motley collection of hybrid populist, national socialist, but also socially liberal concepts that aimed at combining local and regional traditions of pre-modern thought with two versions of modernity, that is, with either liberalism or socialism. However, in East Central Europe in the second half of the nineteenth century this situation was overtaken by nationalism which began to crowd out both the liberal and the socialist form of universalism. Here again, in order to understand the force of the extraordinarily virulent type of nationalism characteristic of East Central Europe, it is necessary to became familiar with the political and economic context.

What was—and partly still is—this context? What were the dominant traits of the political traditions—to use George Schöpflin's (1990) term—of Eastern Europe? The fate reserved for liberalism in this part of the continent after 1989 will remain unintelligible unless we are able to construct a kind of Weberian 'ideal type' of the East Central European mentality. What was the nature of the social and intellectual environment into which liberalism penetrated? What was the structure of the amalgam, so difficult to grasp and to describe, of Sovietism—or, let us say, of Marxist socialism—on the one hand, and of the ideological configurations of agrarian, populist, and, in some cases, even corporative societies, on the other? Only if we are able to interpret this peculiar mixture will we comprehend our central theme more deeply.

Regional Aspects

It is evident from the findings of social and economic historians that, seen from the point of view of its adaptability to economic challenges coming from the West, East Central Europe has to be divided into at least two major macroregions. One is the Balkans, which were for centuries dominated by the Ottoman Empire. The second macro-region—which some scholars tend to further divide—is composed of societies that in the past were part of the Habsburg or the Russian Empire. Sometimes particular areas of Prussia are included among these subtypes.

The Balkan societies used to be labeled 'incomplete societies'. This was explained as a consequence of Turkish rule, which had inhibited the emergence of modern governing elites and a modern middle class. The place of the latter was taken by the military and political elites that had participated in the struggle for liberation and had begun to build the administrative structure of the new nation-state. The majority of the population, however, were still peasants who, although they now were rid of their Turkish landlords, owned only small plots and lived in great poverty. Agriculture in this region only very slowly and with great difficulty changed into a market-oriented enterprise. Equally weak was the class of middle-level entrepreneurs. This situation was made still worse by the circumstance that the bureaucratic and military elites—aware of the precariousness of the economic situation as a whole—strove to enrich themselves as rapidly as possible at the expense of other social strata and, indeed, the nation as a whole. This type of social and power structure was hardly conducive to the formation of a stable and prosperous society.

As for the societies in the second macro-region, there were other factors at work that impeded their dynamic evolution. In the first place, there was a politically powerful aristocracy that maintained its strong position even when modern capitalism began to assert itself. The political influence of the aristocracy was undoubtedly decisive but it is also worth noting its statistical significance. While in pre-revolutionary France the aristocracy constituted a mere one per cent of the population, in Hungary its share was five and in Poland ten per cent. The old social structures and political traditions survived the revolution of 1848 and the subsequent reforms that laid the foundations of the modern Austrian bourgeois state. The societies in this second macro-region of East Central Europe therefore remained to a large degree corporatist, under the strong influence of the court, the aristocracy, the army, and the bureaucracy, while the political position of the middle strata improved only gradually. There were, to be sure, significant differences between the various parts of the East Central European macro-region—for example, between the western part of the Habsburg Empire and Russia. The unified German nation-state also represented a special case. Some scholars believe these differences to be fundamental. For instance, Gale Stokes, the American historian, calls our attention to the consequences of the specific economic development of the Czech Lands, Hungary, and Romania during the seventeenth and eighteenth centuries which came to the surface in the political systems of these countries in the nineteenth and twentieth centuries (Stokes, 1989).

Thanks to, among other things, the earlier involvement of the economy of the Czech Lands in West European markets, the existence of proto-industrial elements, and the rise of a small but very lively urban stratum, free from feudal bonds and dependence upon the nobility, the Czech Lands became a more hospitable environment for the formation of modern capitalist structures than Hungary and Romania. The industrialization wave of the second half of the nineteenth century further reinforced this trend. The development of the modern social structure and democratic orientation of the population was connected with this. In this context, however, it is necessary to emphasize that in this process an important political and social role was played by the relatively successful modernization of Czech agriculture, which, on account of its yields, level of marketization, and other qualities, began to outstrip not only the agriculture of the Balkans, but also that of Poland and Russia. A similarly successful modernization of agriculture, marked especially by the development of modern industrial mills and the machine industry that supported it, took place also in Hungary after 1860. For a number of reasons, among them the already mentioned weakness of the middle entrepreneurial classes and the strength of the aristocracy which determined the core values of Hungarian society, Hungary at the end of the nineteenth century did not start to develop into a modern industrial nation.

Similar constellations of the power positions of individual social strata—that is, a strong aristocracy, and weak middle strata and working class, together with a powerful state, bureaucracy, and army—shaped also Russia, Poland, and the eastern part of the united Germany after 1871. In his critique of Wilhelminian Germany and the German political elites, Max Weber stressed that the most acute danger to which modern German society was exposed was an excessive concentration of power in the hands of the aristocratic upper classes,[3] linked to the army as well as to the high bourgeoisie. A similar social structure could at that time be found in Tsarist Russia and, to a large extent, in the too slowly reforming Habsburg Empire. Yet even under these conditions a capitalist economy emerged, albeit with a considerable delay, in all these large multiethnic states. However, as one analyst of East Central European developments has succinctly observed: "The modern world of business and capitalism was built into these societies as an alien element" (Berend, 1986, 17). It seems that—in another form and as a result of different causes—the same situation is now developing once again, a full one hundred years later, and that the insufficiently developed general social, institutional, and legal preconditions of effective market mechanisms are again imperiling the establishment and stabilization of market economies.

The problem of the modernization of East Central European societies in the second half of the nineteenth and the first half of the twentieth century was further complicated by what we could call 'delayed nationalism'. Ernest Gellner has pointed out the significance of the various "time zones" in which nationalist movements unfolded on the European continent (Gellner, 1983, 88–101). In the German and Italian cases, nationalism meant unification, that is, the inclusion of a number of smaller state units in one national state. This was in harmony with the logic of the evolution of capitalism which in its modern form has tended to favor the creation of ever larger market areas subject to the same 'rules of the game'. Truly liberal economists have always advocated the removal of all political and legal barriers in the way of the free movement of goods and labor. In Central Europe, including Germany, the first part of this liberal economic doctrine—that is, the constant broadening of markets—was accepted, but the second part was rejected by many economic theoreticians, for example, by Friedrich List. An opening-up vis-à-vis the more productive English or French industries was considered dangerous to the weaker, fledgling German industry. For List, the term 'national economy' had a protectionist connotation, which may have been only of a temporary nature, but the German response to West European liberalism also took much more radical forms. Among these, the views of the philosopher Johann Gottlieb Fichte concerning the so-called closed state betrayed an unabashedly anti-liberal stance (Fichte, 1800). German political, social, and economic literature in the nineteenth century abounded in such anti-liberal opinions. Some of them clearly had conservative roots—others were socialist-inspired or socialist-oriented. Comparable reactions to dynamically evolving industrial capitalism could be found, although not so often, in the Austro-Hungarian monarchy.

The national movements in the Habsburg, Russian, and Ottoman Empires were not restricted to the bourgeoisie, lower middle classes, and intelligentsia. Towards the end of the nineteenth century, populist variants emerged with their bases among the peasantry and the lower middle classes. Populism was predominantly anti-liberal and anti-capitalist. It expressed the attitudes of those strata which were afraid of the effects of modernization and capitalism. The majority of populist groups at the same time rejected Marxism, and vied with the socialist movement for the support of the working class.[4]

The liberals in East Central Europe at the start of the twentieth century—weak as they were—had therefore to face two adverse political forces at the same time. In the industrially more developed areas—for example, in Austria, the Czech Lands, and some parts of Poland, Hungary, and Russia—these adversaries were the social democratic parties and the populist-oriented movements. The last-named were, depending on local conditions, often nationalist. However, some social-democratic organizations also succumbed to nationalism and attempted to put a distance between themselves and the originally united international social democratic movement. This can be documented in terms of the history of Czech (actually 'Czecho-Slavic', 'Českoslovanská') social democracy which, following the congress of the Austrian Social Democratic Party in Brno in 1889, began its autonomous existence as a self-contained body within the latter party. On the other hand, a national socialist movement developed in Central Europe at about the same time, which nevertheless espoused some liberal ideas. In the—for the most part—agrarian provinces which belonged to larger multiethnic empires—such as Poland, Croatia, and Romania—however, the main political force was represented by the nationally and democratically oriented movements. Until the time of the acquisition of national independence and the constitution of sovereign nation-states by these ethnic units, many relatively heterogeneous orientations, including the liberal ones, belonged to such movements.

The position of orthodox liberalism of the West European type was generally weak at the turn of the twentieth century. Nationally oriented movements, populism, and socialism proved to be more attractive. The original driving force of the truly liberal groupings that at one time had been strong in Austria and in the Czech Lands began to lose momentum between the 1860s and 1880s, as it was gradually squeezed out by parties of a nationalist or socialist orientation.

In the search for an explanation of the mutual misapprehensions and disappointments of these two camps, another historical development may be helpful. The modernization processes that, already in the second half of the nineteenth century, were unfolding in the western part of Central Europe started to materialize at the beginning of the twentieth century in Russia and in the Balkans. This is evident from export growth statistics and in some cases also industrial production. Hand in hand with industrialization and the marketization of products, social conflicts began to sharpen. Also, the eclipse of older economic and legal institutions became manifest, and a part of the intellectual elites started to fear for the integrity of the communities in which they lived. In some cases—most often in Russia—publications appeared that openly voiced the rejection of—and resistance against— what was coming from the West. The West was accused of oppressing the East European countries and attacked for its alleged decadence. The critical attitude of East Central European intellectuals vis-à-vis the West, liberalism, rationalism, and often even parliamentary democracy, was a complex phenomenon. It was, on the one hand, stimulated by frustration over the fact that the European periphery was unable to accept and successfully assimilate Western modernization; on the other hand, the East willingly accommodated proto-fascist and radically socialist, even communist, ideologies as recipes for the solution of its problems. The antipathy towards traditional Western thought was additionally reinforced by the support given by East European elites to the revolution taking place in European fine arts, literature, and music. The artistic avant-garde was, somewhat paradoxically, understood in the East as a weapon with which to fight the mainstream concept of modernity emanating from the West. Thus, already before the First World War, a large section of the political and intellectual elites of East Central Europe rejected the West European models of the modernization of political and economic systems.

A Complex Code Dating from the Inter-War Period

Views on the impact of the period between the two world wars upon political mentalities in East Central Europe differ substantially. They range from a rather negative assessment by authors such as the British historian Hugh Seton-Watson, to an—on the whole—positive evaluation by scholars such as the Polish-American historian Piotr S. Wandycz. Seton-Watson, in a book written during the Second World War, judges the changes of mentality that occurred in the region which he calls "Eastern Europe" quite harshly: "Most of the political struggles of the East European states during the last twenty years were fought between different small groups within narrow ruling classes, over the heads of the people. These struggles were no more than scrambles for power, for material advantages and personal prestige between ambitious individuals and interested cliques" (Seton-Watson, 1986, 256). Piotr S. Wandycz is less critical (Wandycz, 1992). The existence of such diverse views in the literature could be the result of the individual writers' search for a common denominator in an extremely heterogeneous region. As a result, their interpretation obliges them to resort to listing a number of exceptions. In the context of our discussion of the fate of liberalism, it will be appropriate to distinguish between three main types of political solution to the situation created by the First World War.

(i) Radical left-wing revolution. Apart from the Russian Bolshevik revolution that led to the creation of the Soviet Union, there were unsuccessful revolutions of this kind in Hungary and Bavaria, and attempts at revolutions in other parts of Germany in the years 1919 and 1920. To a degree, the revolution in Bulgaria, which was initiated by a revolutionary peasant movement, was of a similar kind.

(ii) National revolution. These took place especially in those countries where national movements had existed for many decades while these countries were part of large multinational empires. This is valid, above all, for Poland, Czechoslovakia, and Yugoslavia. The fact that the war led to the formation of new nation-states did not determine the nature of the political regimes in these states: Czechoslovakia maintained its democracy until 1938; Poland after 1926 became an authoritarian state; Yugoslavia from 1929 until the Second World War was a monarchal dictatorship.

(iii) A solution produced by radical right-wing movements. The ideological roots of this go back to the time before the First World War, but these movements did not accede to power immediately. Their model can be seen in

Fascist Italy where Mussolini seized control in 1922, but there were similarly oriented, national-conservative regimes in Hungary (established by Miklós Horthy in 1920), in Austria (right-wing corporativism after 1927—the Schattendorf incident), and in Poland (the 'rule of the colonels' after 1935). The royal dictatorships in Yugoslavia, Romania, and Bulgaria were also clearly undemocratic.

Towards the end of the inter-war period, non-democratic regimes prevailed in East Central Europe. The only exception was Czechoslovakia which preserved basic democratic institutions but had to face serious internal difficulties stemming from the ethnic structure of the state. In the 1930s, as a consequence of the political changes in Germany—but also as a reaction to Czech nationalism—the desire for change in the constitutional order grew among the German- and Slovak-speaking populations. The final outcome is well known: the destruction of Czechoslovakia by the Nazis with active support from domestic forces.

We will deal with the consequences of Bolshevism and Stalinism in the Soviet Union for the fate of liberalism in the whole region in the concluding part of this chapter, which will be devoted to the communist regimes in East Central Europe after the Second World War.

For the understanding of the current situation, however, it is important to analyze the fate of those nations which, after initial attempts at democratization, nevertheless metamorphosed into right-wing fascist-type regimes. Their chances of establishing a democratic system were frustrated partly by internal, partly by external causes. Among the unfavorable internal factors we might mention their inability to compromise, as well as persistent group conflicts leading to social fragmentation. These conflicts were further exacerbated by nationalist disputes. Counterproductive conflicts, lasting for many years and leaving important social problems—especially rural poverty—unsolved, spread dissatisfaction among the masses, and led to a loss of trust in the political elites and the ruling classes. None of this did much to promote the loyalty of the citizens vis-à-vis the newly constituted states. The political elites which had stood beside the cradle of these states rapidly lost legitimacy in the eyes of their fellow countrymen. Among the poorest segments of the population, both rural and urban, sympathies grew for the radical Left.

The key role in these widespread transformations of attitudes was played by the internal development of the agrarian parties which represented the dominant political force in the majority of the countries in question. The leadership of these parties ceased to articulate and to defend the interests of the poor farmers who had initially brought them to power. Moreover, they in many cases lacked a clear vision and oscillated between rightist and leftist positions. Nor were they able to interpret intelligibly the situation of the agrarian movement as regards industrialization, the cities, and the industrial workforce.

Political instability caused by group and personal conflicts, the inadequacy of the policies applied, and—in some cases—frequent changes of government, made people clamor for an alternative. The remedy was sought in various forms of undemocratic, anti-liberal, and authoritarian regimes based on 'law and order' and a 'strong hand'. These regimes legitimized their versions of order in terms of the national interest, the need for national unity, and the suppression of internal enemies. They found these enemies among liberally-oriented democrats and socialists, also among representatives of the world of finance, Jews, and nonconformist intellectuals. The governments based on this kind of ideology quickly destroyed all democratic institutions.

One of the external factors which frustrated the development towards democracy of many countries in East Central Europe was their location, socially as well as politically, at Europe's periphery. The modernization processes of the inter-war period were not robust enough to transform these societies from agrarian to industrial ones. As a matter of fact, this was a zone of unsuccessful or halfway modernization, populated by nations with weak economies.

The second important cause of the failure of democracy in the great majority of nations in the "crisis zone of Europe" was their inability to cooperate. The vision developed by personalities such as T. G. Masaryk, the philosopher and president of Czechoslovakia, Oskar Jászi, the Hungarian historian and politician, and others who aimed at the creation of a 'new Europe'—that is, of an association of small states between Germany and Russia—were invariably wrecked by the unwillingness of these nations to work together. Their leaders could not overcome the prejudicial division of their neighbors into 'victors' and 'vanquished' in terms of the outcome of the First World War. Nor were they able to control their mutual jealousies, chauvinism, and disrespect for each other, as aptly expressed by the Hungarian-American scholar Stephen Borsody in his book on the problems of the region (Borsody, 1993). Animosities among the new states were further aggravated by the persecution of ethnic minorities newly created by the retracing of state borders, and by feelings of having been wronged on the part of those who before the war had enjoyed privileged status and subsequently lost it—for example, ethnic Germans in Czechoslovakia.

This inability to collaborate also led to anti-liberal economic policies in the new nation-states. High customs tariffs seriously limited trade and hampered the economic development of the whole region. In addition to political and cultural nationalism, economic nationalism also had negative effects in East Central Europe.

The third category of unfavorable external agents was the general change in European political thought. It should not be forgotten that the development towards authoritarian nationalist regimes in the region was encouraged by the rise of fascist and Nazi regimes in Italy, Austria, Germany, Portugal, and Spain, as well as by the growth of movements of the extreme Right in many West European countries and the United States. The myopic foreign policies of West European democratic powers, especially Great Britain and France, also belong in this category. These powers, afraid of the influence of the Soviet Union in East Central Europe—which they viewed as a kind of buffer zone or '*cordon sanitaire*' between Russia and the West—preferred the creation of allegedly more stable semi-fascist systems to unstable, weak democracies. They refused to recognize that the former were themselves extremely precarious.

The joint impact of all these internal and external factors brought about a tragedy that culminated in the Second

World War and the profound changes which took place immediately afterwards.

Political mentalities and cultures are always the fruit of the experience of entire generations. Also, political communities have a memory of their own. The experience of the inter-war years has marked the collective memory of East Central Europe—discounting a few exceptions—in a rather wretched way. It deepened the mistrust in liberal democracy and its institutions, and put the idea into the heads of these nations that a strong state suppressing group interests and legitimizing its power by emphasizing national unity is the right way of solving the crises and conflicts of modern societies.

From the War to Communism: A Legacy of Inhumanity

It would be difficult to fully understand the specific political mentalities and cultures of the nations of East Central Europe without first recapitulating the main characteristics of the most recent historical period, which, with varying degrees of intensity, shaped the psychology, views, and sociological landscape of the whole region. Since it has been established—beyond doubt and long ago—that without the Second World War no communist regime could have been installed in this part of the continent,[5] we will deal with the war years and those of communist rule as a single entity, regardless of how they might be further subdivided for other purposes.

The spirit of war is anathema to all liberal thought, whether focusing on economics and trade, or on ethics and philosophy. Civil society cannot rest on extreme ways of thinking, on radicalism, or on conspicuous heroism. It emphasizes the values of civil life, tolerance in the process of seeking the truth—it respects even mundane values, as illustrated in the story 'Ordinary Life' by the Czech novelist Karel Čapek.

By contrast, communist movements, especially in their Leninist–Stalinist form, were characterized by organizational and psychological traits most often to be found in military organizations or in wartime.

There is, however, still another—and more cogent—reason why we should link the study of the effects of communist regimes with that of the war. Wars tend to subvert societies and to push individuals into taking radical positions. Both great waves of the communist tide—that is, after 1917 and after 1945—were directly war-related. Let us briefly recall the characteristics of the Second World War. Seen from the point of view of social and individual psychology, it brought about an unprecedented brutalization of human relations that affected also civilian populations. The physical destruction resulting from direct combat included laying waste entire cities, and countless towns and villages. Human losses, mainly on account of the extremely high number of civilian victims, were inordinately great. As in all earlier wars, the war experience reinforced radical and extremist views; individual control and planning of life ceased almost completely. On the other hand, as a reaction to all these horrors, it was also possible to find examples of ethical idealism and social utopianism.

For the purposes of our discussion, the social effects of the war may be even more important. The Second World War produced far-reaching changes in social structure, especially in East Central Europe. The Holocaust and the emigration of Jewish survivors largely signified the extinction of Jewry and Jewish culture in the region, while forced resettlement of German-speaking ethnic groups after the war eliminated German life and culture there. The destruction of intellectual and political elites in the countries occupied by the Nazis is also relevant in this connection. However, many other population groups—for instance, Poles, Hungarians, and Czechs—were also forced to move. The liquidation of the Jews and the migration of the Germans, with the attendant loss of property, led to the enrichment of other groups and to important modifications in their social position. This, for example, was the case with the Czech rural proletariat which acquired land in the border areas of Czechoslovakia that until 1945 had been inhabited predominantly by ethnic Germans. The prosecution and punishment of wartime collaborators had similar effects, albeit on a lesser scale. These vast shifts of ownership, besides stimulating social mobility, also had important political consequences. Yet the mobility which we are discussing is not the same as that characteristic of industrial societies, because it affected a population that was partly still traditional in character, so making it all the more unsettling.

The issues of anti-fascist resistance and pro-fascist collaboration proved to be politically explosive. In general, the war fostered extreme forms of adaptation to brutal life situations: on the one hand, it stimulated courage and a sense of sacrifice; on the other, it promoted cynicism and a willingness to engage in opportunist collaboration with the occupying powers and their puppet governments. The fact that individuals who had fought against the foreign invader and had been interned in concentration camps and those who had openly collaborated might come to live next to each other caused serious tensions in all societies in Europe long after the war. This polarization, of course, did not help the efforts of liberal leaders seeking tolerance. Indeed, what in this context must be particularly stressed is the fact that the psychological, intellectual, and social changes brought about by the war had, on the whole, anti-liberal consequences and opened the door to another radicalism, this time leftist in character.

A large number of studies have already been written on the causes of the rise and disintegration of the communist regimes in East Central Europe. My goal is much more modest: (i) to draw the attention of the reader to the way in which the propagation of communism in this part of Europe was facilitated by the survival of social structures, values, and modes of thought dating from its agrarian and corporatist past; and (ii) to show how forty years of life under communism created new barriers to the development of liberal politics and economics.

The propagation of communism—if we disregard the external influences and concrete historical situation after the Second World War—was in East Central Europe (with some exceptions, such as the Czech Lands, and parts of Poland and Hungary) facilitated by the weakness of the middle classes—especially their entrepreneurial component—and of civil society, the low level of urbanization, the dominance of the state and its bureaucracy, and the imposition of modernization from above. The rise of communism was also helped by the great importance in these societies of informal social networks and social status determined by ascription. If we wished to define this cluster of characteristics most concisely the term '*Gemeinschaft*' would be suitable. Communism in East Central Europe found a favorable soil prepared by a mixture of communitarianism *avant la lettre* and corporatism. Some commentators point to similarities between feudalism and communism: for example, labor relations in the latter are often characterized as a 'new serfdom'.

The Marxist-inspired regimes, while they undoubtedly sought to modernize their countries, by their choice of institutions and methods paradoxically perpetuated the inherited archaic social models. They did, of course, add new components—largely innovations in the control and manipulation of human beings, turning these societies into truly totalitarian ones. These new institutions and power assertion techniques evoked in those who were their objects numerous new forms of individual and group adaptation, and created a complex structure of political attitudes and mentalities. Although there were notable differences from this point of view among the individual countries, it is nevertheless possible to identify a few common features, either directly connected with the basic ideological and organizational principles of the regime or reflecting their unwanted and unexpected consequences.

One of the basic principles of the communist regimes was the uncompromising abolition of private ownership of the means of production, inevitably leading to the establishment of a centrally administered national economy. Central planning was supposed to replace the spontaneous, allegedly non-radical processes of maintaining economic equilibrium, the impact of which upon the average individual was avowedly deemed to be too hard. Public ownership and central planning were inseparably connected: the one could not exist without the other. Society and its 'economic household' were perceived as a kind of combined enterprise—fully integrated and realizing the highest goals of humanity. It was a vision of a modern, socially harmonious, and well functioning super-*Gemeinschaft*. Within its framework, the unity of the political, the ideological, and the economic was to be achieved. In practice, however, it brought about the domination of the economic sphere by the political sphere, as well as the fusion of the public and the private. Ernest Gellner, as he sought to formulate the simplest definition of socialism, stated that "socialism is the command–administrative system of the management of industrial society" (Gellner, 1994, 165). In such a society, no autonomous spheres exist, civil society cannot function otherwise than in the form of dissent, and the fate of individuals—unless they belong to the power oligarchy—is always subordinated to the ends and logic of the political system.

The idea that modern industrial societies, after the abolition of private ownership, would function without problems, harmoniously and truly spontaneously, proved to be one of the greatest ideological illusions of the last two centuries. What really came into existence after the communist seizure of power was an extremely cumbersome, ineffective, and unspontaneous system that, after a short period of initial enthusiasm and some limited growth, began to stagnate. Clearly, its engine was not properly built.

The mode of communism's inner construction, and the need to live in it and become adapted to its nature, gave birth to a number of phenomena which prevented it from successfully competing with contemporary capitalism. However, the disappointing experience of the communist experiment also elicited a number of reactions in the societies that were exposed to it which can be valued positively.

Today, ten years after the collapse of communism, it is evident that in order to introduce democracy and to restore liberal ethics, it is not sufficient to set up classical democratic legal and political institutions. Similarly, it is not enough for the purpose of reviving a robust market economy to abolish central planning, privatize the means of production, and liberalize economic transactions. Among the necessary conditions of democracy is the presence of individuals who think and act democratically, especially among politicians, while a successful market economy is not possible without respect for law and order, trust, the observation of moral norms, and the presence of entrepreneurs who are aware of the need to secure appropriate legal and ethical moorings for their activities.

Thus, both democracy and the market economy require changes in the ways of thinking and values of social actors— one might call it a 'change of heart'. This change, as the experience of all former communist countries shows, is difficult and slow in coming. The difficulty is partly the consequence of patterns of behavior developed in the recent past. The societies now under transformation took over from the previous regime many behavioral forms that are hard to get rid of, including a bureaucratic approach to problems, paternalism, corruption, the shadow economy, a universal proclivity to avoid legal obligations, nepotism, and a lack of loyalty vis-à-vis society. Besides these structural barriers there exist other, more subtle ones—psychological obstacles which can be defined as properties of the social actors themselves: excessive caution and irresolution, unreliability and unwillingness to assume responsibility.

If these barriers are not removed, or at least notably lowered, the former communist nations will run the risk of developing a kind of state democracy, rather than liberal democracy.

The experience of communism did not sink into the collective memory of East Central Europe only as a new set of anti-liberal codes. It also began to produce its own 'anti-toxins', so to speak. One of these is of interest to liberal philosophy. It is—as Ernest Gellner found in *Conditions of Liberty*—the genesis or regeneration of the concept of civil society. The East has begun to redefine the conditions of existence of a liberal society precisely because it once lost them. Gellner labeled it "civil society", underscoring the fact that civil society is the sum of non-governmental organizations and institutions which operate as a countervailing force against the power of the state. Eastern liberals realized, much more keenly than their Western counterparts, what it means to lose the benefit of this counterweight. In the West, it has always been taken more or less for granted and therefore it hardly enters the awareness of Western liberals. This is another example of misunderstanding. The concept of civil society is considered redundant by some Western scholars, who claim that 'liberal society' is all that is needed. They do not seem to perceive—as they have not lived under a totalitarian system—the specific functional edge with which the concept of civil society is endowed.

Another positive product of the communist experience is what we could call the strengthening of the social actors' immunity vis-à-vis totalitarian modes of thinking. A third positive reaction to the system that collapsed in 1989 is connected to this, namely, a critical attitude to all forms of social utopia. This, in turn, is related to an overall critical spirit and political pragmatism (which can be excessive at times). Individual post-communist nations naturally differ in this respect: for example, in the Czech Republic there are strong calls for the 'de-ideologization of politics', whereas in Poland this trend is weak. With some reservations, it is also possible to claim that in the former communist countries the interest of the citizens in political matters has increased since 1989. This seems natural.

In any assessment of the consequences for the idea of liberal democracy of the developments in East Central Europe, we must not overlook the impact of the great societal changes that occurred after the Second World War in the countries we are investigating. The circumstance that their Marxist-inspired regimes endeavored to establish a kind of modern super-*Gemeinschaft*, and that they based this effort on archaic and utopian concepts of the management of industrial society, should not conceal a very important fact. These were regimes that wished to modernize their societies. The principal instrument they proposed to use was industrialization, supplemented by controlled urbanization, an expanded system of education, programmed secularization, and promotion of the equality of women, particularly in respect to access to education and employment. It was, no doubt, a distorted form of modernization, but even in this form it was an agent powerful enough to disrupt the structural foundations of agrarian societies which—with the exception of the Czech Lands and parts of Poland and Hungary—still existed in the East Central European macro-regions at the end of the Second World War. The changes brought about in this way were often very swift, even brutal, but they nevertheless transformed a major part of the rural population into an urban one, and helped emancipate several disadvantaged social groups. It is true that people in Poland often talked about the 'ruralization' of cities, rather than the urbanization of the rural population, and that many intellectuals in Budapest complained about the Hungarian capital having lost its middle-class character owing to the large influx of inhabitants from the countryside. Equally justified is the criticism of socialist industrialization, which put too much emphasis on heavy industry and underestimated the significance of the service sector. Nevertheless, a return to the situation as it existed before communist rule, which would mean abandonment of the cities, de-emancipation of women, restriction of access to education, and so on, is not probable. Thus the accomplished changes give these societies a chance of evolution towards greater freedoms and more participation in political decision making. It is obvious, of course, that other, less optimistic interpretations of the changes listed here can be imagined. The propensity to react less liberally and democratically to the hardships and difficulties of post-communist transformation is strengthened by a collective memory and traditional political culture shaped in the relatively remote past.

Bibliography

Berend, Ivan T. 1986. *The Crisis Zone of Europe*. Cambridge: Cambridge University Press.

Borsody, Stephen. 1993. *The New Central Europe—Triumphs and Tragedies*. Boulder, Colorado: East European Monographs.

Chirot, Daniel, ed. 1989. *The Origins of Backwardness in Eastern Europe*. Berkeley: University of California Press.

Fichte, Johann Gottlieb. 1800. *Der geschlossene Handelsstaat*. Tübingen.

Gellner, Ernest. 1983. *Nations and Nationalism*. Oxford: Blackwell.

———. 1988. *Plough, Sword and Book. The Structure of Human History*. London: Collins Harvill.

————. 1994. *Conditions of Liberty: Civil Society and Its Rivals.* London: Hamish Hamilton.

McFarlane, Alan. 1978. *The Origins of English Individualism.* Oxford: Blackwell.

Mommsen, Wolfgang J. 1984. *Max Weber and German Politics 1890–1920.* Chicago: The University of Chicago Press.

Rupnik, Jacques. 1989. *The Other Europe.* London: Weidenfeld and Nicolson.

Schöpflin, George. 1990. 'The Political Traditions of Eastern Europe', in *Eastern Europe ... Central Europe ... Europe, Daedalus* 119, no. 1 (Winter): 55–90.

Seton-Watson, Hugh. 1986. *Eastern Europe Between the Wars.* Boulder and London: Westview Press.

Shils, Edward. 1982. *The Constitution of Society.* Chicago: The University of Chicago Press.

Stokes, Gale. 1989. 'The Social Origins of East European Politics', in *The Origins of Backwardness in Eastern Europe,* ed. Daniel Chirot. Berkeley: University of California Press.

Wandycz, Piotr S. 1992. *The Price of Freedom. A History of East Central Europe from the Middle Ages to the Present.* London: Routledge.

Notes

1 Some scholars label these value systems 'myths'. We prefer the less normative term chosen by Shils (1982).

2 It is necessary to stress that the 'Great Transition' which took place in Western Europe during industrialization was something out of the ordinary. By contrast, the stagnation experienced by Eastern Europe, its inability to escape from the agrarian type of society, is a more usual historical phenomenon. The fact that capitalism, liberal political systems, and the rule of law originated in Western Europe was probably the result of a number of historical accidents and coincidences, as has already been emphasized by Max Weber and Ernest Gellner.

3 A detailed explanation of Weber's view of this problem is presented by Mommsen (1984).

4 This is especially true of the Russian '*narodniki*', but also of the Hungarian '*népies*' movement and of all German '*völkisch*' movements.

5 For a well-informed interpretation of the political impact of the war, see Rupnik (1989). Chapter 4 of Rupnik's book contains a part dealing with 'War and Revolution', which describes the concrete steps of the Sovietization of East Central Europe.

Liberalism in Central Europe after 1989

Zdeněk Suda

There are good reasons why we should view the turn of the third millennium as a time of great opportunities for liberalism: as a socio-political and economic doctrine, it has successfully faced two major challenges in less than a century. The first of these—I mean the defeat of fascism or the totalitarian political ideologies and movements of the Right in their bid for global power, consummated in the Second World War—is often too readily forgotten, although liberalism's triumph in this particular struggle was as important as in the confrontation with communism. Two victories of this magnitude in the span of one human lifetime are enough to justify liberalism's candidacy for the position of universal social and political philosophy of modern Western industrial civilization.

Reluctant Heir?

That is not to say, of course, that liberalism is actually submitting such a candidacy. It would seem, rather, that the idea of assigning to it this role originated outside the orbit of liberal thought; that liberalism has thus far proved even a little reluctant to claim the inheritance which others appear willing to concede to it. To be sure, liberalism does not explicitly reject a leading role among contemporary intellectual currents. It does not aspire any more or less to such a role than any other school of thought engaged in the interpretation of social reality. Liberalism, however, implicitly disqualifies itself from this function by asserting that it is not a self-contained view of the world, an ideology making possible a consensus on basic social and political values, and that, after all, such a consensus is neither possible nor necessary for maintaining social stability.

However, this disqualification—or self-disqualification—of liberalism needs itself to be qualified. In reality, liberalism can be recognized as ideology-free only if ideology is understood not merely as a definite picture of the world as it is, but also as one of the world as it should be; in other words, not only as a perception but also as a project. As we are all aware, it is in this sense that the term is currently used, which may be due to the recent experience with totalitarian movements and political systems. If, on the other hand, we keep strictly to the meaning assigned to this term by the sociology of knowledge, liberalism meets all the necessary criteria of an ideology. We could even say that liberalism is a 'super-ideology' on account of the extent and the depth of its perspective on social reality. No other doctrine—perhaps only a religion—can from this point of view measure up to liberalism. Liberalism implicitly but unmistakably claims that it knows the basic elements of human nature—present, past, and future.

The Enlightenment Tradition in Liberalism

In order for us to understand how liberalism arrived at this claim, we must go back to the Enlightenment, the last great 'ideological revolution' (in strictly social scientific terms). The most profound change brought about by the Enlightenment in terms of world-views was the prevalence of the notion that the universe—which for them included nature as well as human relations—is intelligible, and consequently predictable and amenable to rational action. Auguste Comte, the founding father of sociology and the last great figure of the Enlightenment, based his definition of the three main steps of scientific action—"voir pour savoir, savoir pour prévoir, prévoir pour pouvoir"—on this principal assumption. However—and this is of the essence in the context of our discussion—the Enlightenment did not claim that the objects of rational perception, understanding, and manipulation—nature and society—were themselves rational. It was liberalism that took this one step further and attributed not only intelligibility but also rationality to human behavior and motivation, at least in the area of economic transactions—that is, in the market. As for the view of the nature of the social world, the Enlightenment tradition actually yielded two offshoots. One of them—to which liberalism also belongs—holds social reforms, social reconstruction, and all kinds of social engineering humanly possible: man is at the same time creature and creator. This in no way signifies, of course, that rational interventions in all sectors of social life are desirable. On the contrary, intimate knowledge of social mechanisms and of the manner in which they operate should, according to liberal thinkers, lead us to abstain from too much interference. The other current of the Enlightenment tradition considers social evolution intelligible and predictable, but at the same time preordained. It will take its course whatever we do. Social policies will be successful only if they respect this predetermined course: political leaders are only 'obstetricians of History'. Marxism is the most important branch of this current.

The Verdict of History

As for the adequacy of the interpretation of social reality which these currents offer, the verdict of History is indisputable: liberalism comes incomparably closer to it than Marxism. The development of societies is not a pre-programmed process determined by some sort of social 'genes'. Social laws, if they indeed exist, are of an entirely different nature from the laws of physics. Human will, choice, and preferences are factors independent of the various social and economic environments, so that the response of different societies to a seemingly identical challenge may be completely different. Marxism also proved to be hopelessly inadequate in its assessment of the sources of human motivation. On the one hand, it postulated some mystical feeling of social loyalty and solidarity, allegedly inborn in every individual, which was supposed to replace, as a motivational force, the drive to attain individual economic advantage, once private owner-ship of the means of production has been abolished. On the other hand, it completely misjudged the disastrous effects of bureaucratic administration of the economy upon the quality of goods and services, and the catastrophic results of com-prehensive central planning in modern industrial systems where flexibility is a crucial condition of survival. It was probably this misjudgment, more than anything else, which consigned Marxism—to use its own vocabulary—to the "rubbish heap of History". After that, liberalism's right to the place of a leading social and political idea in the post-communist era and in the former communist region could hardly be denied, even if it was not explicitly invoked.

Triumph in a Crisis Zone

What appeared to be the triumphal entry of liberalism after 1989 into the regions previously dominated by the official doctrine of the Soviet Union was, in fact, an event of double significance. On the one hand, the principles of a pluralist society, a market economy, and an integrated community of free nations were vindicated in this part of the old continent; on the other hand, they made a comeback in a critical zone where in the past liberalism had several times attempted to establish its influence, although always without success. The most important rival force which had prevented liberalism from taking solid roots in this part of the world was nation-alism. It has been so powerful a foe that even today it might be premature to consider the victory of liberalism as final. This implies that not even at this point can we be certain of an early and smooth completion of the process of political modernization, undisturbed by nationalist and ethnic con-flicts, in the former communist sphere as a whole.

Some will perhaps disagree with this statement on the grounds that liberalism has at least one great victory over nationalism to its credit: the defeat of fascism already mentioned. However, two circumstances must be taken into consideration before we can decide on the validity of this objection. First, the victories and defeats with which we are presently concerned are, in this context, ideological—that is, intellectual and spiritual—phenomena rather than military ones, which the confrontation between the three totalitarian powers—Germany, Italy, and Japan—and the coalition of powers opposing them in the 1940s undoubtedly was. The question we are interested in here is that of the ability of these two currents, nationalism and liberalism, to assert themselves as relevant motivating forces in the political process in East Central Europe, where the balance sheet seems clearly to favor nationalism over liberalism.

The second circumstance which should not be ignored in our evaluation is the fact that nationalism is not identical with fascism, that is, with the totalitarian ideology of the Right. In its 'pure' and general form, nationalism has neither the appeal of, nor the need for, universal solidarity manifest in countries and societies with similar fascist regimes. To put it in concrete terms: Fascist Italy and Nazi Germany viewed any threat to the other fascist systems in Europe as a direct threat to themselves and were ready to intervene directly in such cases, as for example during the Spanish Civil War in favor of General Franco. Nationalist attitudes and moods as such, however fervent or even fanatical, do not *per se* elicit perceptions of common interests among nations and countries. On the contrary, they may increase the probability of conflict between them. That is what happened during the Second World War and what facilitated the victory of the democratic powers (assisted, incidentally, by a totalitarian superpower, the Soviet Union: it was not an accident that the war against Germany, while it was going on, was referred to in the USSR as the 'Great Patriotic War').

But there is more. The democratic West was helped not a little by nationalism in its struggle to contain and to neutralize communist global expansion. This was all the more natural as the doomed communist experiment took place chiefly in the East Central European region, where the nationalist current is extraordinarily virulent. The multiple crises of the communist satellite system were marked by the controversy between the claim of communism to a kind of supranational proletarian class solidarity and the national interests and aspirations of the individual communist party-states. These conflicts brought down all initiatives directed towards the closer integration of these states, especially in the economic sphere, as the failure of Nikita Khruschev's 'international socialist division of labor' project in the 1960s clearly illustrates. It was then that the term 'national communism' was coined. The term itself testifies to the extraordinary power of East Central European nationalism which succeeded in permeating and eventually subverting the movement and the doctrine that had prided themselves on being the heralds of a new age of international, class-based collective identity and solidarity.

Accidental Ally—Implacable Rival

Nationalism in East Central Europe, although it contributed significantly to the failure of both totalitarian attempts— fascist and communist—at securing regional domination, only unwittingly became an ally of democracy. Its earlier historical record—as well as the most recent experience— shows that in reality it has been one of the most dangerous rivals of the liberal democratic current in the process of political modernization in the nineteenth and twentieth centuries. It has played a similarly pernicious role in relation to the contemporary endeavor to achieve a social and political reconstruction after the collapse of communism.

Perhaps the most persuasive example of nationalism's fateful influence can be provided by the modern history of Germany which in fact could be written as a story of recurrent defeats of liberalism by nationalism, of unsuccessful efforts of the liberal movement to impregnate and shape German political culture. These defeats occurred almost invariably at the turning points in modern Germany's development: the abortive liberal revolution of 1848–49; the creation of the unitary German nation-state in 1871, which was achieved not by the liberal, but by the conservative nationalist forces, hostile to liberalism; and during the fifteen years of the hapless Weimar Republic, 1919–33. The vicious circle was broken—let us hope permanently—with the German catastrophe in the Second World War and the new start embodied in the Federal Republic. This 'German miracle' may be of even greater and more lasting significance than the economic phenomenon for which the epithet was originally coined. It also underlines the centrality of Germany as a geo-political factor in the entire East Central European region which, for better or for worse, has shared Germany's destiny.

'Loose Nationalism':
A Central European Specialty

In the past, liberalism in Central Europe has invariably succumbed to nationalism because it could not match its fervor. There was no room for another motivating and mobilizing force. The reasons for the extraordinary fervor of Central European nationalism have to be sought in the specific manner in which the nation-building process unfolded in this part of the continent. Several analysts have pointed out that, in contrast to the development typical of West European societies, national consciousness and perception of national identity in Central Europe preceded the constitution of a unitary state. France and England had existed long before the emergence of the French and English nations, understood as self-conscious collectives adopting nationalist attitudes in the modern meaning of the term; the German nation and German nationalism took shape at least two generations before the creation of the German nation-state. We could borrow from the vocabulary used by Friedrich Meinecke and argue that, while in the West the pre-existing state was subsequently 'nationalized', in Central Europe the nations existed first, to be eventually 'étatized'.

The 'étatization' of nations was a process which had nothing of the gradualness and near-spontaneity of its counterpart. Also, not every nation in this category could successfully complete the process. However, having existed prior to and outside the framework of a state belongs to the experience of all nations in the Central European region. It deeply marked the quality of nationalism in this part of the world, making it 'unrestrained'—that is, unbridled, fierce, like all natural forces *in statu nascendi*. Because of the reverse sequence of stages in the nation-building process, Central Europe could not benefit from the kind of 'division of labor' between nationalism and liberalism granted to the societies of the European West, whereby the former supplied the sense of collective identity and solidarity, and the latter helped create the institutional guarantees of free development and self-actualization of the individual. Central Europe, for the better part of the nineteenth century, was busy shaping and defining its various national identities, which, in the absence of visible geo-political frameworks, was a frustrating full-time job for all the ethnic groups involved. The emancipation of the individual—liberalism's primary concern—was given a low priority. Proof of the prevalence of interest in collective problems in this region is the peculiar notion of national freedom, understood as the independence and sovereignty of the state and altogether unconnected with individual freedom. Following this notion, it is conceivable to view as free any nation living within the borders of a state that is sovereign in the terms of international law, regardless of the type of political regime—absolutist, authoritarian, even totalitarian—to which its members are subject. This most certainly was not a climate favorable to liberal thought.

The pre-existence in Central Europe of fully developed nationalism before the conclusion of the nation-building process bred, among other things, an uncertainty about the actual scope of the various nations—that is, about who belonged and who did not. This uncertainty was particularly acute in the German case. It found its most obvious expression in two different concepts of the German nation-state to be created: the 'Great versus the Little Germany' formula.

Oceans of blood were shed on account of this controversy; even after it was apparently resolved, as the result of two major European wars, in favor of the 'Little' variant, it continued to plague Germany and, indeed, the whole world. It contributed in a significant measure to the unleashing of both global cataclysms of the twentieth century. In any event, it considerably delayed the process of political modernization in the Central European region. However, it may be assumed that, not unlike the long-drawn-out and uneven struggle between liberalism and nationalism, the outcome of the Second World War has put an end to the ambiguity relative to the geographic and demographic extent of the German nation. In principle, it is defined by the borders of today's Federal Republic. If future evolution confirms this assumption the prospects of liberalism and democracy in Central Europe will brighten considerably.

Liberalism's Great Opportunity and Challenge

What can liberal thought contribute to the ongoing process of post-communist reconstruction? Much will depend on what liberalism will identify as its central problem and main point of interest. The liberal debate of the nineteenth century put the emphasis on liberty, understood as 'freedom from' rather than 'freedom for' something—that is, for a goal or purpose. This kind of liberty could also be termed respect for the autonomy of the individual. It made perfect sense, on the assumption that there existed an objective, clearly defined sphere of opportunities within which this autonomy—that is, freedom of choice—could be exercised. The nineteenth-century mind took this sphere for granted. It was not without its problems, however. Already the supremacy of the concern with liberty was challenged by those who stressed equality as a comparably important political and social value. Some political sociologists—for example, Lipset—see in the search for equilibrium between liberty and equality the *leitmotiv* of the social history of the United States, one of the key modern societies and the one most profoundly informed by liberalism.

It seems as if, from this point of view, contemporary liberal thinking has continued the emphasis of the previous century. The most lively debate among liberal thinkers today is focused on the question of liberty, especially the possibility of a universal consensus that would legitimate this liberty. This shift in focus may have been stimulated by the opportunity that now appears to beckon of a universal extension or 'globalization' of liberal democratic philosophy in the wake of the Western victory in the Cold War. If democracy is to become the universal political system of tomorrow, the basic tenets of its doctrine, inseparably tied to liberalism, must stand the test of being translated into the language of other, non-Western political cultures.

Yet this preoccupation with the search for universal consensus on one particular point may obscure the need for liberalism to draw the consequences from another, equally important outcome of the Cold War: the lesson this war has taught us about the true nature and meaning of equality in modern industrial societies. The confrontation of the totalitarian ideology of the Left with the liberal community of thought clarified—once and for all—the question of the place of equality as political objective as well as that of the form of equality compatible with the democratic system of values. There can be little doubt that only equality of opportunity meets the latter requirement.

It would seem, therefore, that the polarity characteristic of the democratic political culture of the nineteenth century persists, only that it is now more starkly articulated. It can still be ascertained, in principle, between liberty and equality, but we would perhaps prefer to label the first as respect for individual autonomy and the second as concern about preserving equal opportunities. We feel that today's liberalism is too engrossed in the discussion about the former and tends almost to forget the latter. The problem, however, is crucial. Should liberalism prove unable to address both issues, it would disqualify itself—this time irrevocably—as the spiritual leader of the post-communist world. In that case it would fail to provide a source of legitimation for the new political, social, and economic order.

The one-sidedness of the current Western liberal debate, absorbed in the quest for a consensus on values and ignoring opportunity—an indispensable life condition of modern society—as well as the implicit commitment of democracy to preserve it, may be found at fault also on other, more fundamental grounds. Liberalism as an offshoot of the Enlightenment cannot disown its link to, and share in, the idea of a social contract. This contract does not guarantee only freedom, or respect for individual freedom of choice, but also sufficient social space for making such a choice. Acceptance of the extreme positions taken by some chapters of the contemporary liberal school, denying the obligations of society in this respect, would be tantamount to reneging on the moral roots of liberalism. The consequences for liberalism—indeed, for Western civilization as a whole—might be fatal, since it is precisely in the realm of the social contract that the Cold War was fought and won, although it may even yet be lost.

Can Weak-State Liberalism Survive?

STEPHEN HOLMES

There is a famous story of a friend of mine who met Robert Frost. He was taking him to see John Kennedy. Frost said "You know, I really like John Kennedy, he is no liberal. You know my definition of a liberal? It is a guy who cannot take his own side in an argument". I am glad to see that that is no longer the case. Liberals seem to be very opinionated in different ways, and I am very happy to join a debate of opinionated liberals who have different opinions about what liberalism is. One warning note for the reader: you should not conclude from this fact that American debates about liberalism are relevant to your circumstances just because they are relevant to ours.

Liberal Order and Spontaneity

Liberalism, in the classical European sense, is a system of coercive authority, not merely a system of spontaneous exchange. The easiest way to bring this home is to point to the very special relations of authority and subordination presupposed by any open society or any civil society. All free societies, in a liberal sense, are places where some people tell other people what to do—that is, where people without guns tell people with guns what to do. Which, if you think about it, is not very logical. Liberal government is—yes—limited government, but this limitedness must not be extended to the point of incapacitation. For crippled or paralyzed or 'hands-off' government would be one in which, for instance, civilian authorities would not control the military—which is not a liberal arrangement in anyone's imagination or definition. I begin my remarks this way because I want—that is what *I* want to do—first of all to focus on the problems of liberalism in this region, broadly defined, as a problem of authority—not as a problem of how to limit the state, or only a problem of that sort, but instead as also a problem of how to create a working functional state. My implicit point of reference—due partly to the fact that I was unaware of the subtitle of the conference when I wrote my contribution, partly to my own background—will be the quasi-anarchical fringes of Eastern Europe where I have done most of my work (particularly the former Soviet Union, but also the former Yugoslavia to a lesser extent). This is not because they are representative of the challenge to liberalism after communism, but rather so that I can prevent the discussion from becoming too Czecho-centric and too 'velvetized'. Furthermore, extreme conditions can help us to focus sharply on crucial political and administrative preconditions of a liberal economy and society—preconditions which are not wholly or robustly present anywhere in East Central Europe. Russia is a magnifying glass which points, in its absurdity, to things you can also find elsewhere.

The premise of these remarks is that liberalism is not an 'all-terrain vehicle', because it cannot create its own preconditions, most notably those which are connected with 'stateness'. That is to say, liberal principles—such as the rule of law or majority decision making, included in liberal democracy—presuppose and answer certain questions (for example, concerning the location of national borders and the identity of members of the community) to which liberalism has no answer. In addition, the relationship between liberalism and stateness is also called into question by the history of liberalism itself. Those enemies of liberalism—such as Solzhenitsyn or Carl Schmitt—who associated liberalism with state weakness have a lot of explaining to do since the most powerful state in world history was the inventor of the liberal system. It is not an accident that the system that created liberal principles took over between one-third and half of the globe.

No State Power—No Property Rights—
No Freedom

I will start with a Bosnian parable, because Bosnia is a particularly pitiful case for liberalism. It is a place where liberalism does not seem to have any answers. It looks like partition is the only answer, bringing about ethnic homogeneity in order to solve the ethnic conflict—this is far from a liberal arrangement. Liberalism's incapacity in a place like Bosnia is expressed very poignantly in its basic attitude towards state borders: borders are totally arbitrary and therefore cannot be changed. They are certainly morally arbitrary. As we know, the borders of the state in which we live were not created by markets, bargaining, or voluntary exchange, but rather by *force majeure*. The Serb residents of Sarajevo, that is, the people who stayed loyally in the city—and in those parts of the city that were bombed, and sniped at, and so on—are (in 1996—*editor's note*) being confronted in their homes by Moslem gangs, armed groups, guerillas, decommissioned soldiers (they do not know who they are), they have guns put to their heads and are told: "Move out of your apartment, leave your goods, we are taking them!" And these good, loyal citizens go to the police and to the courts, and the police and the courts says to them: "Too bad!" The Moslems who are doing this are often victims of the same thing in other cities. The claim to occupancy rights has no value, no validity across the system. The first theoretical point I want to draw is quite simple: property rights, the foundation of any liberal regime, are meaningless if you do not have the government on your side.

Why is economic growth so rare in history? One of the reasons is that wealth accumulators—property accumulators—have been very vulnerable, particularly to two, what one might call 'NGOs': (i) thugs with weapons, and (ii) poor people with matches. If you are a property owner you need the government on your side to prevent these 'NGOs' from destroying your property. A state that cannot intervene in society will not create a market system, but one in which the Mafia— those who use force and fraud—own and run everything. Only when property owners, who are the wealthy, find a reliable protector in the state will a liberal system be established. Needless to say, once this occurs the property owners still have to figure out a way of preventing the state authorities from confiscating their wealth (what came to be known as liberal constitutionalism). A bargain is struck.

All this requires emphasis because history in this part of the world tends to fuel the illusion that the only serious threat to liberty is the overmighty state, a half-truth which obscures many of the most pressing difficulties faced by the advocates of liberalism among the ruins of communism. We will be more conscious of the danger of state weakness here—and this should be an aspect of any discussion about liberalism—if we realize what an immensely difficult task it is to build even a minimal state. To build a state capable of repressing force and fraud, repressing predatory relations among strangers, is not at all easy. I once asked an economist to explain how it was possible to move from a society in which business rivals think plastic explosive is the best way of dealing with competitors, to one that is more like a civil society. "Economics does not explain the non-use of violence", he replied. At least we can rest assured that economics does not overlook any important problems! Liberalism makes a number of assumptions when it deals with the establishment of the liberal market system: for example, that competition has been 'decriminalized'—not in the sense of 'made legal', but rather in that of 'freed from criminal pressures and influences'.

Freedom Is Not Free of Charge

At this point, I would like to 'make a parenthesis' and say something about human rights theory. I have so far dealt mostly with the kind of state needed for markets, but I want to stress the fact that for the enforcement of basic human rights across the board you need not only state authority, but also state solvency. You need state tax-and-spend, the state's extractive capacity, and the power to channel the resources extracted from society into public services. Furthermore, in order to prevent abuses by the police you do not simply need to keep the police out of the private sphere of prisoners or detainees, but you require a monitoring system which is part of the state authorities: the monitors have to be paid—they are state officials. Freedom clearly depends on authority.

Let us take the example of prisoners' rights: prisoners have rights to light, ventilation, and heat in their cells, a toilet perhaps—these things cost money. If the state cannot tax, it cannot provide these things. A state incapable of taxing its citizens cannot implement rights, because rights cost money. People often think that rights are established in some way 'against' the state, generally because one goes to court in order to seek a remedy. But the court is part of the state, its officials are salaried by the state from taxpayers' money, and so forth. This is also part of an illusion that those fighting or campaigning for human rights tend to believe or to insinuate when they present themselves simply as opponents of the state. Put in another way, the world's largest and most effective human rights organization is the liberal state, and people without a state—Kurds, migrating Vietnamese boat people, and so on—do not have any effective rights because they have no institution to protect them.

To return to the economy, liberalism of the Reagan–Thatcher type—and I mean Reagan and Thatcher's words, rather than their deeds, because they were in fact very much state-dependent in many things—liberalism which denounces welfare dependency, red tape, and profit-destroying tax rates, and uses slogans such as "Get the government off our backs", has a lot in its favor in particular contexts, but it is not always to be praised for profound philosophical depth. For property owners, as the Bosnian story reveals, are just as dependent on the government as any single-mother on welfare. Are you against dependency? Well then, give up private property! If you are against creating dependency relations between government and citizens, you must do away with private property as well as welfare programs. Indeed, as the escapees from the butchery of Srebrenica could tell you, if you have an inadequate, constrained, untrained, and ill-equipped army, you are also without property of the kind that could have any wealth-creating effects. That is, if you ask, "do taxpayers pay more for welfare rights or for property rights?", and you include in what is paid for property rights the entire defense budget, it becomes clear that the latter is a measure which is an order of magnitude greater. Not that the expenditure is not eminently justified, but it is not the case that property rights need no government resources and do not create dependency, as the rhetoric in the United States often implies.

The Liberal State as a Source of Trust

All of this is very relevant in Bohemia where we know how property was created in many cases: I am, of course, speaking about Beneš's decrees. Even if we turn away from such extreme circumstances, many of the difficulties of marketization in post-communist societies, as numerous commentators have noted, result from state weakness and incapacity—and not merely the incapacity to make long-term investments in skills and infrastructure, such as increasing the cargo capacity of Bratislava airport. You need a state to do that, but also the basic state functions, such as stabilizing the currency, and enforcing contracts in court and disclosure rules. This is very important—it will not be the market, but the state which increases the airport's cargo capacity. Flights, stockholders' rights, mean nothing if there is no state to make the managers say what is happening, what their inventory is, and what they are doing. This does not happen by itself. Stockholders' rights, therefore, are a very good example of the political function within the economy, which includes breaking up corporate monopolies and creating a reliable system of titles and deeds—this includes preventing those who register titles from taking bribes, which is in fact quite difficult. Governments have to pass and enforce laws on collateral and limited liability companies, and regulate banking in order to guarantee a steady supply of credit. I do not know what all this has to do with liberalism as rationalism. An even more fundamental point about the contribution of the state to marketization was expressed by the manager of a refrigerator factory I met in Yekaterinburg a year ago, who became a *'sobstvennyj'* provider. I asked him: "Do you feel like an owner?", and he replied: "You know, if you do not believe in the future, property is meaningless". Because property is a system in which you invest something now, in order to receive something back later on. Why is property dynamic? Because the results of your investment will accrue to you and your family, or be diffused and ungraspable. If you do not believe in the future, property's function of prosperity creation will fail. That is the incentive for investment, also for human investment. You try to convince a young Russian to go to law school. If he does not know whether the country will still exist in five years' time, he will not do it. That has terrible effects in the long run because the requisite skills are not created. Who creates long time-horizons? Why will I give a *'korruptchik'* a ten-year loan of ten thousand dollars in the United States and not in Russia? Because in the former there is a system that tells me that I will get it back, because I have a long-term rent. The state is not the only organ which can do this—wealth creation in China has a different mechanism, mainly based on the family—but it is one of them. In a place like Russia, where, unlike in China, the family system does not exist, the state is the only body able to lengthen the time-horizons of private actors, to make it possible for them to give them long-term loans. Mancur Olson points out that there have been markets everywhere in the world, throughout history. Every poor country in the world is full of markets, but there is no wealth. Where there is no wealth there is no trust, and there is no trust because the sources of trust do not exist which make particular kinds of wealth-creating exchanges possible.

There Are Some Things the Market Cannot Do

Political unpredictability depresses investors' confidence and spoils the business climate—we know all about that. This is an immense topic which I can only touch upon here. The only other example that usually gets a mention in this connection is the following: in a society where the state is incapable of repressing force and fraud, and where the predominant relations are predatory relations among strangers, individuals' property cannot be guaranteed against theft and they are not going to engage—at least not very often—in mutually beneficial exchanges for fear of being cheated. To put it another way: when I was in Budapest I talked to people about what it was they found unsavory about market exchange. It was not that it violated some residual socialist norms, but rather that they associated market exchange with being tricked: that is, market exchange is based on asymmetrical information and there is no remedy for fraud. This is cheating, and nobody wants to be cheated. Take the case of the Russian who bought a hundred tonnes of cat food and relabeled it as tuna fish. He made lots of money, moved to Cyprus, and lived it up while children died from poisoning. This is, of course, repulsive from any standpoint, not only from a socialist one. If there is no power to bring such fraud before a court of law, people are going to perceive market exchanges as immoral, not because they have some kind of mental deformation inherited from the previous regime, but because such exchanges *are* immoral.

Marketization in East Central Europe is not inhibited by residual collectivism or an inability to understand individual self-reliance. On the contrary, in places like Russia there is hyper-individualism, amoral familism, and an inability to do anything to create a common good. Because anti-fraud law is a common good. And the Russians cannot do it precisely because they have no collectivist capacity—what they have is individualism. This is indeed a paradox. In a society where everything is for sale, including the judges and those enforcing contracts, you cannot have capitalism. Markets require certain things that are outside the market. Why does a post-communist state such as Russia have such a difficult time repressing force and fraud? That is the great question. As an answer—or perhaps just a reformulation of the question—I would put it like this, in vaguely Hobbesian terms: the government cannot impose order on a disorderly society if the agents of the government themselves are 'disorderly'.

To reformulate this point in terms of my trust and time-horizons perspective: how can a government perform the essential function of linking the time-horizons of individual actors, making it possible for them to create wealth and investment in education and a society that functions—a civil society—if the agents of the government have very short time-horizons? So in Russia they are selling weapons to the Iranians and to the Chinese. They are thinking about today, the money they can walk away with. Government officials have a largely private orientation towards corruption and very short time-horizons, so constituting an obstacle to the stability and order—or 'stateness'—required for civil society to function properly.

These officials are motivated by the need to secure their own future, because their bank accounts are abroad. What they are not thinking about is their country's future. And there seem to be—and this is the state's problem in Russia—no institutions within the framework of which the most important social actors can get together and ask: "What do we want to be as a nation, what is our common policy, our common goal; what is the framework within which we are going to act?" This situation creates all kinds of unintended anarchy, and we know that anarchy produces grotesque failures. The deepest problem in Russia is not tyranny, one of classical liberalism's two principal problems, but the other, corruption. Tyranny in the sense of making people conform to a party orthodoxy does not exist at all. The people who control journalists or the media are not attempting to make them follow a party line; all they want is to prevent them from exposing the fact that they have stolen something from, for example, Gasprom.

The inability to create a government which attends to common interests is the problem—this is, indeed, the liberal problem. Whenever you meet an economist you should ask him the following question: "What is the utility of a totally unregulated market in ground-to-air missiles?" I put this question to Václav Klaus, and he paused; he was fond of Gary Becker and did not want to admit that unregulated markets had any limits in their capacity to produce utility. In the end, he replied: "There are certain things markets cannot do". Certainly, they cannot defend the country, negotiate with terrorists, reschedule loans, push back organized crime and narcotics, and so on. The post-communist countries are experiencing the unprecedented situation in which government has even more peculiar and more demanding things to do than ever. For one thing—and this is relevant to the Czech situation—it has to maintain public support to be legitimate. According to Walter Bagehot, in Britain there is the queen and the prime minister: the former is the emotional symbol of the nation, and the latter does all the work. This is similar to the situation in the Czech Republic, but with a president instead of a queen. I am sure that both Havel's position and the legitimacy of the regime are promoted by his ranting against the meaninglessness of television commercials and so on. It is a way of making people who are disaffected somehow identify with the system, even though it annoys Klaus. It would seem that in the Czech Republic there is currently (1996—*editor's note*) a double act comprising Martin Heidegger and Margaret Thatcher.

Inequality and Legitimacy

But how does the government keep its domestic constituency in the face of the following problem: the observable obscene disparity between luxury and misery? That is a psychological problem, especially when those with power have it because they have been voted into power. The obscene disparity between luxury and misery cannot be dealt with adequately by markets and the rule of law. After all, if a general follows the rule book he is likely to be defeated: he must 'seize the day' and deal with whatever dangers come upon him. The statesman is in a similar position. Life is too variable for the rule of law. Of course, that does not mean that the rule of law has no place, but no liberal polities ever survived by following the rule book, because all liberal polities live in a dangerous world. The Czech government, for example, has to deal with dozens of disparities, not as severe as those in Moscow, of course, but similar. It also has a legitimation problem. This cannot be solved by the market mechanism, if it can be solved at all. Certainly, Havel has not solved it, it seems, although he has tried to do so by picturing the regime in a particular way. Machiavelli says that if you want to have a successful revolution you should call it a reformation, making people think that they are simply returning to something they had before. So Havel says "let us go back to the old, hardworking Bohemia". But how many of those hardworking bourgeois Bohemians were Germans and Jews? The old Bohemia is gone. This is not the point for Havel, however, who uses this kind of language because a return to Europe is a way of covering up the narrative most threatening to the legitimacy of the government, its incorporation into a sort of 'Greater Germany'. The Czech Republic's status of provider of spare parts for other European economies does not do much to legitimize the regime. The talk of a return to Europe, which is working to some extent, has not achieved its effects by means of millions of spontaneous market actors engaged in exchange.

The issue of legitimacy is particularly important because property lacks legitimacy in all post-communist systems. This is a historically unique state of affairs. But the basic principle of a liberal property system—'give back what is stolen'—cannot be applied in countries where state assets were visibly gobbled up by people who happened to be in the right place at the right time. The legitimation of property in the West is probably the result of amnesia—we cannot remember who stole what from whom, since it happened so long ago. Our principle is that property is legitimate because it was earned or inherited in accordance with a set of rules known to all. So there is a deep problem with legitimating property. You cannot legitimate it in terms of its origins. Voucher systems are fine, but in the end they did not regulate the distribution of property justly. Legitimation is a problem, particularly because people feel they have been forced to tighten their belts, to accept austerity measures, to give up their pensions, not to buy the antibiotics they need because the budget is empty, while all those in government are living in big houses, racing motor boats, and driving beautiful cars. It is difficult to take when the people who are telling you tighten your belt are 'fat cats' who have become so on your back. You were dazzled for decades, you did not protest, you obeyed the law, you did your job, and after all that they 'broke the contract'. How can the system be legitimized under these circumstances? By means of results. The economy must be made to boom, German capital must be brought in, the streets must look better, public services have to be provided, and the people must feel that they are benefiting. Unequal ownership can be justified only in terms of its contribution to the 'common weal'. Governments are successful to the extent they are able to make the population believe this. This is a responsiveness problem, not a market problem. It is also the problem in the former DDR: quite apart from whether it is possible to make people feel better off, there are a number of other ways in which they can be persuaded to accept the legitimacy of the new system.

Liberal and Illiberal Bargains

For the sake of contrast, let me mention also that political support can be obtained by making a bargain of a certain kind, an illiberal bargain. Nationalism says: you support us and we will revenge historical wrongs and attack the historical enemy, who has put us into our present position. The mature liberal bargain, by contrast, is that we provide public services—roads, bridges, schools, clean water, food handlers and monitors, and other public goods—and you pay taxes. In a way, democracy is a way of reducing the number of enemies. Democracy lowers the amount government officials steal and increases the amount they spend on public services. In Russia, by contrast, you have a pathological bargain which is neither nationalist nor liberal: it is a bargain between unaccountable government and untaxable wealth, in which the rest of society can die in a pseudo-Darwinian process of exclusion. The question is, how does one get from this situation to a liberal one? To return to the Bosnian case, the Bosnian government regards the thugs with guns as better bargaining partners than civilians who obey the law. How do you get the government to feel it is better off making a bargain with those who get rich without force and fraud? Liberalism has to have public support from at least some social groups—it does not necessarily have to be the majority. And it has to be civilians—after all, the men with guns are dangerous to the government, too. In this way a dynamic can be established which leads towards the more civilized bargain already mentioned. On this basis, further bargains, such as a social bargain concerning welfare, can be reached, after persuading the wealthy to agree to be taxed to support the poor, which will most easily be achieved when the rich believe that they need the cooperation of the poor, as in wartime.

State weakness can also be a problem because of the requirement that a decent state shelter members of cultural minorities. A liberal state cannot just pull out of the economy and social life if that leaves minorities vulnerable to majority repression—think of the Gypsies. If the government is too corrupt, disorganized, or stupid to deliver individual protection to members of a minority group, it creates an incentive for those at risk to 'draw the wagons into a circle' and subordinate themselves to unelected leaders who promise them protection on illiberal principles: that is, the bosses are not questioned, no disagreement is allowed, and defectors are mutilated or killed. In other words, liberalism—if it does not deliver individual protection to members of vulnerable groups—creates an incentive for primordial ascriptive group formation of a totally illiberal kind. If you believe that primordial groups are a threat to liberal values, provide the necessary protection, but also make people feel they are part of society. Take the trial of O. J. Simpson. The 'not guilty' verdict was clearly the result of many African Americans not believing that they are part of society. In the United States, if African Americans are unwilling to cooperate in the jury system great problems must inevitably ensue. This is another example of the social bargains that are necessary for effective state action in a liberal context.

Neo-Liberalism, Post-Communist Transformation, and Civil Society

ILJA ŠRUBAŘ

One of the substantial components of the post-socialist transformation is the transition from Marxism to neo-liberalism. This could also be defined as a transition from the dogma of planning to the dogma of the free market (Przeworski, 1992). In light of this we are confronted with two pressing questions: (i) is neo-liberalism becoming an alternative post-socialist world-view?; (ii) is the neo-liberal theory of society really capable of analyzing social reality as adequately and reliably as it claims?

Radical Economism

Let us start with the first question. Why has the brand of liberalism developed by Hayek been so appealing to the post-socialist countries?[1] At first glance, the simplest explanation is pragmatic: the transformation of a planned economy into a market one is not an economic issue only, but also a social one, and therefore requires a theory which combines these factors. The existence of a need, however, tells us nothing about why a particular concept is selected to meet it. Various alternatives spring to mind, from Keynes to Mueller-Armack's ordo-liberalism—which clearly has a liberal background—or to Sir Karl Popper's 'open society' project. Why is Hayek's neo-liberalism so appealing in the post-socialist environment? How did 'real socialism' clear the ground for this kind of thought? What are the patterns of thought that emerged during the real-socialist period which can serve as a link?

One should not assume that a system of ideas that is the extreme opposite of its predecessor cannot have anything in common with it, other than being its negation. Quite the contrary: the transition from one extreme to another points to the fact that both relate to a common reality or principle, to which, however, they apply interpretations and methods of a radically different kind, often, indeed, precluding one another. What, then, is the common principle connecting the Marxist and the neo-liberal perceptions of reality?

I will argue that the connecting principle of both doctrines is the conviction that the main functions of society are controlled by an economic mechanism. This conviction, which determines both Marxist and neo-liberal thought, springs from common historical roots, going back to the early period of the development of civil society. At that time—that is, at the end of the seventeenth and during the eighteenth century—the different analyses of society which became sources of liberal thought asserted that it is political economy which, in Marx's terms, represents the determining part of the anatomy of society, and that a scientific analysis of the way societies function implies an analysis of their economic core. Marx, as we know, drew his faith in the determining power of the economic mechanism from the liberal economics classics, and on this faith he founded his expectation that a collectivistic correction of this mechanism would lead to the emergence of a society of a new kind. Both the liberal–individualistic and Marxist–collectivistic variants of economic radicalism therefore are based on the premise that economic systems—each of which generates a social formation of a particular kind—can be precisely defined.

Economic reductionism is therefore the first factor inherent in both systems. There is, however, a radical difference in the consequences drawn by the two doctrines from their common horizon of thought. For Marx, the possibility of analyzing the economic anatomy of civil society means that it is possible to know its system as a whole and thus also to radically transform it through systemic changes in its economic structure. In Hayek's neo-liberal thought the Marxist approach is an example of inadmissible holism. The central outcome of his analysis of the market anatomy of civil society is the thesis that, although the system can be described, and coordinates and balances individual interests and objectives, it is not possible to analyze it in sufficient detail for us to be able to define a model for determining the behavior of all its participants. Quite the opposite: the invisible hand of the market is, in this perspective, an outcome of social evolution. It represents a solution which allows the coordination of subjective, individual goals that mostly remain mutually unrecognized by market participants. Any attempt at systemic intervention in this mechanism—that is, intervention restricting individual freedom of decision to the advantage of collective interests—disturbs this spontaneous coordination of society and must be rejected.

Paradoxically, during the process of post-socialist transformation the close affinities of the two concepts based on their shared radical economism are becoming evident. The success of the intended transformation must, on the one hand, rely on the validity of Marx's postulates, according to which planned manipulation of the economic base is not only possible but actually necessary for implementing essential changes in society; on the other hand, the objective of this planned process has to be a spontaneous coordination of social processes by the market which finds, theoretically, its fundamental justification in the argument about the unfeasibility of such planned reforms.

Despite their diametrically opposed positions, these approaches obviously display common features which can be studied further. They both encounter the problem identified by Durkheim as the "extra-contractual conditions of contracts", and by Parsons as the "utilitarian dilemma" (Durkheim, 1975, 266; Parsons, 1968). Both authors point out that theories drawing on the economic determination of behavior and society sooner or later reach a point in their argumentation where purely economic motivation to social action proves unsuitable to explain its evident collective features, and it becomes necessary to establish the rules of action—as criteria for the acceptance or rejection of one economic system or another—on the basis of extra-economic criteria. For Marx, this means the emergence of the issue of 'appropriate consciousness', that is, of the correct interpretation of historical events in the perspective of a revolutionary class—which implies, of course, an ideological deformation of the line of argument, inherent to the Marxian system. Since a detailed scientific prognosis concerning the motivation to perform a concrete individual action in response to a general economic situation is not possible, there is an opening for dogmatic statements on what is and what is not a historically correct class consciousness—and that irrespective of the factual course of events and history.

Hayek must solve a similar problem. He emphasizes the randomness—from a theoretical point of view—and mutual ignorance of individual objectives. The emergence of a spontaneous market as the result of the sum of individual actions represents for him the evolutionary solution of the issue of order. Nevertheless, a number of collective interests emerge in response to this order—in the form of monopolies, trade unions, and so on—and successfully oppose its presumed individualistic essence. The neo-liberal rules aiming at the preservation of individual liberties by resistance to collective pressure cannot therefore be derived without further explanation from the working of this spontaneous market mechanism. This is where Hayek's argumentation is bolstered by the indispensable thesis of the power monopoly of the state, developed—and at the same time restricted—by liberal normative principles. These must be imposed from outside, however, since they cannot be established as inherent in social reality itself, and therefore often stand in direct conflict with this reality, that is, with actually existing individual interests.

Hayek's neo-liberal concept, which seeks to found the "constitution of liberty" of the individual on spontaneous order, is therefore forced to postulate its principles in a dogmatic way, and to define all the historically arising individual interests which do not agree with these principles as interests that threaten liberty and social order. In this respect—similar to Marx's theory—it ceases to be an analytical theory and becomes a normative and prescriptive one, defying the test of falsification.

Dogmatic in their immanent bias, a feature inherent in both variants of radical economism, it is possible to detect a second substantial aspect which they have in common. In both cases they represent an ideology in Mannheim's sense, that is, a system of ideas drawn up as the legitimization of a particular political practice, and therefore conceptually structured in a way which excludes their falsification, and denies the validity of the ideas of opponents by referring to their social or class position. Both conceptions support their own validity by means of economic determinism, presented as an outcome of scientific analysis. On the other hand, they are both forced to abandon this determinism, and therefore also the scientific–analytical claim attached to it, in order to be able to postulate the normative principles of their political doctrines. This fundamental contradiction in their structure is the source of their inclination to subject the results of scientific analysis to absolute normative claims, to their own ideologies.

Evidently, the popularity of Hayek's model in the post-socialist societies cannot be explained merely in terms of their present endeavor to find an analytical theoretical system on which the transformation process could rest. By its radical economism, its inclination to dogmatize, and its unconcerned, dismissive attitude towards concrete individual and group interests, Hayek's neo-liberalism fits without difficulty into particular patterns of the Marxist and real-socialist tradition. In these terms, a conception so different in its intentions becomes, due to the structure of the argument, so familiar in post-socialist conditions.

Economics—A General Theory of Society?

Let us now approach the question of the extent to which Hayek's neo-liberalism, as a scientific theory of society, adequately reflects social reality and the genesis of its order. We have seen that Hayek perceives this genesis as a function of the invisible hand of the market and places its analysis in the field of economic theory.

This is where the ambivalent approach to the problem of social order, inherent in this type of theory of action, comes to the surface. On the one hand, an order is always the result of individual rational action; on the other hand, it is evident that this result is just a matter of chance, since it was not intended by the actors. True, the mystery of how the actions of individuals could give rise to common rules—social norms—which then control these actions has been formulated as a problem and symptomatically labeled the 'function of the invisible hand'; nevertheless, it has not been resolved. This shortcoming has been pointed out by Talcott Parsons, in connection with the dilemma of utilitarian (that is, liberal economic) theories of action. Parsons arrives at the conclusion that the explanation of the spontaneous emergence of a social order cannot be founded merely on the purpose-seeking rationality of individual interests, coordinated by the market, but that it must relate also to the social genesis of common normative rules which legitimate the purpose and means of economic action.

Parsons' theoretical argument focuses our attention upon another, more empirical explanatory shortcoming of the neo-liberal theory. Given that one of the essential factors in the autogenesis of the social order in modern European societies is the mechanism of the market, it seems astonishing to note that liberal theories, on the one hand, continuously report deviations from the optimal functioning of the market, caused in the course of history by the emergence of various 'collectivistic' normative systems; and, on the other hand, point out that the liberal principles of a political set-up cannot be derived from the spontaneous functioning of the market alone. Although liberal theories register and reject collectivistic deformations of the market, pointing out their dysfunctional consequences for society, they are evidently not able to explain why these deviations in the working of the market occur so often, while liberal principles have to be introduced externally by the power monopoly of the state.

This is where the liberal theory of society encounters analytical barriers, given on the one hand by its methodological individualism, and on the other by the need to distance itself from the collectivistic interpretations which, in its eyes, are built into the stance of its radically economistic Marxist competitor. The utilitarian theory is here fighting battles that fit best into nineteenth-century discourse and attempting to avoid having to prove the universal validity of its principles by an ahistorical analytical approach to social reality. The notion that the liberal model is an adequate description of the functioning of social mechanisms in modern civil societies is therefore false.

The Dialectic of the Liberal Spontaneity of Order

Let me provide some empirical evidence for this statement. The fact that the liberal model is not an adequate representation of the functioning of society does not, of course, mean that it is not itself a part of this reality and does not have an impact on it. This leads to a number of unintended consequences. The function of the market, which is—according to Hayek—the core of modern societies, requires private ownership and therefore presumes social inequality. The maintenance of such inequality is not merely an issue of state or economic power but—as Max Weber points out—also an issue of their legitimacy as granted by social normative systems. One of these systems—observed sociologically—is liberalism itself. Its merit in the development of modern society in its early stages consists in the implementation of two social techniques which do provide such a legitimization. The first rests on the definition of social conflicts as the legitimate expression of views which seek their resolution in discourse, that is, in a parliamentary manner. The second ensues from the assumptions necessary for the market economy—that is, from the necessity of private ownership on the one hand, and from the need for the equality of market participants as free parties to contracts on the other. The legitimation of material and social inequality by means of instituting equality under the law represents the other basic legitimizing technique of liberal concepts, but also their fundamental normative contradiction.

This second technique of legitimation is evoked by Hayek, too, as a tool protecting the market as a spontaneous mechanism of the social order. In this neo-liberal version, however, this principle becomes much more problematic and contradictory than in its original form. The main bearers of spontaneous innovation—and therefore guarantors of progress—are the 'independent' market participants or the owners of capital, who can best withstand group and government pressures and preserve their individual freedom, creativity, ability to assume risk, and so on. On the other hand, the market participants who are dependent on the owners of capital—that is, the majority of people in modern civil societies—understandably share an interest in the collective promotion of their social security at the expense of independent owners, despite the fact that the possibility of ensuring their social security rests on the latter's creativity (Hayek, 1983, 144ff.). The neo-liberal principle of freedom—that is, the freedom of the individual from power and social pressure—demands the protection of the interests of the 'independents' against the 'dependents' and the appropriate limitation of the possibility of collective pressure being exerted in an undesired direction. In this respect liberal principles must stand against the abuse of power by the democratic majority because that, as we know, belongs to the 'dependents' (Hayek, 1983, 127ff.). The power of the majority, according to Hayek, achieves its limits at the moment when individual freedom could be threatened by the legislative adoption of a demand which is the outcome of the collective pressure of the 'dependents'. For Hayek, most measures characteristic of the social policies of modern welfare states represent such undesirable legal acts.

If we start again from the premises that the mechanism of the market is a necessary integrative agent of modern societies, whose working requires and reproduces material and social inequality, the question arises whether the legitimation of this mechanism, as proposed by Hayek, really contributes to its maintenance. Is it not that the spontaneous development of a social order, based on market mechanisms, implies rather the creation of the welfare state as a new model of its legitimation?

Let us look at the way in which 'collective pressures'—which in the liberal perspective threaten individual independence and freedom—emerge, and ask about the role played by these pressures: (i) in the implementation of the formal equal rights on which the liberal model is based, and (ii) in the further development of the legitimizing mechanisms of modern market societies.

Historically, the liberal concept of individuals being equal under the law was applied to citizens whose claim to individual freedom rested on their economic independence. A society of independent individuals, resolving its group conflicts by parliamentary means on the basis of political participation and representation, is therefore at the origin of 'bourgeois' society, which founds its claims to civic status on property— as reflected in the history of suffrage in Europe. Material inequality is here projected directly onto legal inequality, differentiating between the 'dependent' and 'independent' in Hayek's sense. This principle, however, cannot be enforced universally within the market system, from which civic property—and therefore also civic independence—stems. The market demands the freedom of movement of capital and labor, and therefore also freedom of contractual obligation, in terms of which both capital and labor are equal. Legal equality of contractual subjects and their—also legal— inequality at the level of political representation therefore contradicted the liberal principle of civic equality which was well established within the framework of the early historic realization of liberal doctrines.

In his study of the legitimacy of the capitalist state Habermas points out that it was not until conflict arose with the non-integrated dependent groups of civil society, especially the working class, that the universal integrative capability of the liberal ideal of civil equality was realized (Habermas, 1973). It was only under the pressure of this conflict that this principle became generalized during the nineteenth century and expanded its validity to all social strata at all levels of law. The order of modern European societies is certainly indebted to liberal thought for the norms anticipating such a generalization. Without the collective pressure of the 'dependents' challenging the originally socially limited application of these norms, however, they would not have attained general validity for society as a whole—something which has meanwhile become a fundamental liberal axiom. The increasing collective pressures on the development of capitalist societies represented, therefore, not a departure from the market economy and liberal principles but their logical historical implementation.

From the beginning of the twentieth century, the development of the market economy began to reach a stage of concentration of capital which demanded the planned coordination of economic activities by masses of administrative staff and managers. The consequence has been an enlargement of the dependent classes by the 'new middle strata'. The absolute dependence of the majority of the population on the functioning and dysfunctioning of the market has given rise to expectations of state support on the part of both labor and capital. Capital demands preferential treatment and services for the sake of maintaining employment; employees demand protection against their absolute dependence on capital. The result is that the state is forced to assume roles which earlier had been alien to it. These are the pressures from which the welfare state was born as an instrument protecting and legitimizing the market order (and social inequality as its precondition). This has taken place not despite, but as a consequence of, the autonomous role of the market and its unintended effects on the social order.

The protecting mechanism of the welfare state may be praised or criticized without changing the efficiency of its functioning. The swings in the preference given to 'dependent' or 'independent' social groups which may be observed in the policies of the Western states, do not imply the victory of one or the other party and its characteristic ideology, but are merely the expression of weight-balancing in the structure of the legitimization system of civil market societies at their present stage of development. To attempt a solution to this social conflict by preferring the ideology of one or the other party would be a dangerous anachronism. It would mean a step back from the equilibrium of the mechanisms which—in Hayek's terms—were developed by the spontaneous evolution of civil societies for their own protection. On this basis, just as socialism did not survive its Marxist implementation, capitalism would not have survived the nineteenth century were it merely the implementation of the liberal doctrine as interpreted by Hayek.

Bibliography

Durkheim, Emile. 1975. *Über die Teilung der sozialen Arbeit*. Frankfurt am Main: Suhrkamp. (English edition: *On the Division of Labor in Society*.)

Habermas, Jürgen. 1973. *Legitimationsprobleme im Spätkapitalismus*. Frankfurt am Main: Suhrkamp.

Hayek, Friedrich A. 1983. *Die Verfassung der Freiheit*. Tübingen: Mohr. (English edition: *The Constitution of Liberty*. London and Chicago, 1960.)

Parsons, Talcott. 1968. *The Structure of Social Action*, vol. I. New York—London: Macmillan.

Przeworski, Adam. 1992. *Democracy and the Market*. Cambridge: Cambridge University Press.

Note

1 The current chapter draws mainly on his programmatic work *The Constitution of Liberty* (1960).

Constitutional Transformation in Post-Communist Central Europe: A Liberal Revolution?

ALLISON STANGER

Introduction

Even after the return of reconstituted former communists to power throughout much of East Central Europe, it is not uncommon to see the world-shaking events of 1989 identified as a liberal revolution. Given developments in the region over the past few years, it is worth taking some time to consider whether that label is, on balance, misplaced.

Citizens of the West—especially Americans—extrapolating from interpretations of their own history, associate liberal revolution with the promulgation of a new constitution, one which institutionalizes the break with an undemocratic past by protecting individual rights and providing the ground rules for the conduct of post-authoritarian politics. In this perspective, liberal revolution is fundamental political and economic change embodied in law.[1] Yet the transition to democracy in Poland, Hungary, and the former Czechoslovakia did not follow this trajectory. Rather than immediately abrogating constitutions devised by their former oppressors, the democratic opposition in each of these countries endorsed the existing communist charter as a stop-gap measure until a new basic law could be drafted and ratified. Post-communist elites in each country, that is, sought to bring democratic constitutions into being without violating the spirit or letter of the fraudulent documents they aimed to replace. Andrew Arato has described this approach as the "method of radical continuity" (Arato, n. d., 110).

In Hungary, given the timing of the round-table talks and the reform nature of the communist regime, the members of the democratic opposition really had no other option than to follow this path. In Poland, Solidarity also had to labor under the possible threat of Soviet intervention. Yet Czechoslovakia's Velvet Revolution took place after the fall of the Berlin Wall under quite different circumstances. Czechs and Slovaks, it would seem, had at least the potential to choose their strategy of constitutional change.

While the Polish, Czecho-Slovak, and Hungarian opponents of the outgoing order were ultimately successful in amending the old regime's constitution beyond recognition, all found the task of agreeing on a new constitutional framework to be more, rather than less difficult as the initial revolutionary euphoria evaporated. Thus, more than six years after the official collapse of communism in Europe, democratic Hungary continues to be governed by a heavily amended version of its former communist constitution, while Poland is ruled by what was first promulgated as an interim agreement, the so-called Little Constitution. Both countries are still attempting to draft and ratify constitutions that are more than an unsystematic product of the less savory aspects of transition politics. Czechoslovakia no longer exists, in no small part because the rules that the makers of the Velvet Revolution chose to inherit exacerbated rather than ameliorated conflict between the federation's two members.

The present chapter has two principal aims. In the first part, I take a careful look at the shape of constitutional politics in the immediate aftermath of communism's formal collapse, and suggest some reasons for the similarities sketched above. I largely focus on the attempt to build a new political order using wholly legal means in the former Czechoslovakia, but I draw comparisons with parallel developments in Poland and Hungary throughout. In the second part, I evaluate the costs and benefits of the method of radical continuity and attempt to account for its adoption. I argue that Civic Forum's explicitly anti-revolutionary approach to overthrowing communist power was an improvised extension of pre-existing dissident strategies, a product of what Jerzy

Szacki has aptly labeled the "proto-liberal" approach to political change (see Szacki, 1995, 73–117).

The Constitutional Politics of Anti-Communist Revolution

The governing coalition that emerged from the Czecho-Slovak round-table differed from its earlier Polish and Hungarian counterparts in one critical respect: when the dust cleared, the opposition had effective control of both domestic and foreign policy. With respect to matters of constitutional import, therefore, the makers of the Velvet Revolution had unprecedented power to remake the institutions of the communist regime. Yet the marked difference between the character of the Polish, Hungarian, and Czechoslovak round-table talks is the extent to which constitutional change was not a prominent topic for discussion in Prague. Oskar Krejčí, then advisor to Premier Ladislav Adamec and a government participant at the Czecho-Slovak round-table talks has characterized the situation in the following provocative terms: "power was lying on the street and no one wanted to pick it up".[2] Surprisingly enough, both the opposition and the government were in tacit agreement that the point of departure for the transfer of power would be the communist constitution, albeit for quite different reasons.

The accommodating behavior of Civic Forum's leadership on this issue becomes all the more curious when viewed in light of the fact that they had an alternative draft constitution already in hand. At Havel's request, a new federal constitution, dated 5 December 1989, had been hastily drafted by Pavel Rychetský.[3] Thus, Civic Forum's conservative position on legal matters cannot be entirely explained by a desire to buy time to formulate its demands more precisely. To the best of my knowledge, the Polish and Hungarian democratic opposition were not similarly armed. Given that their demands for constitutional amendments were all accepted with little resistance, and that the balance of power was in their favor, why did the makers of the Velvet Revolution from the outset embrace such a conservative approach to the necessary transformation of the country's basic law?

In framing an answer to this question, there are at least four potential explanations whose relative merits need to be assessed. Let us first consider what one might label the 'common-sense explanation'. As the deferred negotiations on the distribution of powers in the new democratic era would later painfully demonstrate, the question of the federation's future form was a potentially divisive one in the former Czechoslovakia. One might argue that the leadership of Civic Forum did not want to risk dividing the movement before the June 1990 referendum elections had rendered their power legitimate. Thus, they wisely avoided taking up the question of the democratic common state's form until the gains of the Velvet Revolution had been irreversibly locked in.

Although this proposition is appealing at first glance, upon closer inspection it fails to square with the available evidence. What is in hindsight ironic is the extent to which most Czech dissidents were at first only marginally aware of what Czechoslovak communists at the time might have re-ferred to as the 'Slovak problem'. One need only look as far as the infamous 'hyphen' debate in March–April 1990, when the Czech side was at first genuinely surprised at the vehe-mence of Slovak views on the future name of the country. The minimal interaction that had taken place under com-munism between Czech and Slovak dissident circles also produced some absurd moments in the round-table talks. At one point in round four, for example, like a good equal-opportunity employer, Adamec had to warn the Civic Forum negotiators that there were not enough Slovaks in their pro-posed government (Hanzel, 1991, 161ff.).

Second, in explaining Civic Forum's conservative ap-proach to constitutional renewal, the hard-line nature of the Czechoslovak communist regime must be taken into ac-count. It was difficult, at the time, to imagine that the appa-ratus would accept substantive change without a fight. While the fear level at the Polish and Hungarian round-table talks was also palpable, given that both sets of negotiations took place before the fall of the Berlin Wall, this must be weighed against the mitigating factor that the price of a crackdown was higher for reform communists than it was for unreconstructed party members of the Czech and Slovak variety. Put another way, where the reform Polish and Hungarian communist regimes attempted to hijack the cause of constitutional transformation and claim it as their own reform agenda, the minions of the outgoing hard-line Czecho-Slovak order did not feel the same pressure to pose as the agents of legal change. Since a crackdown could not be ruled out in the former Czechoslovakia, demanding too much all at once seemed to jeopardize the negotiations themselves, and the dialogue with the regime was something that Civic Forum sought to keep going at all costs.

Third, in many respects, Civic Forum was understandably wholly unprepared for the breathtaking pace of possible change. In Timothy Garton Ash's oft-cited words, it took ten years to make the revolution in Poland, ten months in Hungary, and ten days in Czechoslovakia (Ash, 1990, 78). Czechs and Slovaks did not have the luxury of self-consciously reflecting on the course that the revolution was taking while they were negotiating; there simply was not enough time.[4] Viewed in this context, it is perhaps unsurprising that, when in round two of the negotiations Ladislav Adamec unexpectedly asked the opposition to propose candidates for ministerial positions, Civic Forum first refused to do so, presenting the regime with a list of names only a full week later. Communist negotiators criticized the movement's initial reluctance to contribute to the dialogue on the new government's composition. Adamec complained that Havel and his compatriots wanted power without responsibility (Hanzel, 1991, 70–72, 158 ff.).

Finally, and perhaps most importantly, Civic Forum's indisputable leader does not seem to have at first believed that a new constitution belonged at the very top of the democracy movement's list of priorities. It is easy to lose sight of this fact, given that President Havel would later devote almost all his attention—some would say excessively so—to the effort to retire the inherited constitution. While Havel commissioned the drafting of an alternative federal constitution, he did not press for its immediate implementation as a provisional replacement, nor did he spearhead an initiative to refine the Rychetský draft. Instead, he waited until after the June 1990 elections to take up in earnest the task of constitutional renewal. Why?

One obvious response is that the new president had plenty of other things to think about. Yet this common-sense explanation again does not tell the whole story. In his dissident writings and early presidential speeches, Havel repeatedly stressed that laws or systems, in and of themselves, can really guarantee nothing of value at all. Good laws alone can never create the quality of life on which human dignity relies, for democracy is more than a collection of formal rules. For Havel, genuine political change could be effected only by the transformation of individuals and their interaction with political power and one another, not by systemic change.[5] This supposition underlies Havel's argument in 'The Power of the Powerless' that violent political revolution was unacceptable to the dissident not "because the idea seems too radical, but on the contrary, because it does not seem radical enough" (Havel, 1989a, 93). These long-held beliefs framed Havel's initial approach to politics in practice, particularly with respect to constitutional issues. As a result, the old dissident strategy of "demanding that the laws be upheld ... an act of living within the truth that threatens the whole mendacious structure at its point of maximum mendacity", as Havel once put it, carried the day (Havel, 1989a, 98).

These ideas were not, of course, unique to Prague, although Havel perhaps expressed them most eloquently. Adam Michnik's "new evolutionism" and the subsequent Polish idea of a "self-limiting revolution" embraced the same basic assumptions. Rather than affirming complete allegiance to the Western political and economic model, many intellectuals in Prague and Warsaw instead envisioned a 'third way', a new order that was in its fundamental features both post-communist and post-capitalist. In his exceptional book *Liberalism after Communism*, Jerzy Szacki deploys the term "proto-liberalism" to describe this body of dissident thought, one characterized by its explicitly 'anti-political' approach to politics. Instead of seeking to topple the post-totalitarian order by confronting it directly, proto-liberals challenged the system they sought to replace through the force of their own individual examples. Citizens of what Havel called the "parallel polis", therefore, renounced conventional revolutionary tactics, both because these were the weapons of their oppressors and because these methods stood absolutely no chance of successfully challenging the Party's grip on all aspects of daily life. Designed to sustain and nurture the democratic opposition under the threatening shadow of totalitarian power, proto-liberalism never constituted an explicit political program. It provided a blueprint for interaction with the old regime, yet said nothing about how to dismantle old institutions or build new ones. It provided a stance, but not instructions on how to proceed after that stance had produced results (Szacki, 1995, 77–82).

This is why the question of whether or not Civic Forum might have chosen a standard liberal approach to founding new constitutional arrangements is ultimately more complicated than it initially appears. The actual balance of power on the ground suggests that Civic Forum had alternatives. Viewed in this light, the decision to postpone the quest for a new constitution might be attributed to a failure of leadership. Yet when the belief systems of the negotiating dissidents are factored into this equation, the range of alternatives narrows dramatically. Simply put, Civic Forum's leadership could have gone another way, but they would have had to become different people overnight for that alternative route to have been selected. They would have had to adopt immediately and without hesitation the outlook of ordinary politicians, after having spent years endeavoring to transcend politics as it was currently practiced. One of the reasons power went begging for a while in Prague was that those who were best equipped to seize control and shape the transition were initially the least interested in exercising conventional political power.

The Costs and Benefits
of Proto-Liberal Revolution

In his provocative book *The Future of Liberal Revolution* Bruce Ackerman argues that the immediate aftermath of revolution provides liberal democrats with a unique opportunity, what he calls "the constitutional moment", when circumstances are optimal for laying the legal foundations for a democratic order and mobilizing the requisite broad popular support for the constitutional initiative. Timing in tackling major constitutional controversies is critical, for the opposition to authoritarian rule will remain united only for a finite period after it has become clear that a new order is in the making. The gains of liberal revolution need to be 'locked in' early on, before more self-interested factions are able to hijack constitutional politics and exploit it to secure their own ends. "Without decisive leadership, the constitutional moment passes in vain" (Ackerman, 1992, 3), and it is very difficult, if not impossible, to recreate it.[6]

In common with the cases of Poland and Hungary, the case of the former Czechoslovakia supports Ackerman's hypothesis. As Ackerman might have predicted, the decision to follow the letter of communist constitutions, never designed to function in conditions of genuine liberty, facilitated the bracketing of the more difficult constitutional questions for resolution at a later date. While postponing these hard tasks allowed democratizing elites to focus on other pressing problems, it also meant that fundamental constitutional questions would have to be confronted after the salient cleavages dividing post-communist societies had fully crystallized into rival political groupings. Once those new divisions had emerged, the goal of securing a new constitution to replace interim arrangements was rendered all the more elusive. The ironic result is that if new constitutions ever become a reality in Poland and Hungary, former communists will have engineered their promulgation, not the individuals who brought the old regime crashing down.

The case of the former Czechoslovakia, viewed in comparative perspective, provides a curious example of ethnic differences fueling the resuscitation of constitutionalism. Constitutional deadlock at the federal level served as a catalyst for constitutional revolution at the republic level. Ackerman's constitutional moment may have passed for Czechoslovakia, but this has had the effect of recreating opportunities for securing a clean legal break with the past in each of the member republics. In this sense, both Czechs and Slovaks were granted an opportunity to learn from their past mistakes that was not available to their Polish and Hungarian counterparts, facilitating, rather than undermining, progress towards the rule of law. By redefining the state, we might say, constitutional democracy was given a second chance in the Czech and Slovak Republics.

Ackerman's framework highlights the negative consequences of proto-liberal approaches to constitutional replacement. A sacralized constitution—the fruit of the Anglo-American model of liberal revolution, of course—guarantees neither democratic consolidation nor the development of constitutionalism. Obviously, there are a number of other factors that are of importance here. Yet the proto-liberal approach to constitutional change—the method of "radical continuity"—does pose hazards that must be acknowledged. To begin with, it is difficult to get on with the business of ordinary politics when the rules of the democratic game are seen by a majority of the players to be in some way flawed or as having been forged in a less than democratic fashion. Furthermore, when the new order is forged as a bargain between democrats and non-democrats, the distinction between authoritarian and democratic politics can all too easily be blurred in the eyes of the regime's newborn citizens. Finally, it is easier for old elites to retain their positions under cover of the rule of law when the rules that they created are presupposed to be legitimate until proven otherwise.[7] Regardless of its content, a sacralized constitution plays an important substantive and symbolic role in any democratic transition. In closing the regime question, it provides a firmer foundation for consolidating democracy.

Yet the proto-liberal approach to constitutional revolution is not without its positive qualities, first among these being that all of these transitions were accomplished without violence. All attempts to break radically with the past—be they sacralized constitutions or lustration policies—are more likely to unleash violent opposition. Although it had a host of unintended consequences, the method of radical continuity was a strategy that minimized the probability of bloodshed. It would be difficult to overvalue this achievement. Furthermore, as Stephen Holmes maintains, one of the strongest arguments against exhorting post-communist political elites to approach constitution making in the standard Western manner is that they face a range of problems—from the assignment of first property rights to privatization and the question of how citizenship is to be defined—which liberal principles cannot easily resolve (Holmes, 1993). Liberal constitutionalism, we might say, presupposes a set of initial conditions that never did and still do not pertain in post-communist Europe. Ironically, this simple fact renders liberalism nearly as mute as proto-liberalism in solving basic transition problems.

Along parallel lines, I have argued that the Polish, Czecho-Slovak, and Hungarian revolutions would have had to take place later than they did and that the dissidents who made these revolutions would have had to become different people overnight in order to successfully seize the constitutional moment, as Ackerman urges. Proto-liberalism's strengths in the battle against communist oppression indeed became weaknesses when the previously powerless suddenly became powerful, yet it is surely unreasonable to demand that those imprisoned and tormented for years should instantaneously have become fully cognizant of their newly acquired power and seek to exploit it.

Under these circumstances, liberal revolution in communist Europe would only have been possible if it had somehow been imposed by the West, in a sweeping application of the post–Second World War German model. The newly democratic regimes of Central Europe would have had to become political dependencies of the West after having long been political dependencies of the East. It is hard to see how this scenario might have contributed to the development of the rule of law, let alone how it could have been implemented politically. Ackerman's book, in the end, is extremely useful in that it can be deployed to delineate some of the trade-offs between different approaches to regime transformation. Four years after its publication, however, when scholars have a clearer sense of how each of these revolutions were actually made, it seems curiously beside the point.

Conclusion

The experience of exercising real power has rendered 1989's proto-liberals an endangered species. Chronicling the changes in the belief systems of these individuals, while worthy of sustained study, is beyond the scope of this inquiry. The evolution in President Václav Havel's views, however, is perhaps indicative of a larger trend, and worth painting in broad brushstrokes here. In 1989 and 1990, as we have seen, Havel consistently insisted that the transition to democracy adhere to the letter of existing law, so as to avoid what he described on numerous occasions as a "dangerous state of dual law". By late 1991, however, faced with an escalating crisis in Czech–Slovak relations, he was willing to turn a blind eye to actions that adherence to full legality might not permit if they promised to contribute to the preservation of the common state. To cite just one example, in the high-level discussions that took place in November 1991 at Havel's summer retreat at Hrádeček, the president argued with those who criticized his proposal for drafting and ratifying three new constitutions (Czech, Slovak, and Federal) on the grounds that it was illegal, maintaining that strict adherence to the letter of existing law would logically prohibit the adoption of any new constitution (*'Poločas rozpadu'*, 1994, 63–64). With this position, Havel had obviously traveled some distance from the dissident strategy of simply demanding that the laws be upheld.

In conclusion, to answer directly the question posed by my title, I would have to answer "no". The upheavals of 1989 were not liberal revolutions, for they were neither made by liberals in the Western sense of the term, which encompasses economic as well as political orientations, nor did their early policies conform to the classical model of liberal revolution. Given that their point of departure and the circumstances in which they unfolded have no direct parallel in Western political development, we should not be surprised to see these transitions taking a different trajectory to the one the West might originally have expected.

Bibliography

Ackerman, Bruce. 1992. *The Future of Liberal Revolution*. New Haven: Yale University Press.

Arato, Andrew. 1994. 'Constitution and Continuity in the East European Transitions', *Journal of Constitutional Law in Eastern and Central Europe* 1 (1).

Ash, Timothy Garton. 1990. *The Magic Lantern*. New York: Random House.

Hanzel, Vladimír. 1991. *Zrychlený tep dějin*. Prague: OK Centrum.

Havel, Václav. 1989a (1978). 'The Power of the Powerless', in Václav Havel, *Living in Truth*. London: Faber and Faber.

———. 1989b (1978). 'Politics and Conscience', in Václav Havel, *Living in Truth*. London: Faber and Faber.

———. 1990. Speech to the first freely elected Federal Assembly (29 June), in Václav Havel, *Projevy: leden—červen 1990*. Prague: Vyšehrad.

Holmes, Stephen. 1993. 'Back to the Drawing Board', *East European Constitutional Review* 2, no. 1 (winter): 21–25.

n. a. 1994. 'Poločas rozpadu: Přepis stenografického záznamu ze setkání nejvyšších ústavních činitelů u prezidenta Václava Havla na Hrádečku dne 3. listopadu 1991', *Slovenské Listy*.

Suk, Jiří. 1995. 'Vznik Občanského fora a proměny jeho struktury (19. Listopad—10. prosinec 1989), *Soudobé dějiny* II (January).

Szacki, Jerzy. 1995. *Liberalism After Communism*. Budapest: Central European University Press.

Notes

The author would like to thank Vojtěch Cepl, Michael Kraus, Andrew Moravcsik, and Anne-Marie Slaughter for thoughtful comments on an earlier version of this paper.

1 While acknowledging that different interpretations of liberalism's foundation exist, for the purposes of this paper I have defined liberal revolution in Anglo-American terms.

2 Oskar Krejčí, remarks at the Conference on Czechoslovakia's Dissolution, CERGE-EI (28 June 1996).

3 *Občanské Forum předkládá československé veřejnosti a ústavním orgánům republiky první návrh nové Ústavy*, 5 December 1989. Document in author's possession.

4 On Civic Forum's initial lack of an explicit program and the requisite internal organization to implement it, see Suk (1995), 28–31.

5 See, for example, Havel (1989a), especially pp. 95–100, and Havel (1989b), especially pp. 153–57. See also President Havel's speech to the first freely elected Federal Assembly, 29 June 1990, in Havel (1990), pp. 151–83.

6 See Ackerman (1992), especially pp. 3, 46–50.

7 All these arguments have appeared in the ongoing Hungarian debate. See Arato (n. d.), pp. 121–22.

Law, Tradition, and Liberalism in Practice: Quo Vadis, East Central Europe?

SVETOZAR PEJOVICH

Purpose, Definitions, and Concepts

When assessing the prospects of liberalism in post-1989 East Central Europe,[1] one question that immediately comes to mind has to be: Why should we care? To provide an answer we can pursue two alternative approaches: (i) we can exchange views about classical liberalism and debate its values; or (ii) we can analyze the costs and benefits of liberalism in practice. The first approach would focus on discussion of abstract values, while the second would emphasize the analysis of the social institutions required to link a set of ideas with the real world. Only the second approach could contribute to our stock of knowledge. Why?

After several decades of ideological brainwashing, it is difficult and perhaps impossible for East Europeans to separate values and cognition. This is a reasonable proposition because many intellectuals in the free world have the same problem. Durkheim, Galbraith, the 'American Austrians', Vaněk, and many other scholars have been marketing their own concepts of 'social values' among the public as if those values were cognitive statements about our world. The moral disaffection which all those mentioned have for the prevailing social system means that they prefer another state of affairs to the one actually observed. The late Professor Brunner wrote: "The sacrifice of cognition is particularly easy to detect in the objections to the market system induced by discrepancies between one's desires, glorified as social values, and the result of market processes. However, our ability to visualize 'better' states, more closely reflecting our preferences, yields no evidence that this state can be realized" (Brunner, 1970, 563).

I think that most of us would agree that the right of ownership, freedom of contract, and the rule of law are three basic institutions of capitalism.[2] Those institutions generate their own incentives and transaction costs, affecting human behavior in specific and predictable ways. They (i) emphasize the rights of the individual over those of the group; (ii) create the environment in which all individuals are encouraged to pursue their own interests, make their own decisions, bear the costs of their decisions, and seek their private ends in competitive markets; and (iii) put a premium on the rules that reward performance, cultivate risk-taking attitudes, promote the development of individual liberties, and make the keeping of promises become a source of wealth.

It is, therefore, misleading to consider capitalism as an 'alternative mechanism' for the allocation of resources. Capitalism is a way of life, or a process, in which individuals voluntarily interact in pursuit of their private ends and, in doing so, create an order. An important positive aspect of this spontaneous order is that the value of scarce goods in their alternative uses is determined by the only possible source of value, the individual. As Professor Buchanan puts it: "Economic performance can only be conceived in values; but how are values determined? By prices, and prices emerge only in markets. They have no meaning in a non-market context ... where the choice-influenced opportunity costs are ignored" (Buchanan, 1976).

It is clear that capitalism 'delivers the goods'. We observe that capitalist countries have consistently provided more individual rights and higher standards of living for their citizens than non-capitalist countries. One implication of this fact is that the theme of the present volume is quite proper. Indeed, if we care about the quality of life in East Central Europe we should care about the prospects of capitalism in the region.

The purpose of the present chapter is to analyze the factors that could enhance the prospects of capitalism in East Central Europe.

Institutions, Transaction Costs, and Efficiency

In pursuit of survival,[3] people interact with one another, their interaction being molded by the institutions that constitute the rules of the game. Social activity then involves human interactions on two levels. The first is the development and specification of institutions. The second level of social activity involves human interactions within the prevailing institutions. The former is a matter of the rules of the game, while the latter is a matter of the game itself.[4] Clearly, the game depends on the rules. To discuss the prospects of capitalism in East Central Europe requires an analysis of the process of institutional change in the region.

The prevailing institutional framework in a society consists of formal and informal rules, all of which carry their own incentives and transaction costs.[5] Formal rules are constitutions, statutes, common law, and other government regulations. A major common trait of formal rules is that they are externally enforced.

Informal rules include traditions, customs, religious beliefs, and so on. They are part of an inheritance which has passed the test of time. Informal rules are often referred to as the old ethos, or the hand of the past, or the carriers of history.[6] The enforcement of informal rules is internalized in the benefits and costs of specific activities. Those costs can range from loss of reputation to rejection by friends and neighbors.[7]

Academic research and empirical evidence have established that different institutional structures generate different transaction costs. By freeing resources for alternative uses, institutions that have lower transaction costs contribute more to the production of wealth than institutions that have higher transaction costs. One implication of this is that institutional changes and the production of wealth are linked via the effects of the former on transaction costs.

The interaction of formal and informal rules is, I believe, a critical factor affecting transaction costs. If and when formal rules are in tune with informal rules, the incentives both create will tend to reinforce each other. A harmonious inter-action of formal and informal rules reduces the transaction costs of maintaining and protecting the rules of the game, and frees some resources for the production of wealth. But when formal rules are in conflict with informal rules, their respective incentives will tend to raise the transaction costs of maintaining and enforcing the prevailing institutional en-vironment, and to reduce the production of wealth in the community.

Observation supports this proposition. The interaction thesis explains the costs of resources that were required to maintain and enforce the old regimes in East Central Europe. It also helps to explain the differences in economic development between Catholic and Protestant countries in Europe, the differences in economic development between North and South America, and the differences in the costs of enforcing the right to life in religious and less religious communities.

The formal rule introduced in order to limit the maximum speed on American highways to fifty-five miles per hour was clearly in conflict with the driving culture of most American motorists and raised enforcement costs. Prohibition laws in the United States were clearly in conflict with the country's prevailing tradition of social drinking. Al Capone and his like served the important social function of giving people what they wanted—at a price. Eventually, the high transaction costs of maintaining and enforcing prohibition laws convinced the government to eliminate the conflict between formal and in-formal rules concerning the consumption of liquor.

The rise of ghettos in American cities reflected a ten-dency on the part of members of various ethnic, racial, and religious groups (all of whom lived under the same set of formal rules) to stay together with individuals whose behav-ior they could predict. Civil rights laws enacted in the second half of the twentieth century have raised the costs of living in ghettos. Street riots, zoning issues, civil disturbances, and various forms of real or—in my view, more likely—perceived discrimination could be thought of as predictable conse-quences of upsetting the prevailing interaction of formal and informal rules in American cities.

To conclude, Professor North has observed that similar formal rules tend to produce different outcomes:

> The US Constitution was adopted with modifications by many Latin American countries in the nineteenth century, and many of the property rights laws of successful Western countries have been adopted by Third World countries. The results are, however, not similar to those in the United States or other successful Western countries. The enforcement mechanism, the norms of behavior, and the subjective models of the actors are not [the same].
>
> (North, 1990, 101)

Pursuing the interaction thesis we can say that institutional changes upset the prevailing interaction of formal and informal rules, and, in the process, create new incentives affecting transaction costs. The efficiency of institutional changes then depends on whether those incentives lower transaction costs,[8] that is, the effects of institutional changes.[9]

The Interaction Thesis and the Transition Process

The end of socialist rule in 1989 created a strong demand for institutional changes. New leaders in the region were confronted with two critical issues: (i) how to choose new institutions, and (ii) at what rate the new rules of the game should replace the old ones. As we look at the post-1989 developments in the region—that is, the transition process—we observe significant differences among East European countries in dealing with both issues. By mid-1990, pro-collectivist parties were doing well in most East European countries. Why?

For several decades East Europeans were forced to live under a system that tolerated neither a free market in ideas nor contacts with the rest of the world.[10] As socialist rule ended, East Europeans were in no position to quickly identify alternative institutional arrangements and/or to evaluate their expected consequences.

I believe that ordinary people in East Central Europe were in favor of capitalism as they perceived the system.[11] But, owing to the Iron Curtain, they knew very little about how and why the system worked. They certainly could not understand such basic traits of capitalism as risk bearing, self-determination, and self-responsibility. The average person identified capitalism with bountiful supplies of goods and large incomes with which to buy them. The benefits of capitalism were somehow to be captured with neither a change in work ethic nor a reduction in the prevailing welfare programs.

Initially, Western scholars, such as Jeffrey Sachs, and East European 'dissidents' designed institutional reforms that are known as the 'big bang approach' in the transition to capitalism. They were in a hurry to promote institutional changes that were alien to the beliefs and behaviors embedded in the fabric of community life in East Central Europe (especially the farther one travels to the East).

By failing to create a harmonious interaction of (new) formal and informal rules, the transition process (and especially the 'big bang approach') quickly disillusioned people about capitalism. From the standpoint of ordinary people in East Central Europe, the transition process then became a substitution of one set of institutions for another, neither of which they had chosen for themselves. It is probably best to say that 'forced' transition is not capitalism but violent neo-classical economics, which is in fact a much closer substitute for *dirigisme*.[12]

I think that it is naive to assert that East Europeans have rejected capitalism. They have yet to experience the system. East Europeans reject the transition process which they have wrongly, but predictably, identified with capitalism.

Law and Tradition

Socialist rule in East Central Europe subjected the rule of law to the will of the ruling elite and seriously undermined people's confidence in formal institutions. However, the old ethos was a powerful fortress behind whose walls extended families were able to hide and survive the depredations of socialist institutions without giving up their customs and shared values. One unintended effect of socialist rule, then, was to preserve the region's informal rules.

As socialist rule ended and its formal institutions were destabilized, East Europeans needed a stable set of rules for carrying out transactions among themselves and with the rest of the world. Predictably, they began to fall back on the only set of rules they knew: customs and tradition. Informal rules in the region are not homogenous, but they have many common characteristics.

First, the intellectual tradition of East Central Europe has remained largely free of such ideas as classical liberalism and methodological individualism. Second, the prevailing concept of the community in the region is not one of a voluntary association of individuals who, in the pursuit of their private ends, join and leave the community by free choice. Individuals are expected to subordinate their private ends and to cooperate with other members of their community in pursuing shared values.

Evidence is plentiful that the old ethos has affected the behavior of ordinary people in the transition process. The gains from the change were seen as a redistribution of wealth rather than as rewards that individuals receive for creating new value. State authorities preferred to block the activities of individuals who earned large profits instead of encouraging others to emulate them in open markets. Members of collective farms in Russia have been threatening to marginalize farmers who want to 'go private', a credible threat in the countryside with little communication with the rest of the country. Small shop owners in Ukraine are treated as thieves. In general, the accumulation of private wealth in East Central Europe (again, the more so the farther one travels to the East) is considered suspect.

Perhaps the most important point about the old ethos in East Central Europe is that communities have developed customs and common values along ethnic lines. While there are three major religions in East Central Europe (Islam, Catholic, and Orthodox), a person's ethnic origin generally defines his religion, which works to reinforce the differences in customs and values among ethnic groups. Interactions within any specific group are thus subject to rules of behavior that do not necessarily promote economic exchanges across ethnic lines.

As initial post-1989 leaders in East Central Europe, with considerable support from the West, used the strong hand of the state to achieve the transition from socialism to capitalism, they replaced the old conflict of formal and informal rules with a new one.[13] Two groups of people exploited this otherwise harmonious interaction of formal and informal rules, and contributed to the rise of pro-collectivist (anti-free-market) parties in East Central Europe: (i) the former local party nomenclatures, and (ii) older workers and retirees.

Local Nomenclatures

As socialist rule ended in East Central Europe, former leaders had an interest in seeking ways to preserve their power and privileges. Their acquired skills qualified them for new careers in a bureaucratic environment; therefore, a free-market, private-property system was a threat to their private well-being. To preserve the value of their former professional qualifications, the former communists, while paying lip service to free-market reforms, had to support the creation of a state-centered system. They knew that enforcing the perception of an external threat among their respective ethnic groups would give them a good chance to stay in power. Most former communists, then, quickly transformed themselves into nationalists,[14] not a difficult thing for them to do because nationalism and socialism have one important common trait: the collectivist mode of looking at the world.[15]

Indeed, most leaders in the multi-ethnic states of East Central Europe in the early 1990s were non-reformed communists, such as Milošević in Serbia, Kučan in Slovenia, Mečiar in Slovakia, and Kravchuk in Ukraine. The case of Czechoslovakia in the early 1990s is an important example. In their quest to retain power, former communists in Slovakia adroitly exploited Slovak nationalism, eventually separating the country into two sovereign states. In contrast, the Czechs, with virtually no former communists in positions of power, are treating ethnic issues as a nuisance that could only interfere with getting the country on the road to recovery.

Older Workers and Retirees

East Europeans had no opportunity to save and invest in 'owned' assets during socialist rule. Instead, the state provided them with assets specific to a non–private-property economy. Those assets consisted of (i) a variety of welfare benefits such as job security, allowances for children, medical benefits, and subsidized housing, and (ii) the economy of want.

Retired people and older workers (forty-five years of age plus) find the returns from those assets irreplaceable. Hence they have incentives to oppose the transition from socialism to capitalism. Older workers see capitalism as a threat to their current and future benefits from the system-specific assets. They fear, and with good reason, that the remainder of their working life will not be long enough to allow them to replace those benefits with private savings and investments.

Retired people have also seen a decline in the value of their pensions and other benefits. Moreover, in the economy of want retirees were an important asset to their families in two ways: (i) they had time to wait in line for consumer goods; (ii) they specialized in knowing what, where, and when goods would be available. Thus, retired people raised the real incomes of their extended families. As scarcity prices replace price controls, retired people fear that they will become a liability to their families.

Predictably, older workers and retirees perceive the transition from socialism to capitalism as a real threat. They did not purchase the assets mentioned above by choice, but that was all they were given. Thus, a major segment of the population in East Central Europe opposes the transition process for reasons of self-interest, whatever their ideological preferences might be. The evidence is consistent with this proposition. Young people, who have made little or no investment in the old system's specific assets, are strong supporters of the transition to capitalism, while older workers and retired people tend to support pro-collectivist parties.

Implications of the Transition Process

Some spontaneous institutional changes have occurred in East Central Europe. For example, privately owned firms have emerged in most countries, although private-property rights do not yet enjoy entirely credible legal guarantees.[16] However, exogenous institutional changes have dominated the transition from socialism to capitalism. Let me point to a few reasons why those institutional changes have reduced the production of wealth by way of higher transaction costs.

(i) Exogenous changes require an activist government as a means of imposing and maintaining them. In East Central Europe, the role of the strong hand of the state in the transition process is usually justified by reference to the 'public interest'. The public-interest argument assumes that the social welfare function exists, that public decision makers (could) know it, and that they can be trusted to realize it. Neither presumption is derivable from empirical knowledge.

(ii) Another consequence of exogenous changes is a contraction in the social opportunity set.[17] A dissipation of resources is predictable for two reasons. First, the strong hand of the state interferes with "the constraints that are voluntarily arrived at when individuals are free to impose restrictions upon themselves" (Alchian and Woodward, 1988, 65). Second, public decision makers do not and cannot possess reliable information about the economy's possible dynamic responses to exogenous institutional changes.[18] In many East European countries, unemployment and inflation forced a contraction in the social opportunity set.

(iii) Finally, the people who impose exogenous changes and those who implement them are not the same. The latter have considerable discretionary power in interpreting the intent of policy makers. They are also motivated by their own incentives and private ends that are likely to differ from those of their superiors and can be held in check only at the price of increasing their superiors' monitoring costs.

A transition process that creates a conflict between formal and informal rules is unlikely either to fulfill its purpose or to endear capitalism to East Europeans. The rising strength of pro-collectivist parties is therefore not surprising.

Conclusion

An alternative approach to institutional changes in East Central Europe is to let people choose their own way of life, and to let capitalist institutions win support through their performance in the competitive market for institutions. That is, instead of building capitalism by fiat, East European leaders should provide, by fiat, a legal environment that would allow people to try out all sorts of contractual arrangements in the production of wealth, and institutionalize those that pass the market test. This approach to the transition process would require a credible guarantee of equal protection of all property rights (including cessation of subsidies for non-private firms), equal fiscal treatment of all incomes, efficient financial markets, open entry and exit for economic agents in all markets, and, very importantly, free access to foreign goods and capital

The setting up of this framework could be quite difficult. It appears to be especially difficult to give credible constitutional guarantees in a region in which the rule of law is totally alien to most citizens. Yet, whatever the difficulties, I conjecture that the total cost of creating competitive markets for institutions in East Central Europe would be less than the future costs of accepting bureaucratic control of the transition process.

The competitive market for institutions would give East Europeans a chance to identify alternative arrangements, try them out, adjust to their consequences, and select those they prefer. Thus spontaneous institutional changes could help them to slowly choose capitalism. Indeed, we already observe thousands of small private firms which have spontaneously emerged throughout East Central Europe in spite of the absence of credible legal guarantees of private-property rights. Many will not last, but some will grow. While their economic significance is still modest, such private enterprises are the breeding ground for entrepreneurs, a work ethic, a capitalist exchange culture, and positive attitudes towards capitalism in general. They educate ordinary people to appreciate a way of life that rewards performance, promotes individual liberties, and places a high value on self-responsibility and self-determination.

To conclude, I do not know what are the prospects of liberalism in East Central Europe today. However, I believe that substituting cognitive knowledge for valuations, and analysis for preferences would convince most of us that enhancing the prospects of liberalism in practice is a worthwhile endeavor.

Bibliography

Alchian, A., and S. Woodward. 1988. 'The Firm is Dead. Long Live the Firm', *Journal of Economic Literature* 26.

Brunner, K. 1970. 'Knowledge, Values and the Choice of Economic Organization', *Kyklos* 23.

———. 1987. 'The Perception of Man and the Conception of Society: Two Approaches to Understanding Society', *Economic Inquiry* 25.

Buchanan, J. 1975. *Freedom in Constitutional Contract*. College Station: Texas A&M University Press.

———. 1976. 'General Implications of Subjectivism in Economics'. Paper presented at the conference 'Subjectivism in Economics', Dallas, Texas (December).

Jensen, M., and W. Meckling. 1979. 'Rights and Production Functions', *Journal of Business* 52.

North, D. 1990. *Institutions, Institutional Changes and Economic Performance*. Cambridge: Cambridge University Press.

Notes

1 Liberalism means individual liberty, openness to new ideas, tolerance of all views, and the rule of law. Liberalism and methodological individualism go hand in hand. The latter says that the individual is the only decision maker in society—that is, to understand decisions made by government agencies, corporations, and other organizations it is necessary to recognize decision makers in those organizations, pay attention to their private ends, and identify the incentives and transaction costs in terms of which they work.

2 Professor Buchanan said the following about the interaction of the common law and economic life: "The object of the never-ending search by loosely coordinated judges acting independently is to find 'the law', to locate and redefine the structure of individual rights, not *ab initio*, but in existing social–institutional arrangements … Law is a stabilizing influence which provides the necessary framework within which individuals can plan their own affairs" (Buchanan, 1975, 46–47).

3 The United States Constitution speaks of the pursuit of happiness; neo-classical economics postulates the maximization paradigm; I prefer the word 'survival'. The point is the same. Human behavior is purposeful, that is, given the individual's preference structure, "the relative evaluation of a positively valued object diminishes with its increasing quantity, and trade-off or substitutability occurs in all directions" (Brunner, 1987, 372).

4 Institutions are the legal, administrative, and customary arrangements for repeated human interactions. Their major function is to enhance the predictability of human behavior, mostly by way of affecting the transaction costs of contracting. The continuity of expectations requires stable and credible institutions. Frequent changes in the rules of the game raise the costs of long-term contracts relative to interactions that have a shorter time-horizon.

5 Transaction costs are the costs of all resources required to transfer property rights from one economic agent to another. They include the costs of making an exchange (for example, discovering exchange opportunities, negotiating exchange, monitoring, and enforcement), and the costs of maintaining and protecting the institutional structure (for example, judiciary, police, armed forces).

6 Formal rules cannot chase out informal rules; they can only suppress them. They coexist in either harmony or conflict.

7 The current abortion debate in the United States is an attempt to replace the prevailing informal rule, which allows women to have abortions at the cost of medical assistance plus their social rejection by some friends, with a formal rule that would substantially increase the costs of unwanted pregnancies.

8 In a recent paper Professor Colombato argued that institutional changes may occur with or without a shock. By and large, Colombato says, the exogenous shock tends to be beneficial, for it destroys or weakens

rent-seeking games. On the other hand, the endogenous change may create more opportunities for rent-seeking.

9 Such an analysis is beyond the scope of this chapter. But a few general remarks may be useful. Informal rules change slowly and spontaneously, mostly in response to changes in the game (for example, social acceptance of birth control pills and single motherhood). Clearly, informal rules are not a policy variable. On the other hand, formal rules *are*. Common-law judges, legislators in rule-of-law countries, regulators at all levels of government, despots, and dictators have the power to create new rules and to modify existing ones. The effect of these changes on the interaction of formal and informal rules depends on the existence (or nonexistence) of objective constraints on the power of rule makers to pursue their own private ends and the incentive structures within which they work. For example, democratic elections in rule-of-law nations raise the rulers' costs of pursuing their private ends, and, in doing so, create incentives to lower transaction costs.

10 Yugoslavia was the only exception.

11 I fully agree with Professor Macey that it is more accurate simply to say that East Europeans were *against* the old system. However, sometimes we choose to follow our sixth sense.

12 I owe this point to Professor Colombato.

13 It is true that capitalism had to face similar problems in many other countries with strong collectivist traditions. However, Japan, South Korea, and Taiwan—among other countries—have given their people freedom to experiment with alternative institutional arrangements. People responded by exploiting various opportunities and adopted those that passed the market test. Eventually, most of those countries ended up with a blend of capitalist institutions and old traditions. The Czech Republic, thanks primarily to Václav Klaus, is the only East European country that belongs to this group.

14 In general, nationalism represents the conviction that the community's common good transcends the private interests of its members. This implies that individuals can attain their full potential only through their nationality. Nationalism is thus incompatible with individual liberty and competitive markets.

15 It is important not to confuse patriotism with nationalism. Patriotism means attachment to a community and its traditions. It is compatible with a voluntary association of diverse individuals who choose to live together, like the United States and the United Kingdom. Unlike nationalism, patriotism is consistent with individual liberty, pursuit of private ends, and cultural diversity.

16 Most state factories in East European countries have little chance of surviving in competitive markets. Yet, we observe that ordinary people do not attribute the dismal performance of those firms to the decades of communist mismanagement. Instead, they say that the free-market, private-property economy is not working either.

17 The social opportunity set is not confined to standard goods and services. It also includes all socio-economic and socio-political institutions (see Jensen and Meckling, 1979, 470–72).

18 Human interactions continuously create and disseminate new knowledge. The interpretation and assimilation of this knowledge by different individuals keeps changing opportunity sets and expectations about the future. To assume that individuals' utility functions are given is thus misleading. Utility functions are continuously modified by the action-choosing process.

Contributors

Karl Acham is Professor of Sociology and Head of the Department of Sociology at the University of Graz and Chair of its Division of Sociological Theory, History of Ideas, and Philosophy of the Social Sciences. He is the author of several books and numerous articles on the philosophy of history, sociological theory, social philosophy, sociology of culture, and related areas. He has been a visiting professor in Canada, P. R. China, Japan, Brazil, India, and Germany, and is a member of the Austrian Academy of Sciences.

Catherine Audard teaches moral and political philosophy at the London School of Economics and at the École des Hautes Études en Sciences Sociales in Paris. Her most recent book is *Anthologie historique et critique de l'utilitarisme* in three volumes (Paris, 1999). She is also the author, in collaboration, of *Individu et justice sociale* (Paris, 1988) and *Le Respect* (Paris, 1993). She has published numerous articles on utilitarianism, liberalism, and justice, in various journals and collections. She has recently published a new French translation of J. S. Mill's *Utilitarianism* (Paris, 1998).

John Crowley is a research fellow at the Fondation Nationale des Sciences Politiques in Paris. He also lectures in political science at the Institut d'Études Politiques and several other Paris institutions. He is the author of *Sans épines, la rose. Tony Blair: un modèle pour l'Europe?* (Paris, 1999).

Marion Gräfin Dönhoff, born in East Prussia, is a well-known writer and journalist. In 1946 she started to work for the Hamburg weekly *Die Zeit*, and in 1969 she became its chief editor. Since 1973 she has been the publisher of *Die Zeit*. In 1966 she was awarded the Theodor Heuss prize, and in 1971 the German Booksellers' prize. She is the author of several books, including *The German Federal Republic in Adenauer's Era* (1963), *Civilize Capitalism. The Limits of Freedom* (1977), and *Childhood in East Prussia* (1988).

Michel Girard is Deputy Director of the Department of Political Science at the Université Panthéon-Sorbonne (Paris I). His main interests are theory and methodology of international politics, foreign policy analysis, and European integration. Among other writings, he is the co-editor of *Theory and Practice in Foreign Policy-Making* (London, 1994) and the editor of *Individualism and World Politics* (London, 1999).

Robert Grant is Reader in English Literature at Glasgow University, and Visiting Research Fellow at the Social Philosophy and Policy Center, Bowling Green State University, Ohio. He is the author of *Oakeshott* (1990), and of one hundred essays, articles, and reviews in literary and philosophical journals and symposia. Some of these are currently being reprinted in *The Politics of Sex and Other Essays* (1999). He has lectured widely in the USA and Eastern Europe.

Stephen Holmes is Professor of Politics at Princeton University and Adjunct Professor of Law at NYU Law School. From 1985 to 1997, he was Professor of Politics and Law at the Law School and Political Science Department of the University of Chicago. His fields of specialization include democratic theory, the history of liberalism, constitutional and legal change after communism, the Russian legal system, and comparative constitutional law. He is the editor-in-chief of the *East European Constitutional Review*. He is the co-author (with Cass Sunstein) of *The Cost of Rights: Why Liberty Depends on Taxes* (1999).

Bedřich Löwenstein is an interdisciplinary historian and was until 1969, researcher at the Institute of History of the

Czechoslovak Academy of Sciences. He has published several studies on the preconditions of Nazism in Germany, including *Bismarck* (Prague, 1968) and *The Middle Ages of the 20th Century* (Prague, 1969)—this book was printed but immediately pulped. He emigrated in 1979 and between 1979 and 1994 he was Professor of Modern History at the Free University, Berlin. His main recent works include *The Project of Modernity* (1987), *Problemfehler der Moderne* (1990), *Annäherungsversuche* (1992), and *We and the Others* (1997).

Jiří Musil is Professor of Sociology at the Central European University in Budapest and Warsaw, and at Charles University in Prague. He was the first Academic Director of the Prague College of the CEU. He is a member of the 'Academia Europea' and 'Academia Scientiarum et Artium Europaea', and a founding member of the Czech Learned Society. His main fields are urban and regional sociology and sociology of culture. He has published and edited 13 books, including (with W. Strubelt) *Räumliche Auswirkungen des Transformationsprozesses in Deutschland und bei den östlichen Nachbarn* (Opladen, 1977) and *The End of Czechoslovakia* (Budapest, 1995).

Svetozar Pejovich is Professor of Economics at Texas A&M University, College Station, and Research Fellow at the International Center for Economic Research, Turin, Italy. Professor Pejovich holds a law degree from the University of Belgrade and a Ph.D. in economics from Georgetown University in Washington, DC. In addition to over one hundred articles in scientific and other journals, Professor Pejovich has published and edited 16 books. His main research interests are the economics of property rights, new institutional economics, and law and economics.

Sandra Pralong is an advisor to the President of Romania. She set up and ran the Soros Foundation in Romania between 1990 and 1993. Romanian-born but Western-educated, Pralong holds an MBA from the University of Lausanne, Switzerland, an MALD from the Fletcher School of Law and Diplomacy at Tufts/Harvard, and is a doctoral candidate in Political Science at Columbia University, NY. She is the author of several articles on ethics and politics, and has co-edited the volume *Karl Popper's Open Society after 50 Years*, published by Routledge.

Thomas Scheffer gained his doctoral degree in Göttingen with a study on 'Kant's Criterion of Truth'. He was an assistant in a DFG-project on 'The immanent morals of the German fundamental law', directed by Professor Alexy in Kiel.

Allison Stanger is Associate Professor of Political Science at Middlebury College in Vermont, USA. She is the co-editor and co-translator (with Michael Kraus) of *Irreconcilable Differences?: Explaining Czechoslovakia's Dissolution*. Her essays on European politics and culture have appeared in the *East European Constitutional Review*, the *New England Review*, the *Oxford International Review*, *Lateral* (Barcelona), and *Literární Noviny* (Prague).

Ilja Šrubař is Professor of Sociology at the University Erlangen-Nürnberg. He studied philosophy, sociology, and history in Prague and Frankfurt am Main, where he was awarded his Ph.D. He has taught at the University of Konstanz and at the Humboldt University in Berlin. His fields of interest include the theory and history of sociology, particularly the so-called phenomenological approach, and the sociology of East European societies.

Zdeněk Suda is Professor Emeritus of Sociology at the University of Pittsburgh, specializing mainly in branches of political sociology with the focus on East Central Europe, and the sociology of work and of education. He has also devoted considerable attention to the problems of modernization and globalization. His principal publications are *La division internationale socialiste du travail* (Leyden, 1967), *Zealots and Rebels: History of the Communist Party of Czechosslovakia* (Stanford, 1980), and (as editor) *The Globalization of Labor Markets: A Challenge to the Social Contract* (Prague, 1994).

Name Index